HOW TO DRAW ANIMALS FOR KIDS

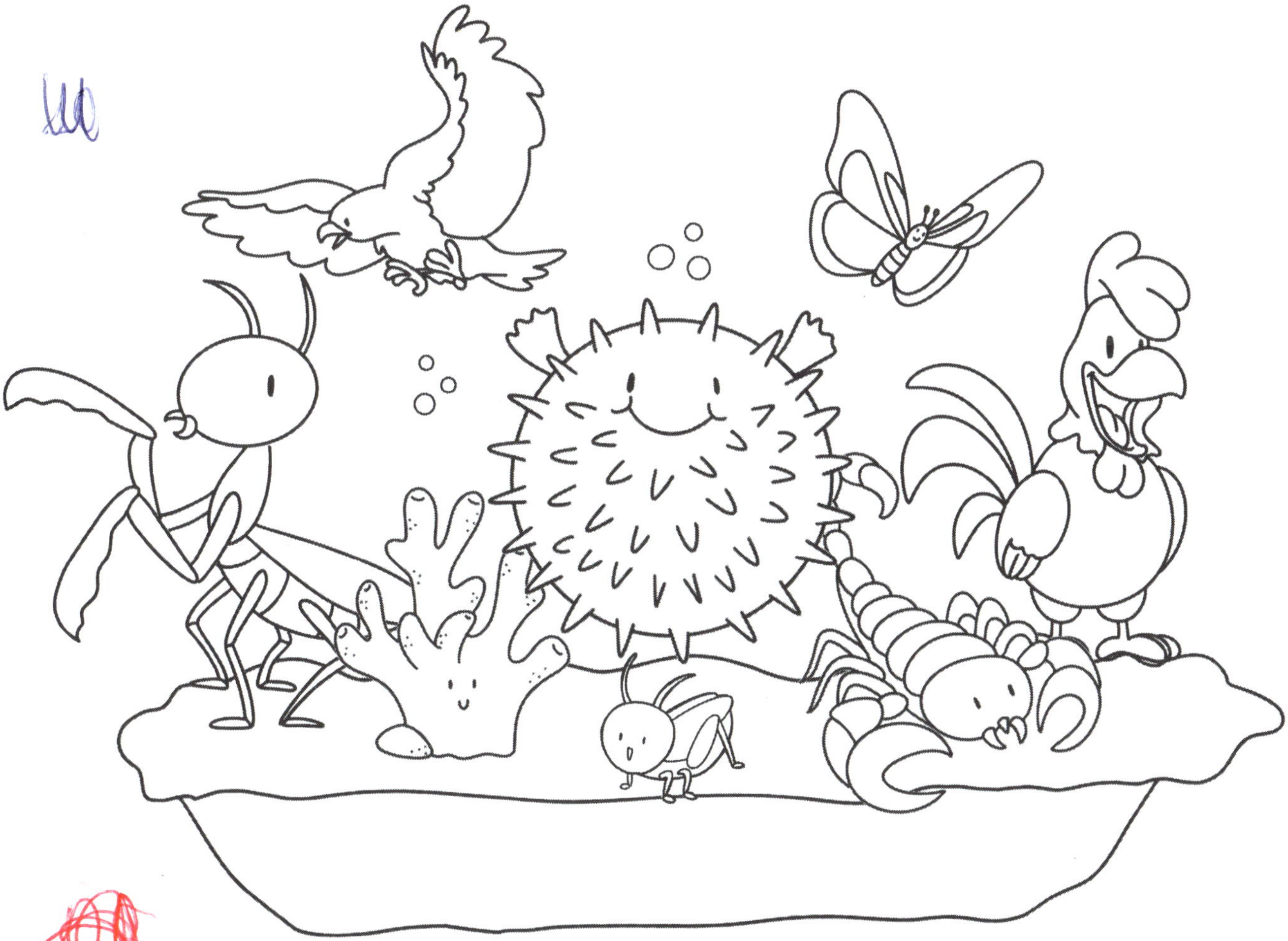

TIPS TO USE THIS BOOK

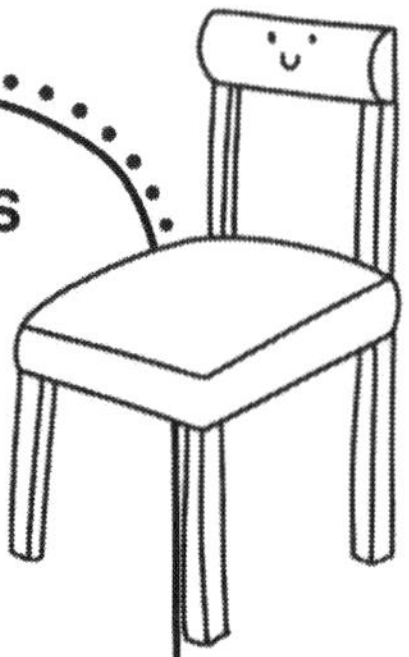

1. Keep the correct sitting posture on a chair which has a straight back and the appropriate height.
2. Prepare a pencil and eraser; depending on your styles, you can also use markers or pens.

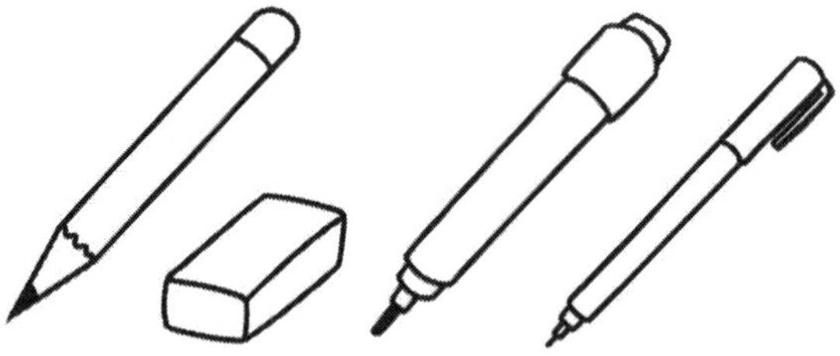

3. When drawing, the first strokes you draw should be light so that it can be easily corrected if there are mistakes or easy to erase when there are excess strokes.
4. Draw accordingly to the instructions by following the arrows then complete your work in the practice section of each page.
5. After finishing a drawing, you can start coloring it any way you like.

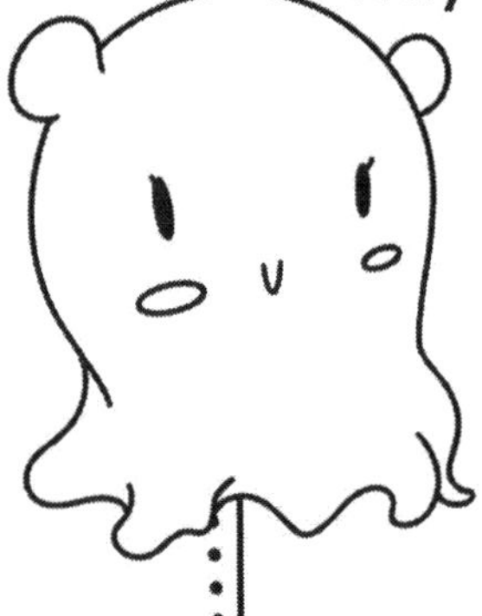

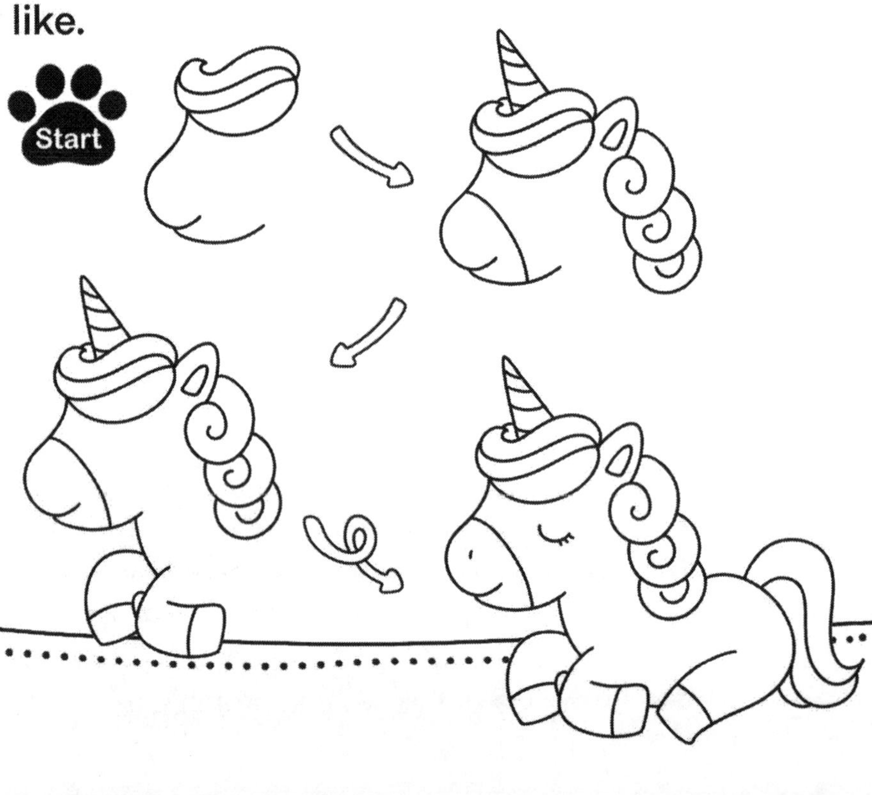

WHAT'S iNSiDE

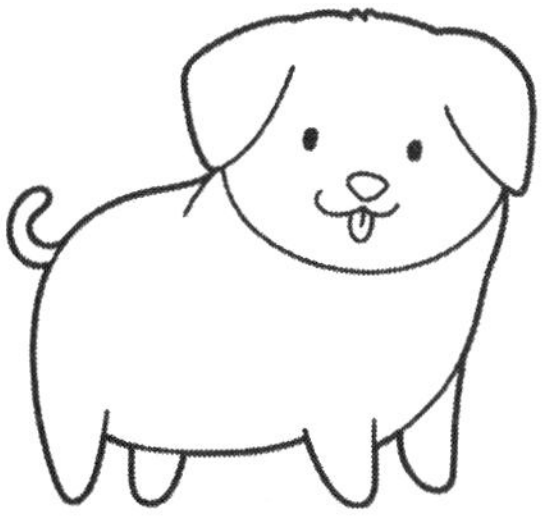
Dog

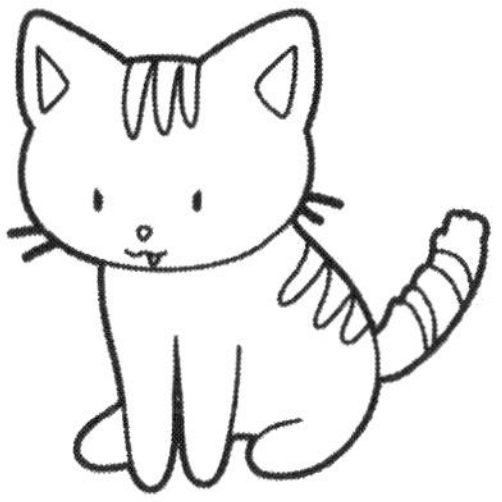
Cat

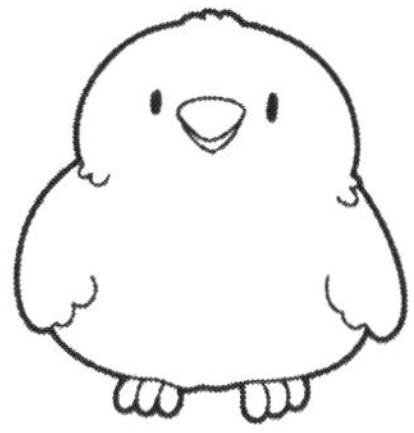
Chick

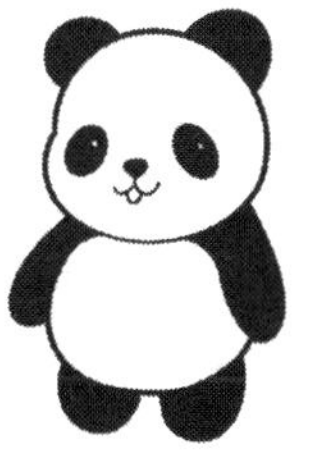
Panda

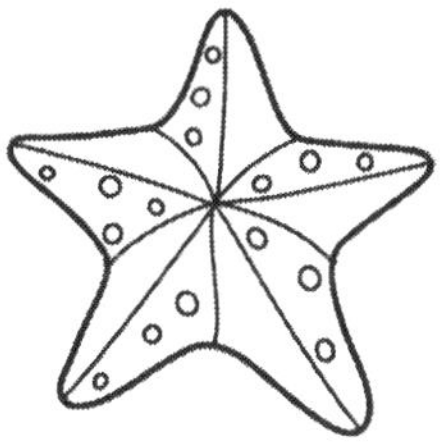
Starfish

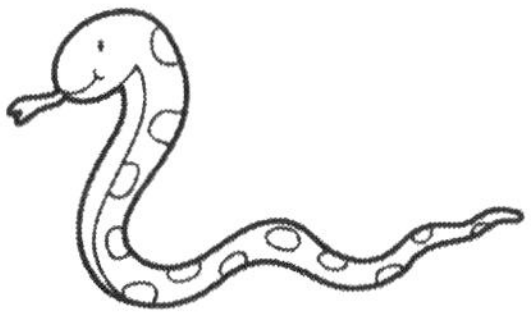
Snake

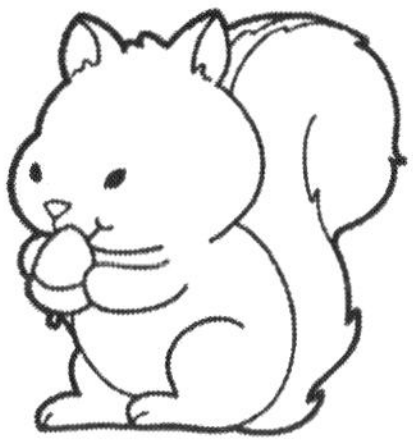
Squirrel

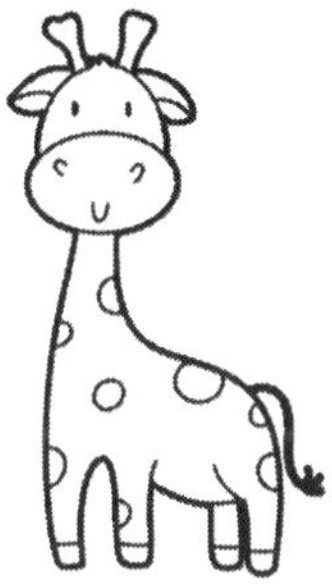
Giraffe

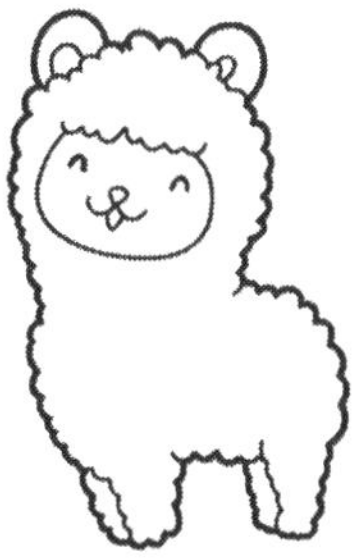
Llama

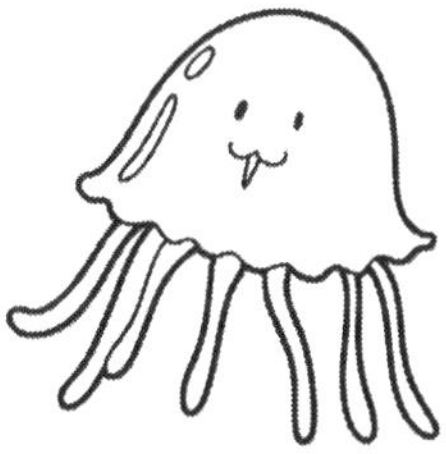
Jellyfish

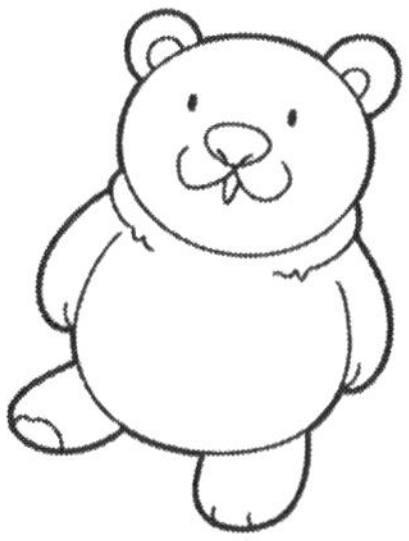
Bear

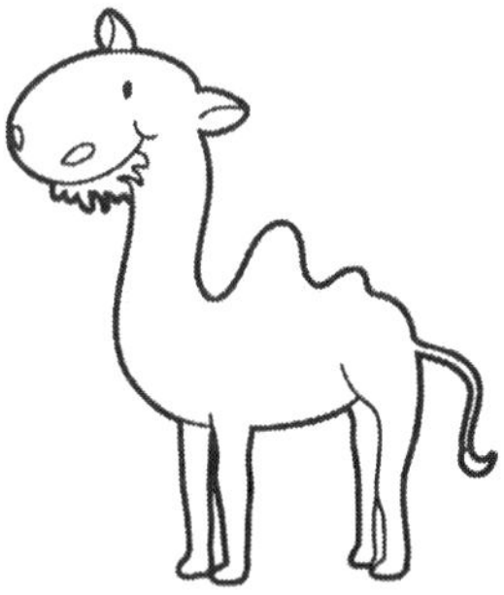
Camel

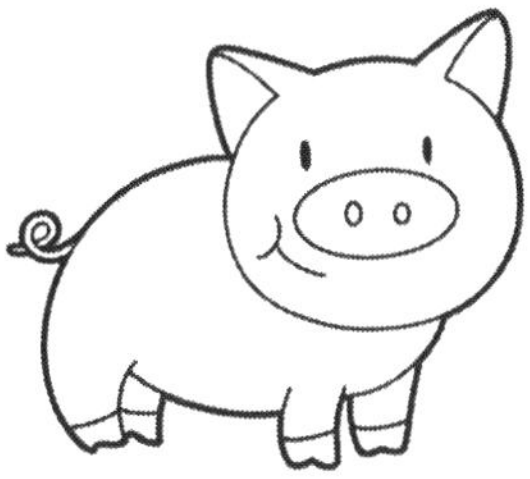
Pig

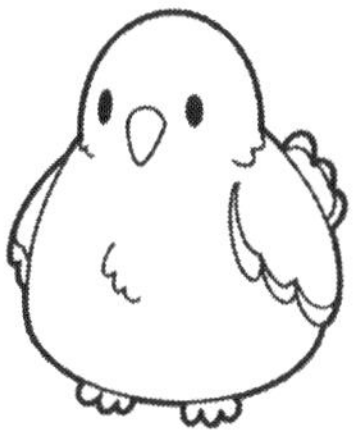
Dove

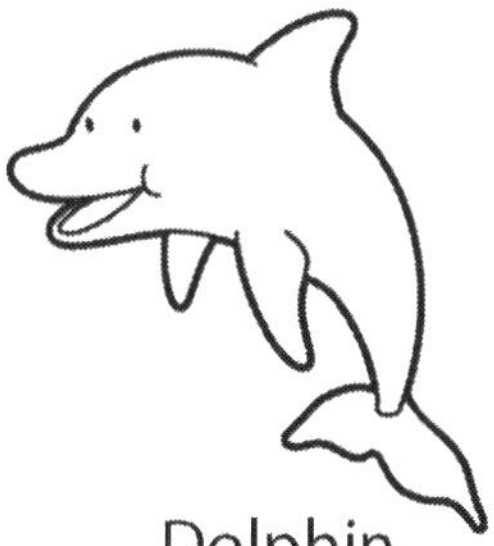
Dolphin

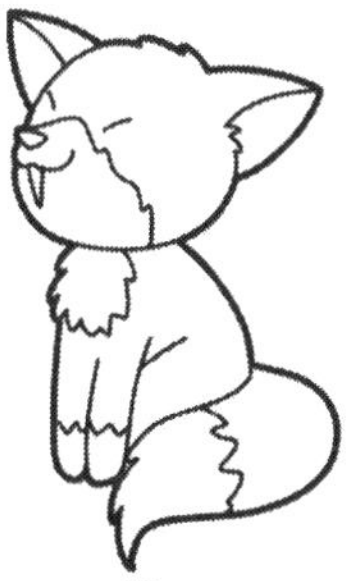
Fox

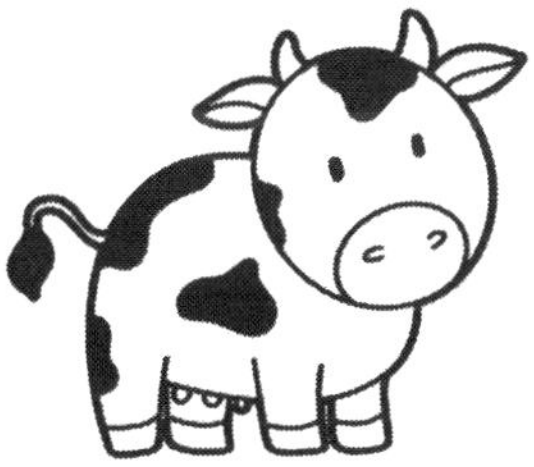
Cow

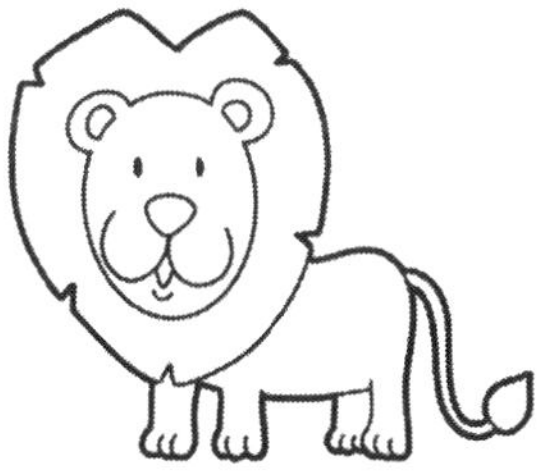
Lion

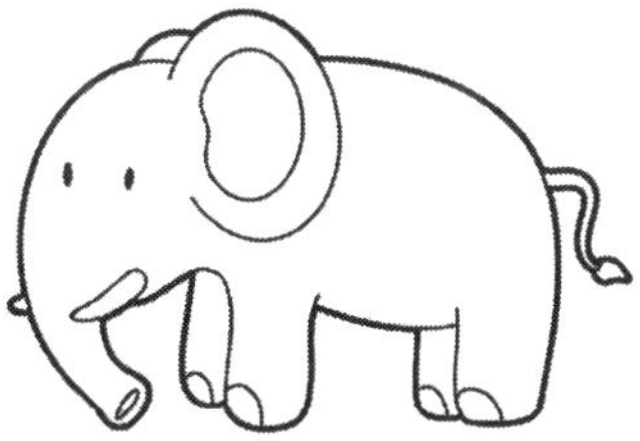
Elephant

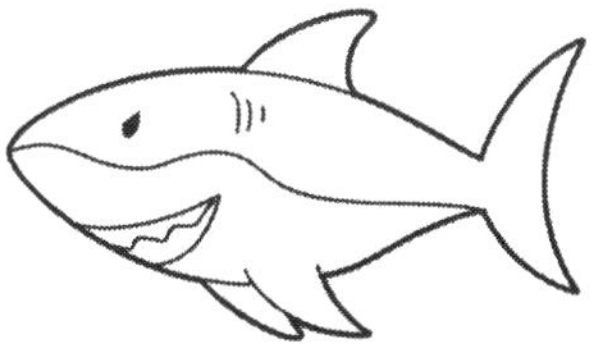
Shark

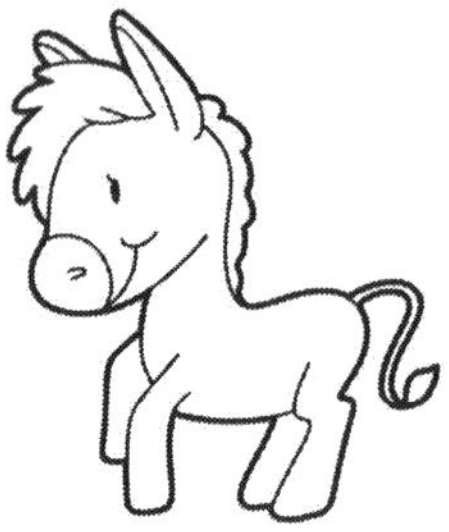

Donkey

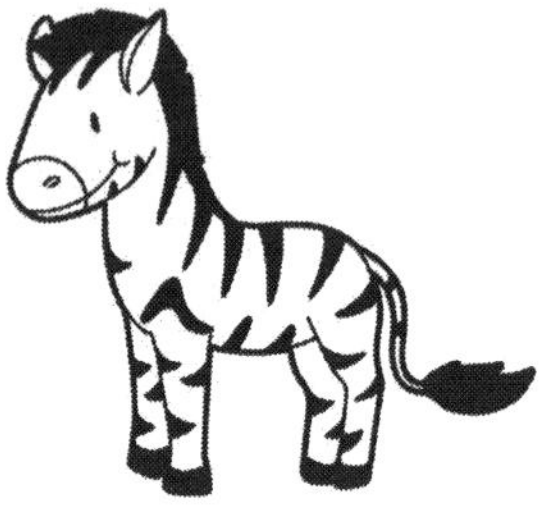

Zebra

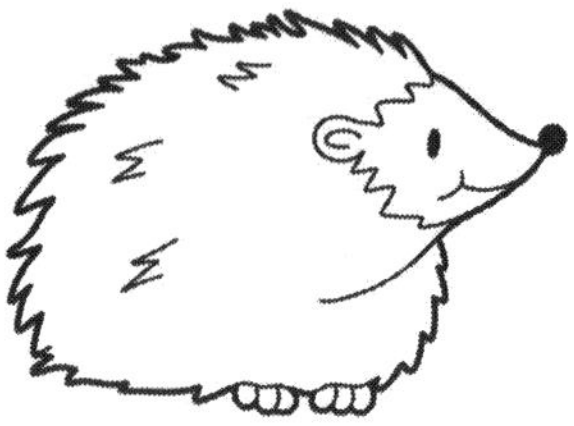

Porcupine

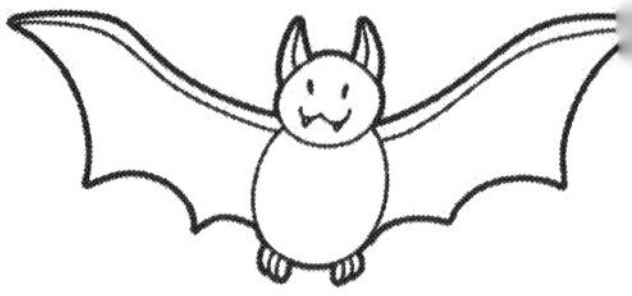

Bat

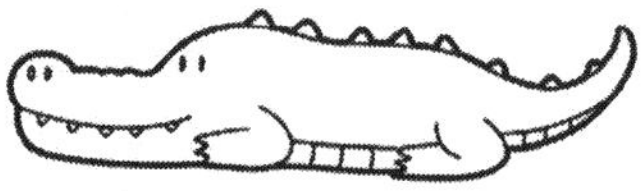

Alligator

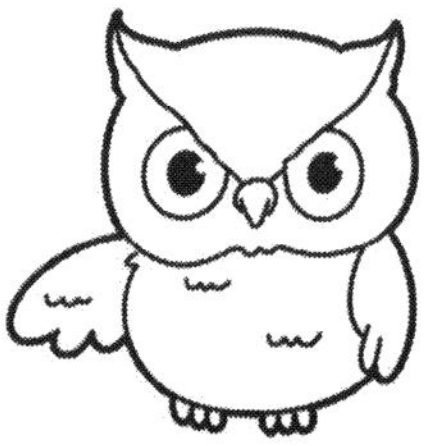

Owl

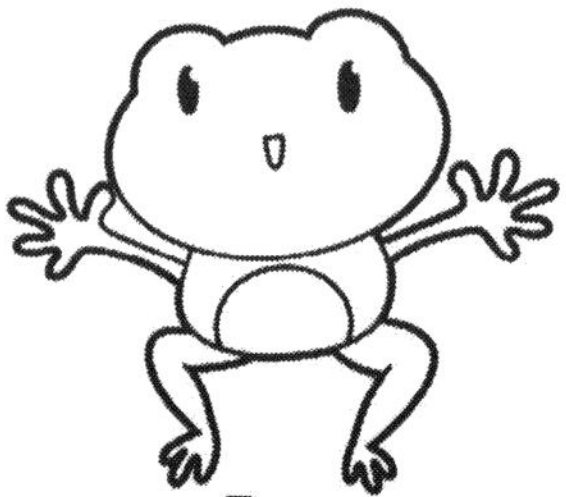

Frog

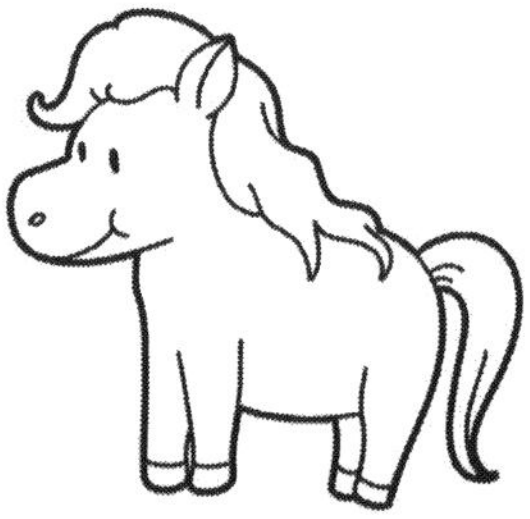

Horse

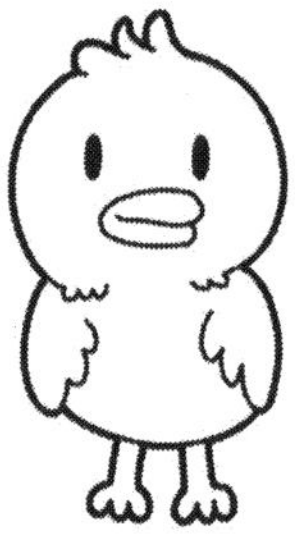

Duck

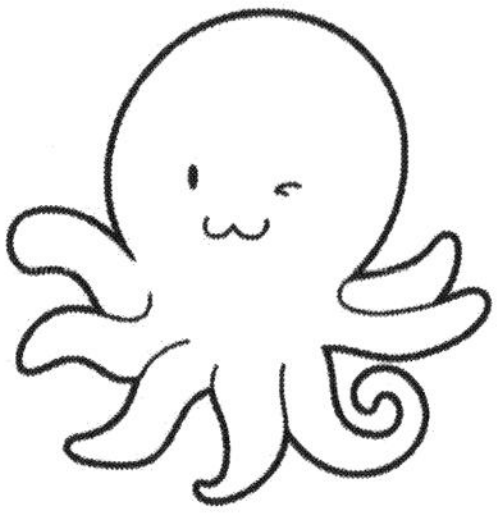

Octopus

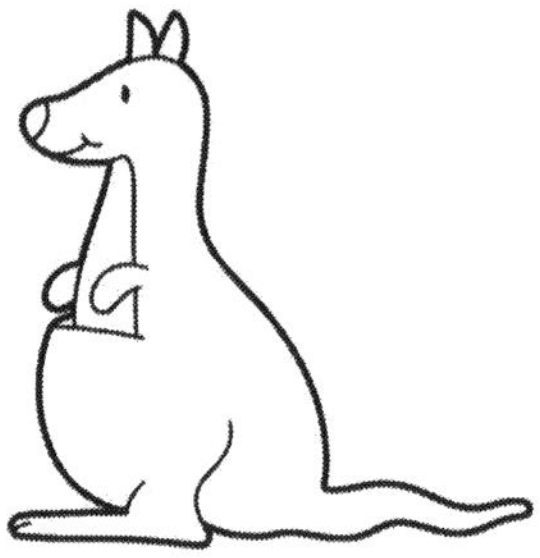

Kangaroo

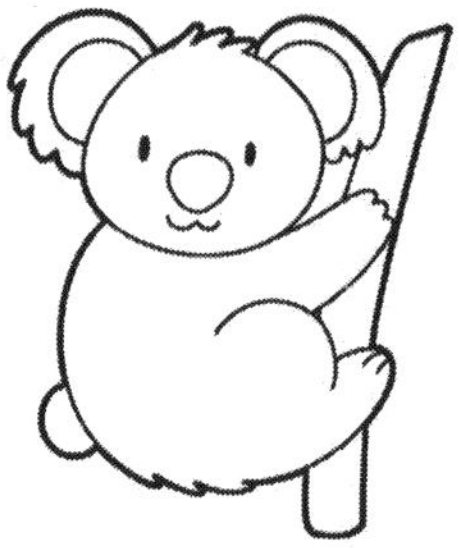

Koala Bear

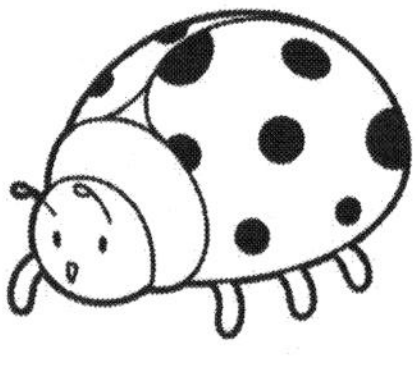

Lady Bug

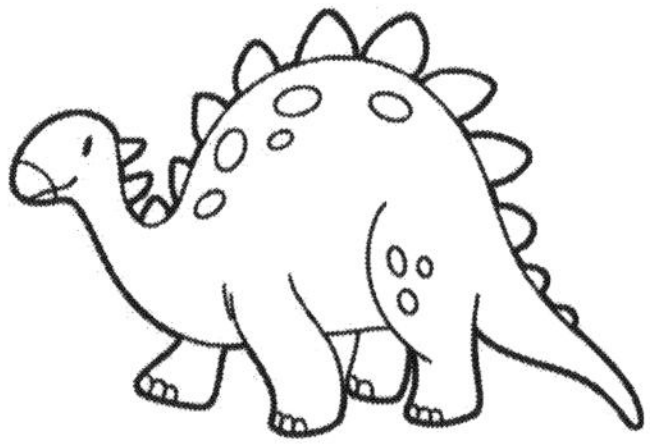

Dinosaur

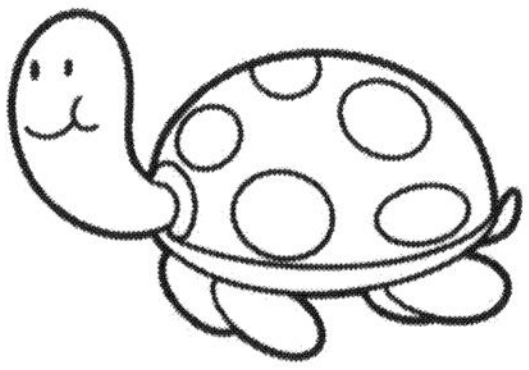

Turtle

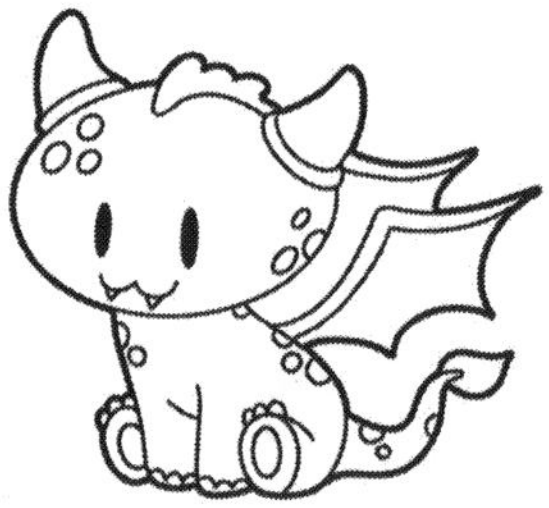

Dragon

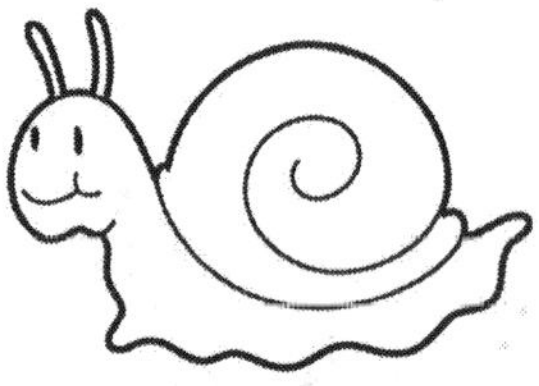

Snail

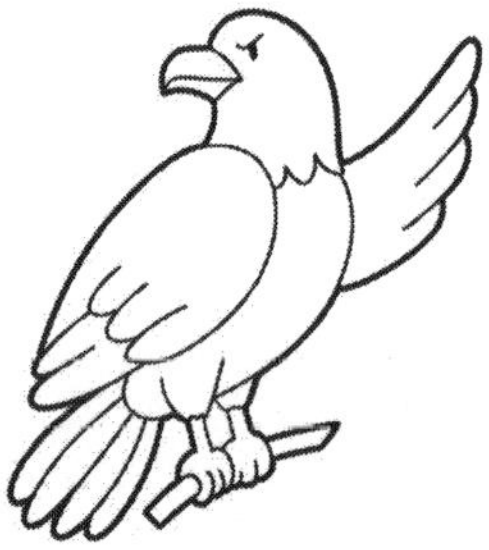

Eagle

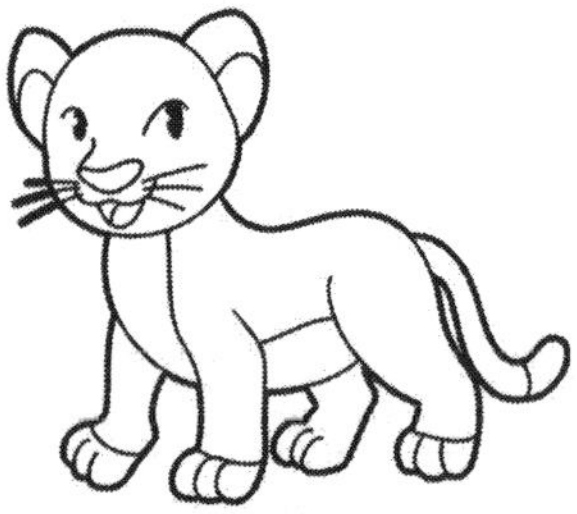

Puma

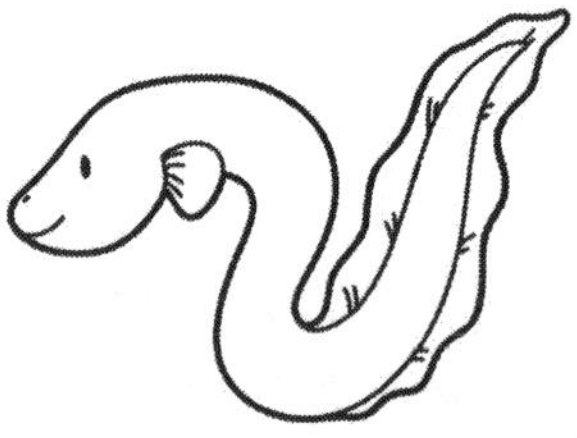

Eel

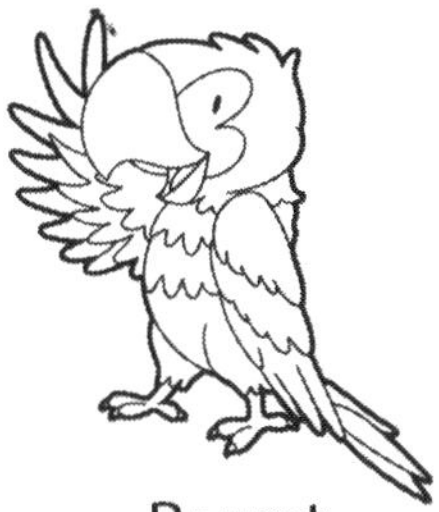
Parrot

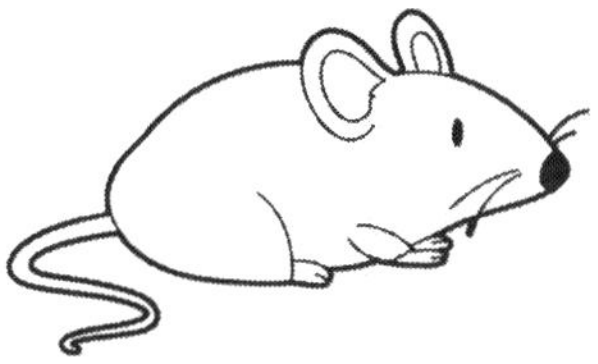
Mouse

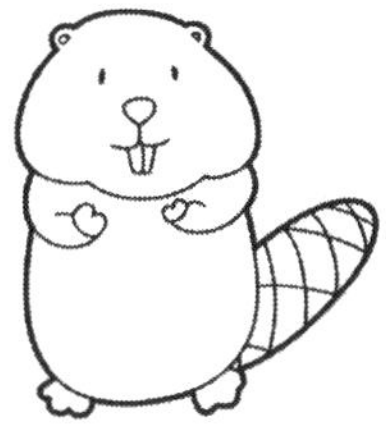
Beaver

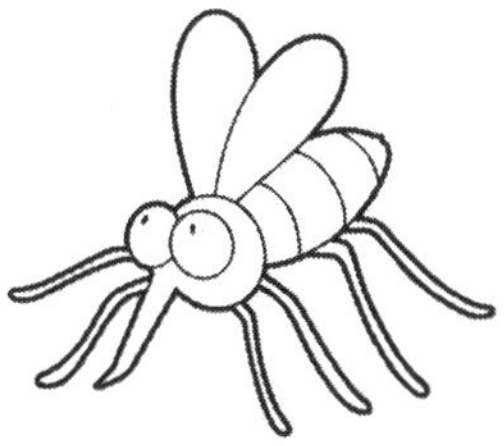
Mosquito

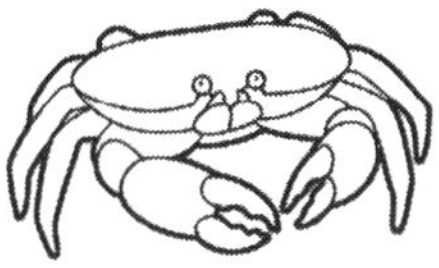
Crab

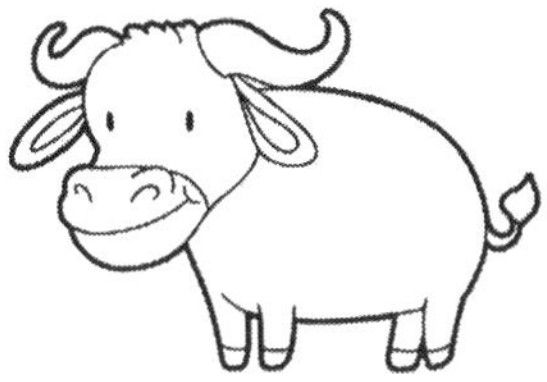
Bufflalo

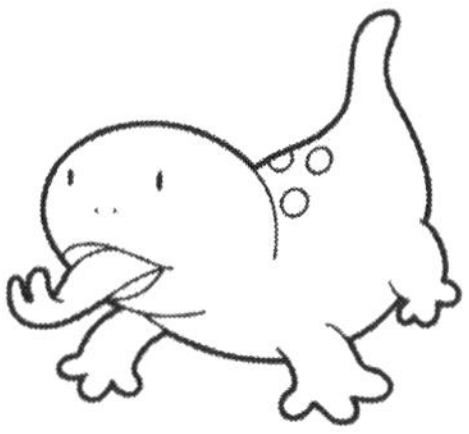
Lizard

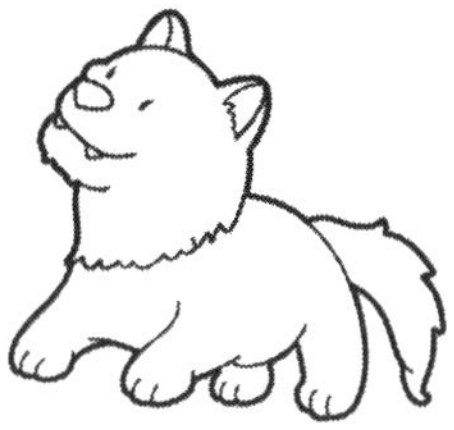
Wolf

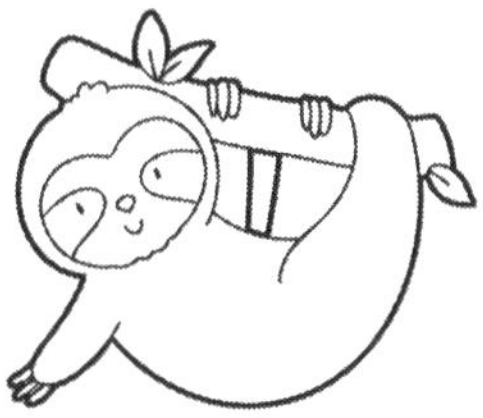
Sloth

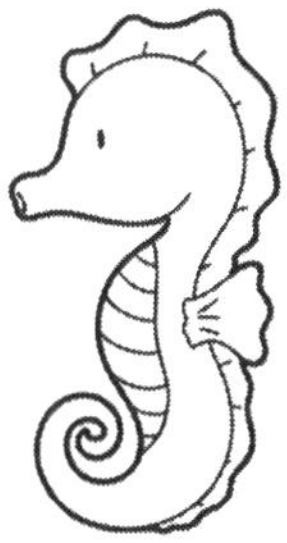
Seahorse

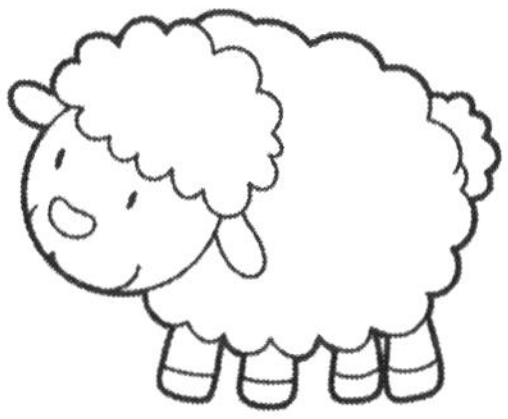
Lamb

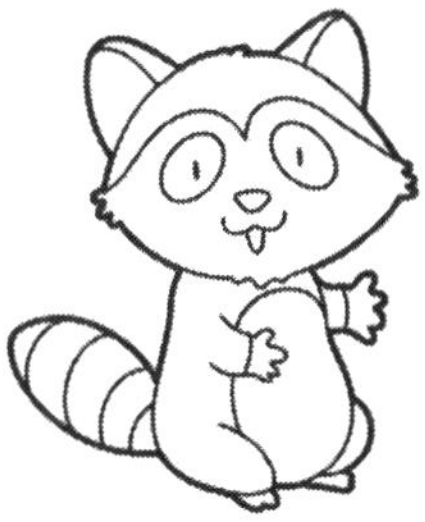
Raccoon

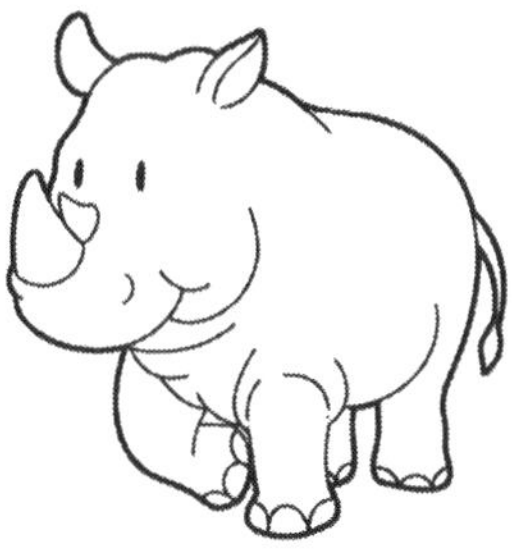
Rhinoceros

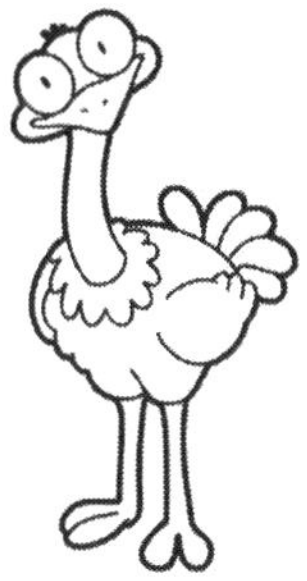
Ostrich

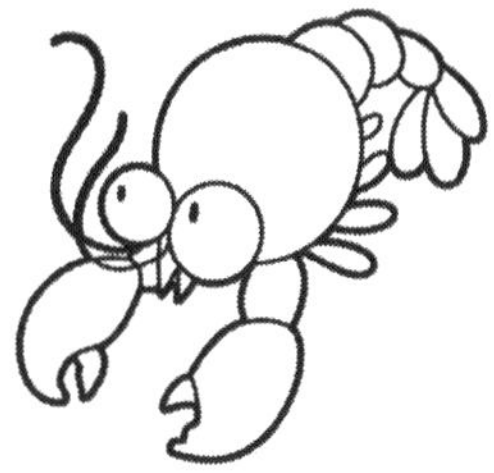
Lobster

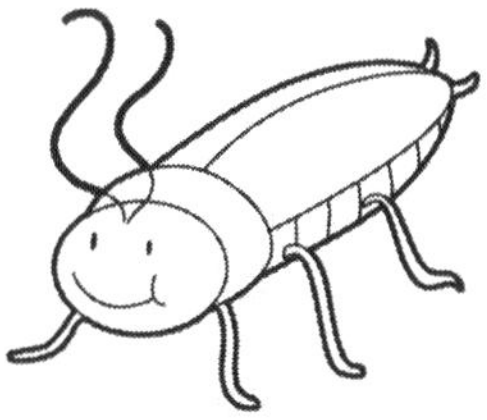
Cockroach

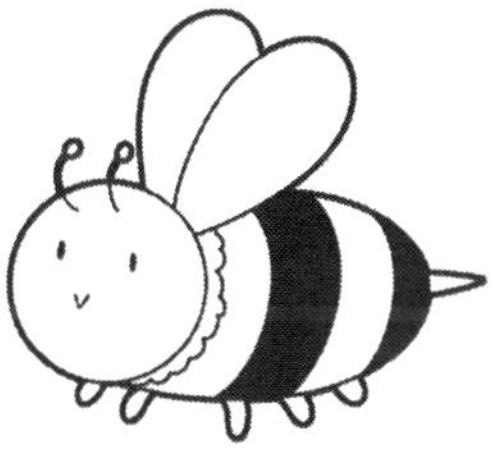
Bee

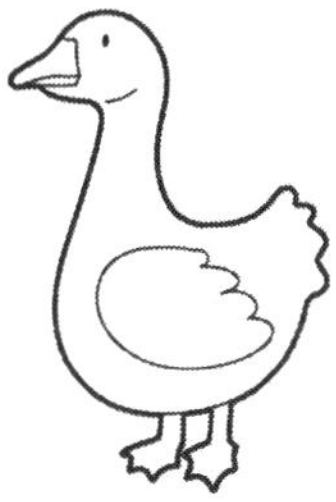
Goose

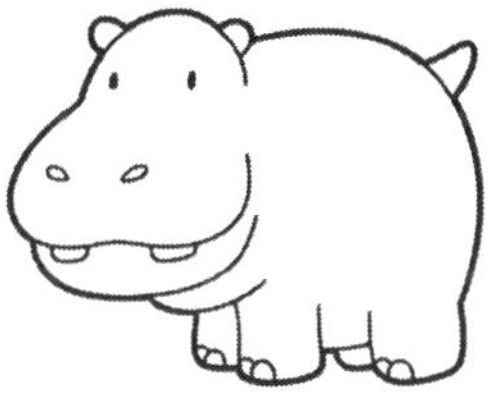
Hippopotamus

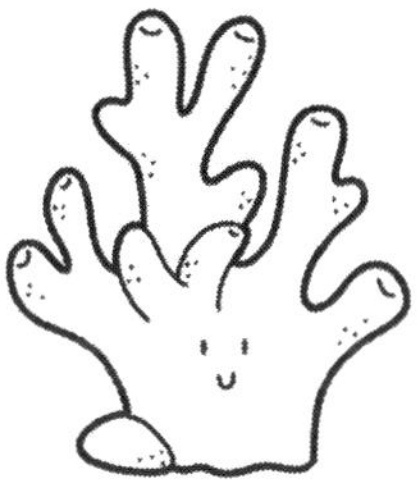
Coral

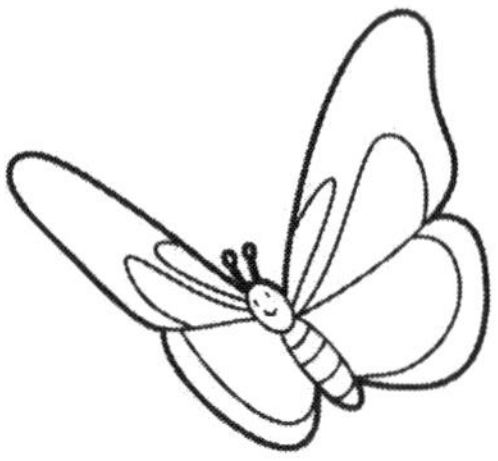

Butterfly

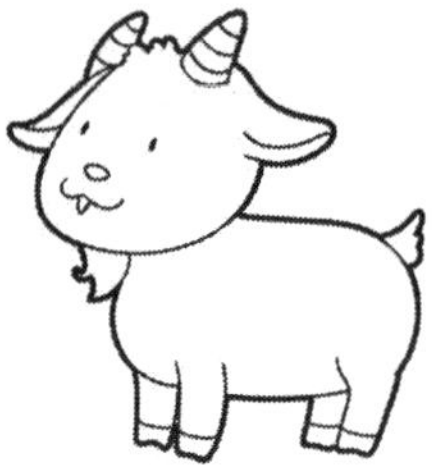

Goat

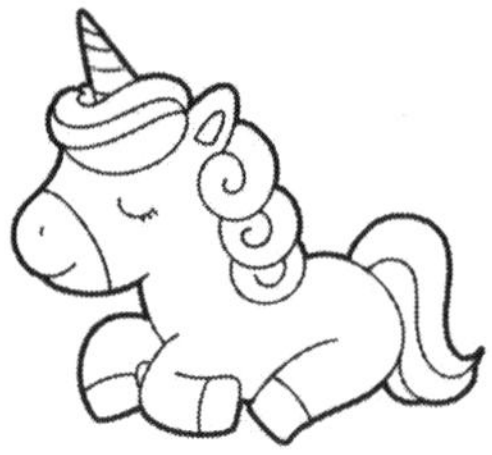

Unicorn

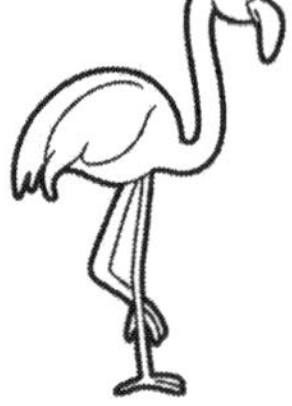

Flamigo

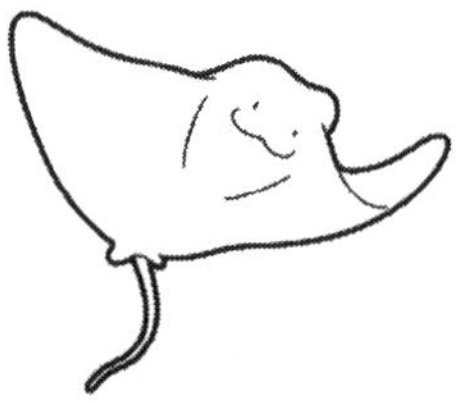

Stingray

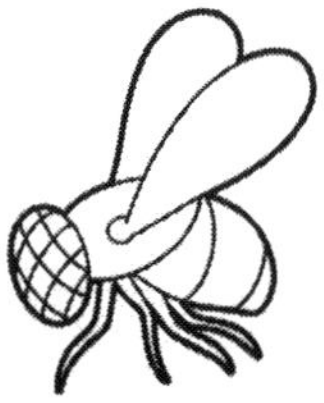

Fly

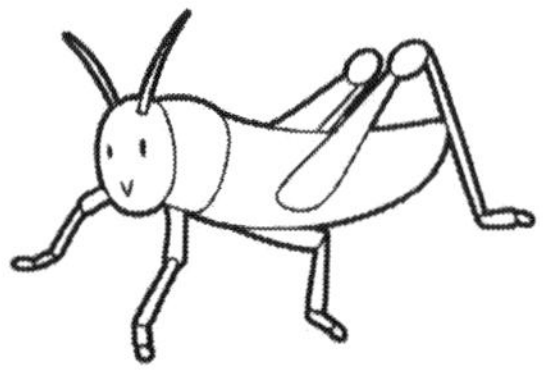

Grasshopper

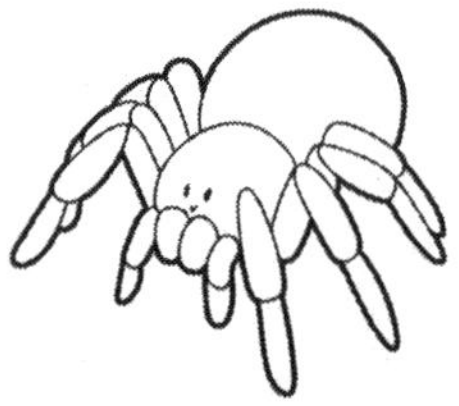

Spider

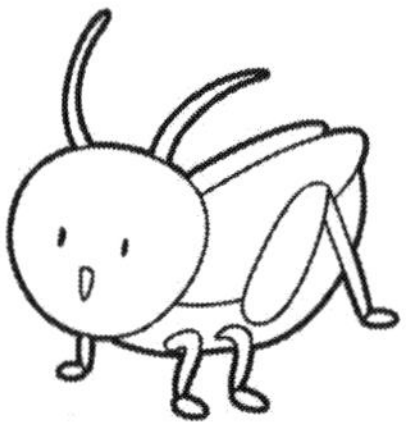

Cricket

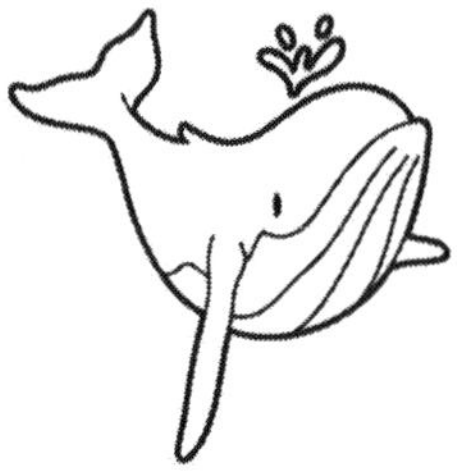

Whale

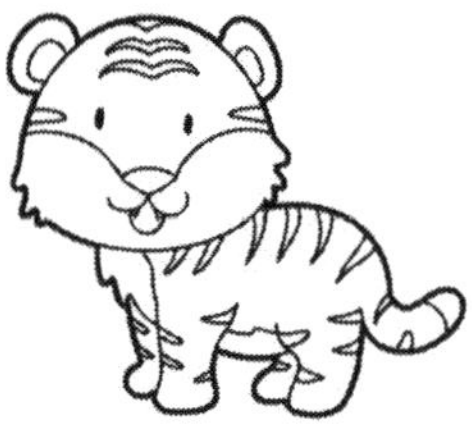

Tiger

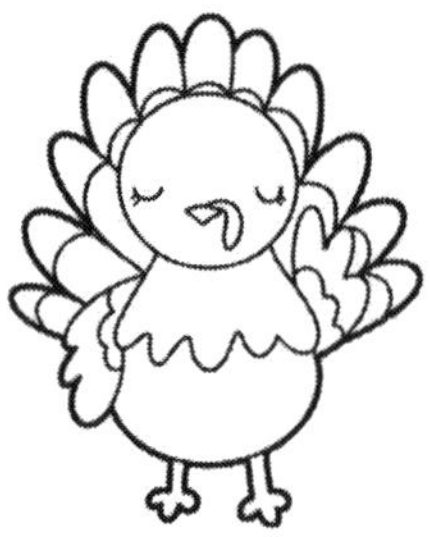

Turkey

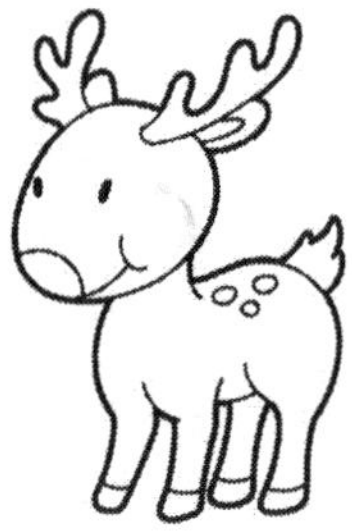

Deer

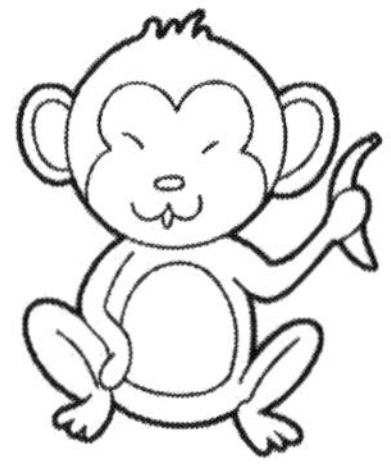

Monkey

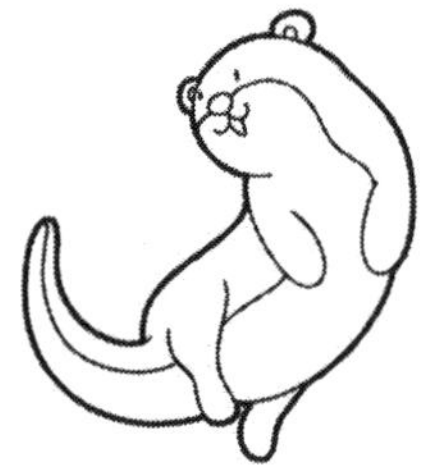

Otter

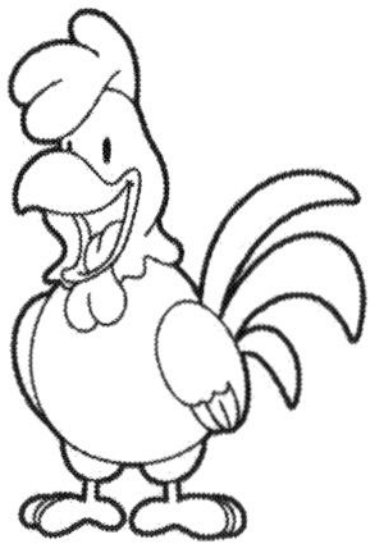

Rooster

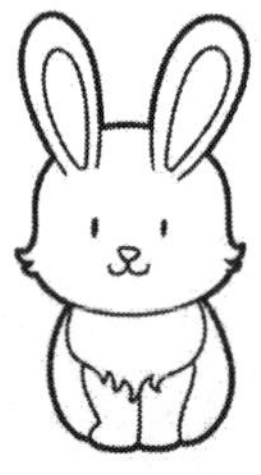

Rabbit

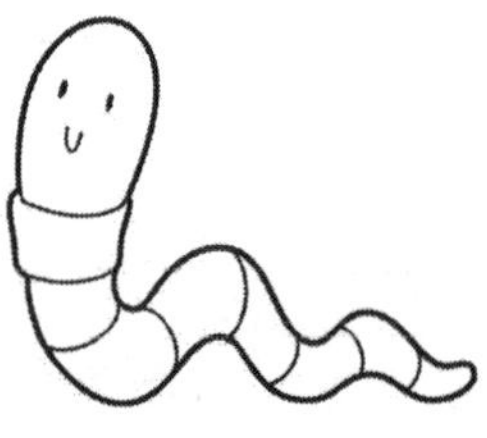

Worm

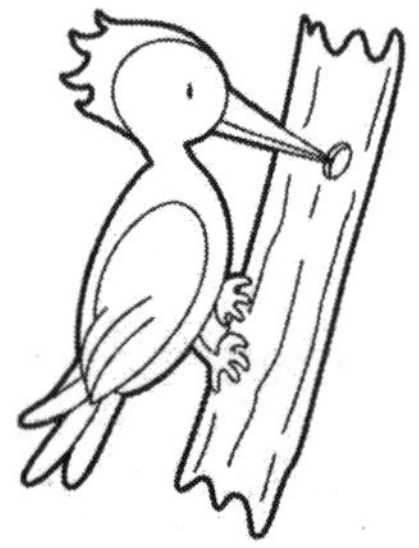

Woodpecker

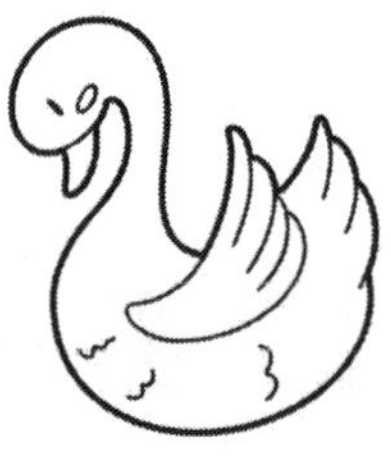

Swan

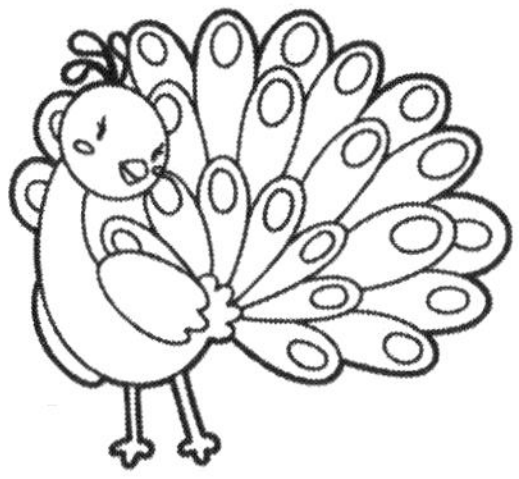

Peacock

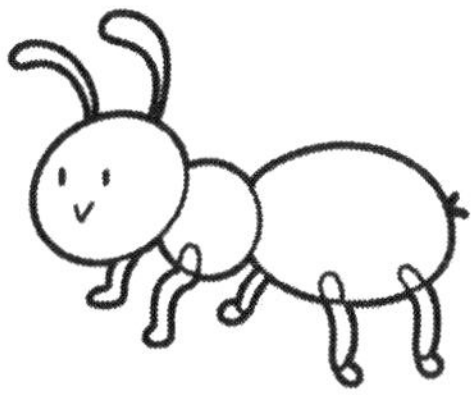

Ant

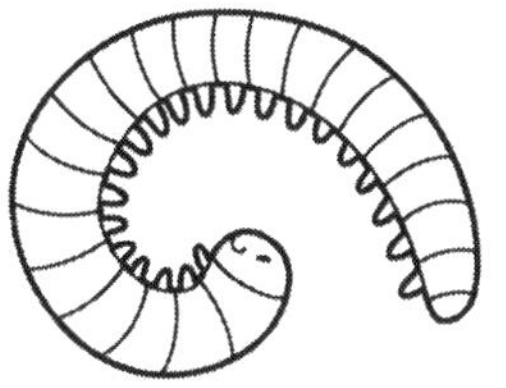

Milipede

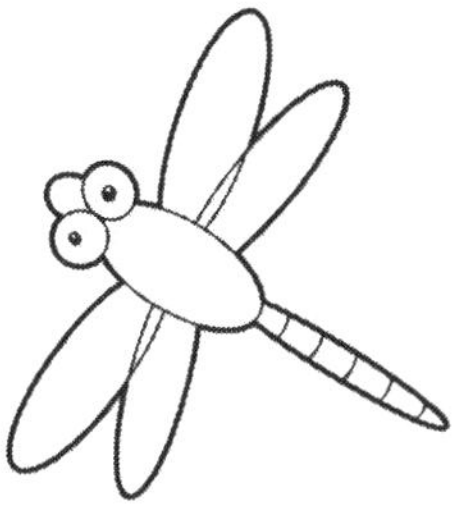

Dragonfly

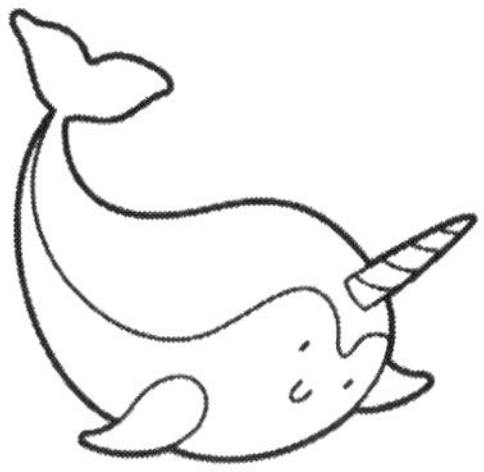

Narwhal

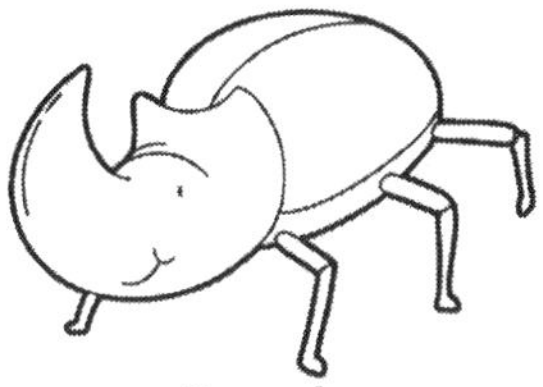

Beetle

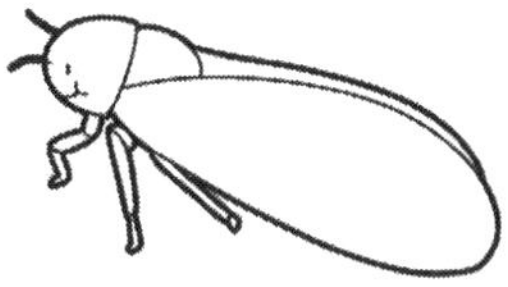

Cicada

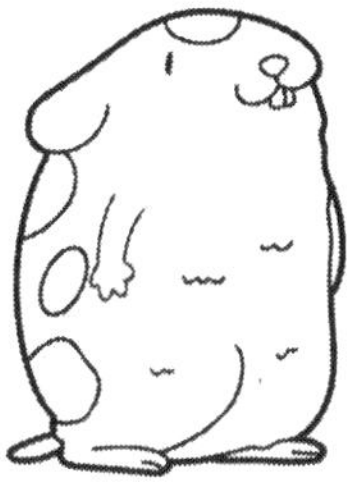

Hamster

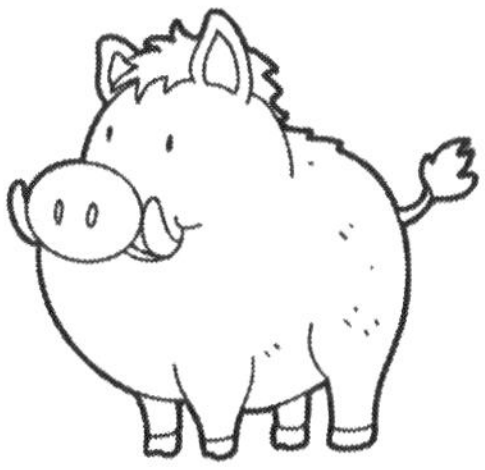

Boar

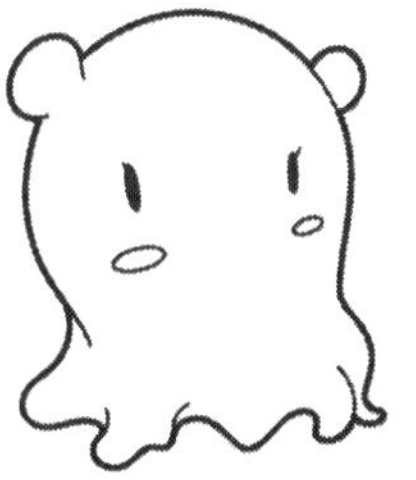

Dumbo Octopus

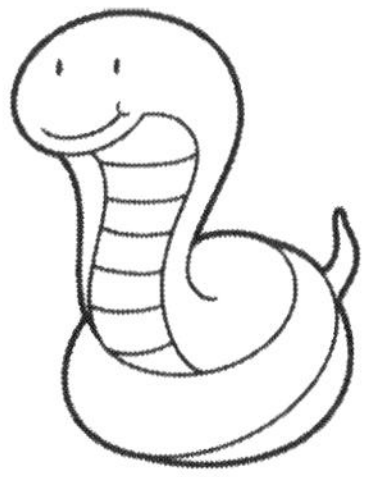

Cobra

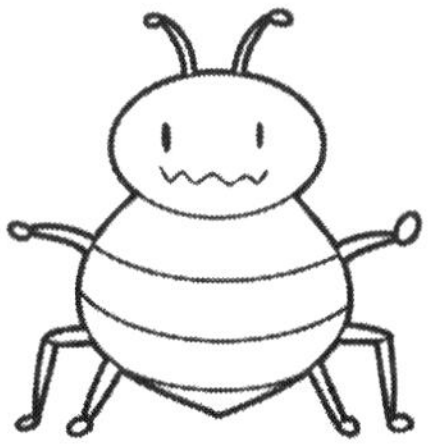

Flea

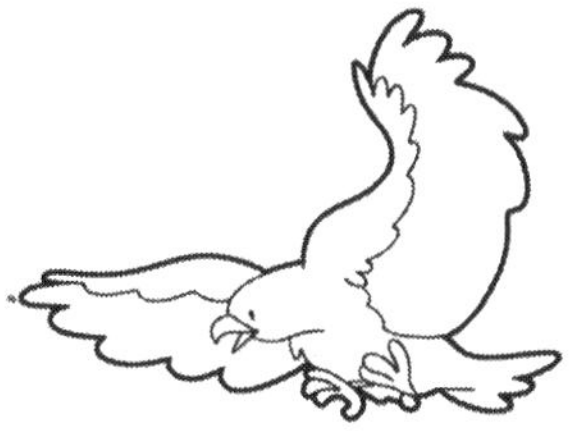

Falcon

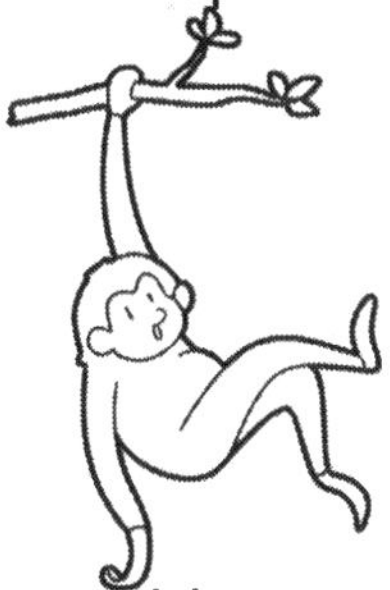

Gibbon

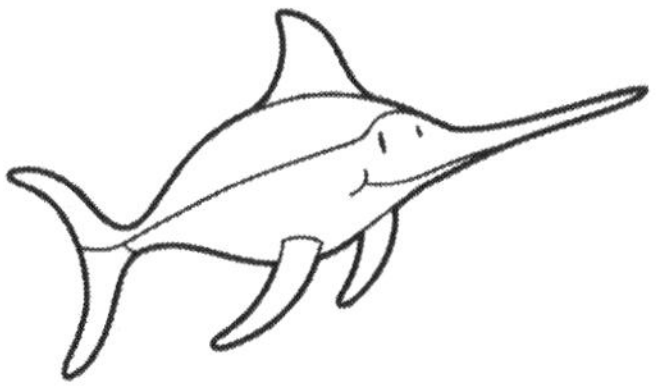

Swordfish

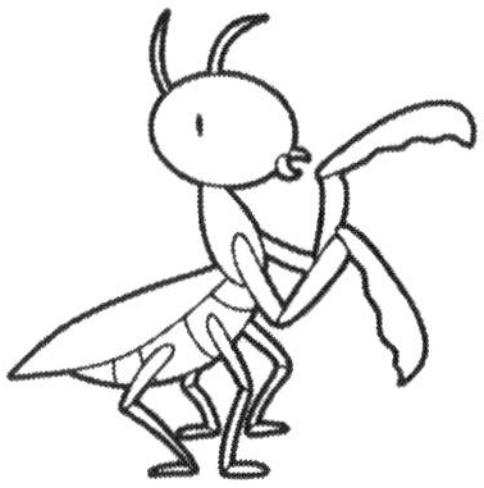

Mantis

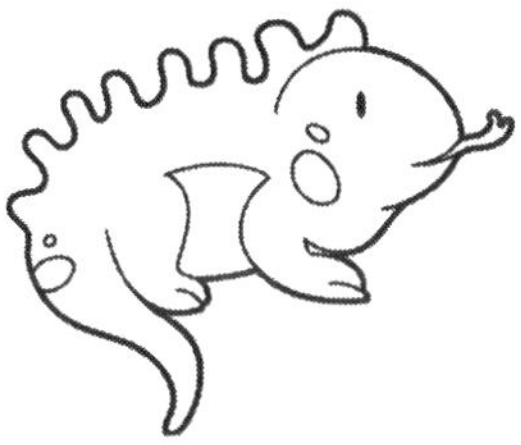

Iguana

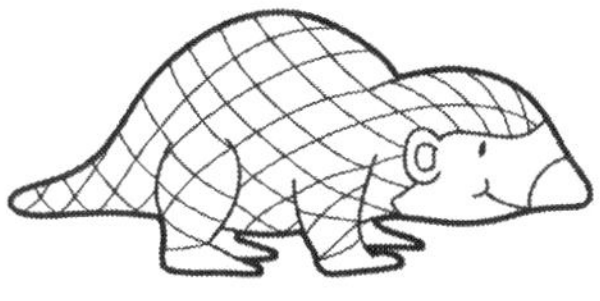

Pangolin

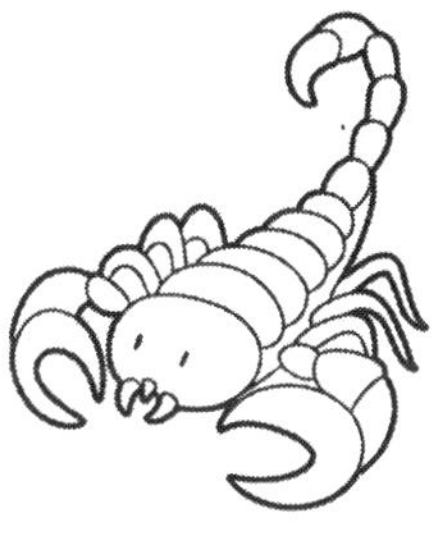

Scorpion

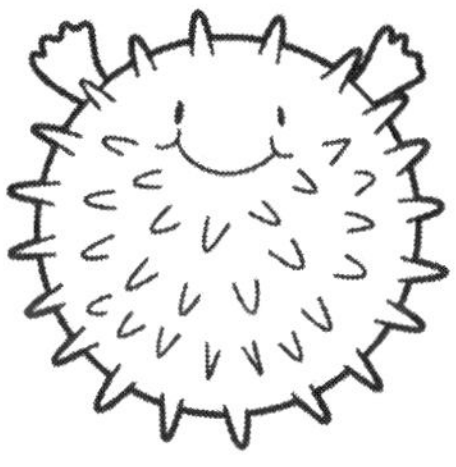

Pufferfish

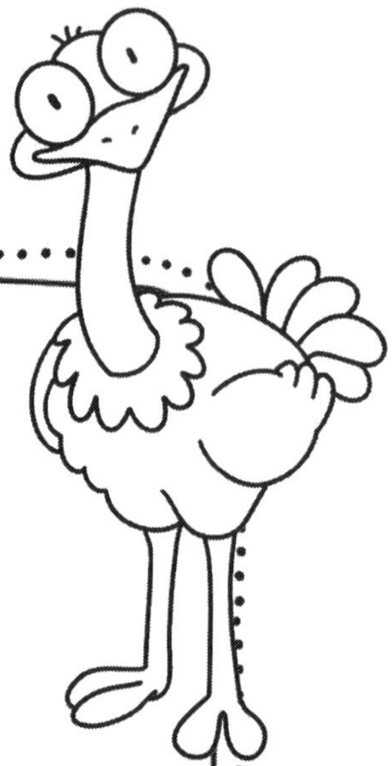

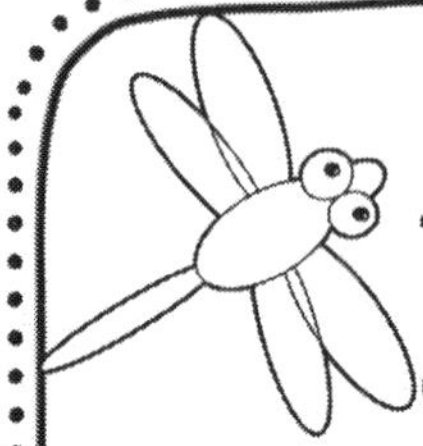

There are many things that you can draw at anytime.
Do not worry if you cannot draw perfectly because nobody can. Practice makes perfect, so keep practicing!!!

LET'S CHECK iT OUT!

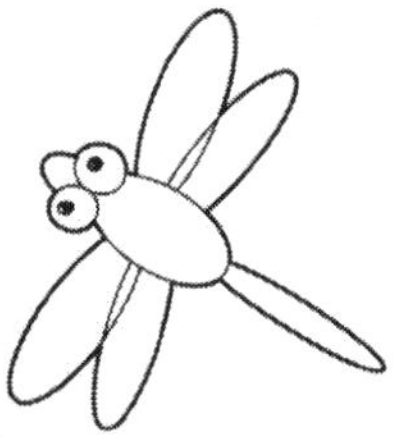

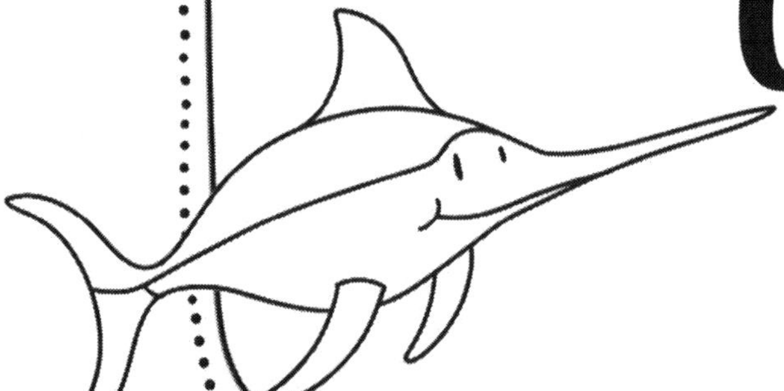

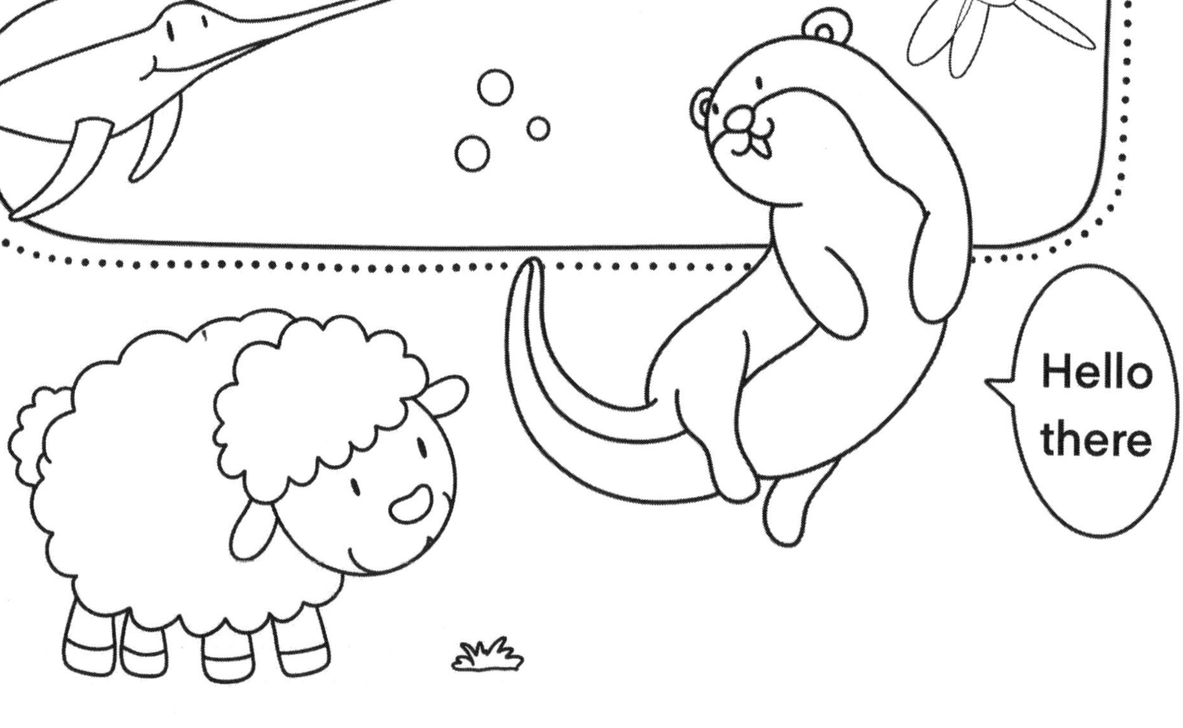

Dog

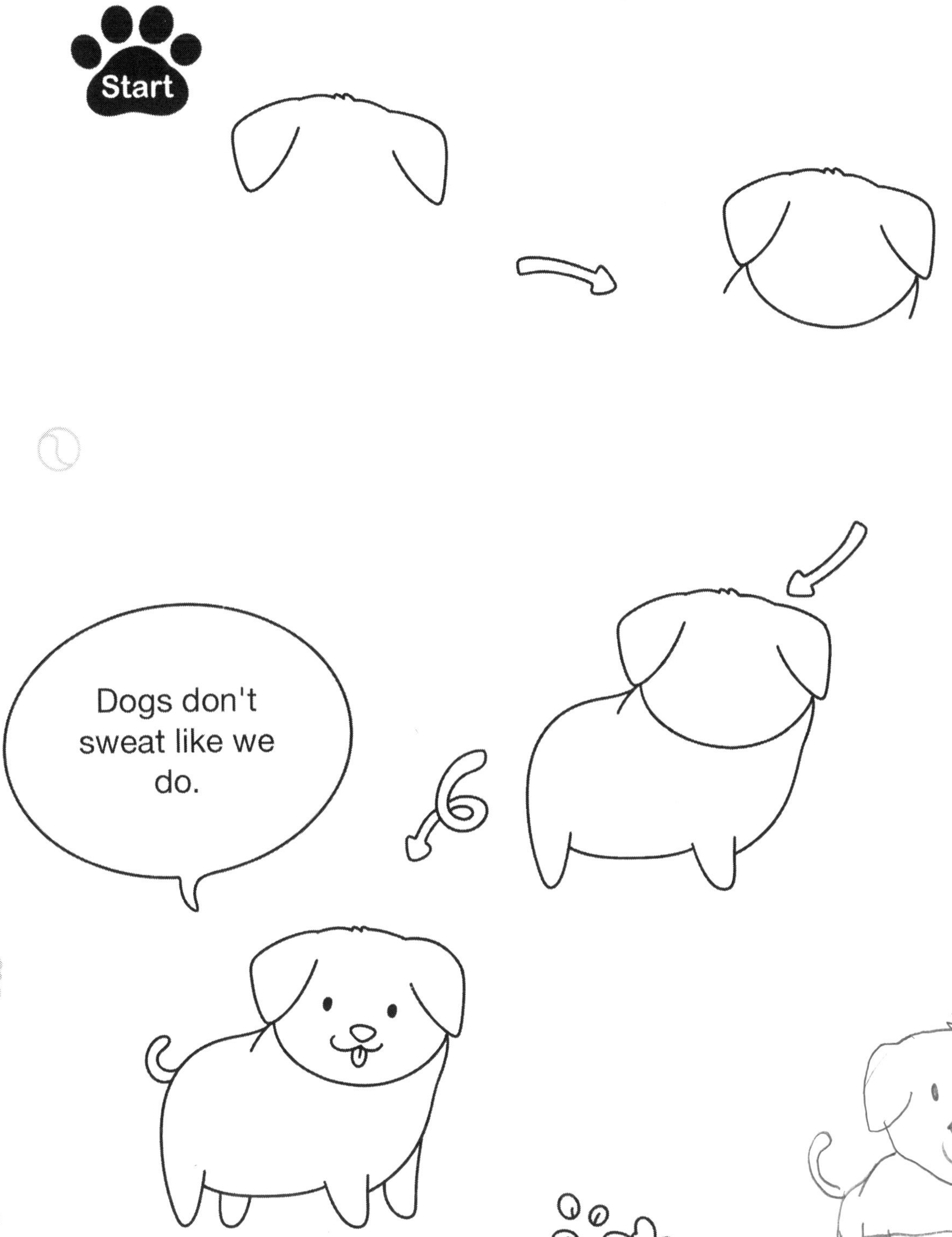

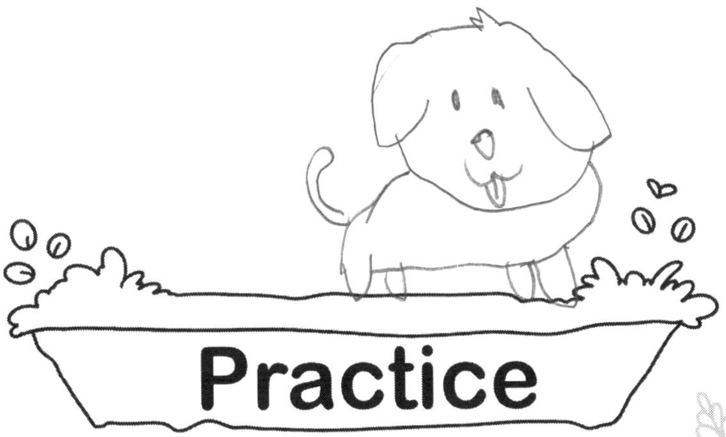

Cat

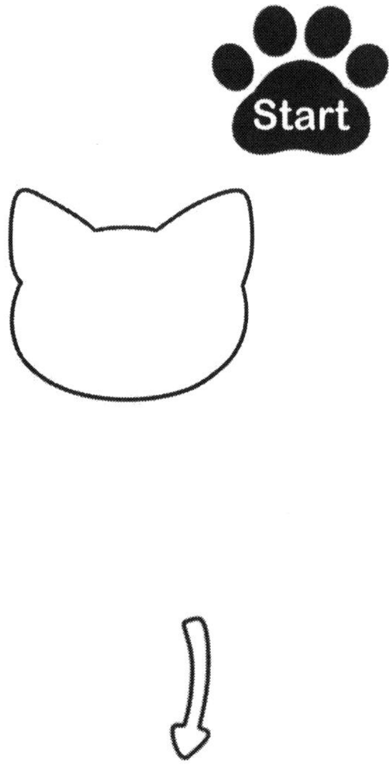

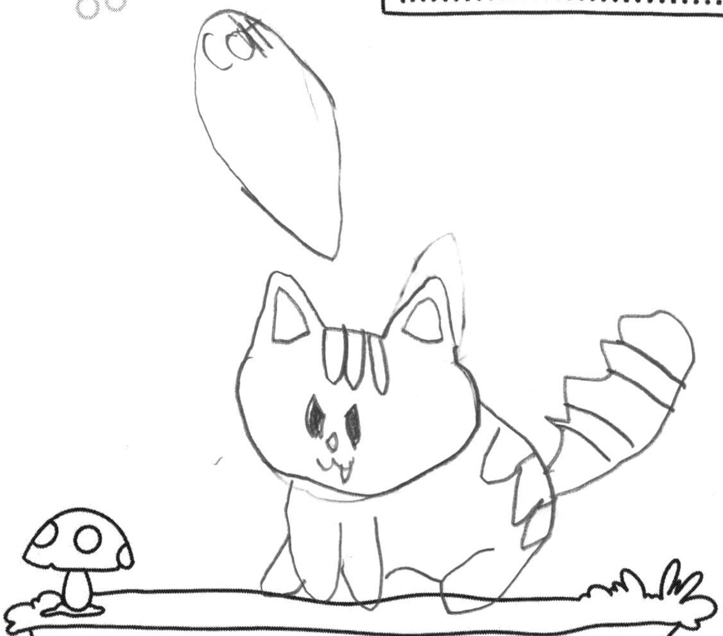

Practice

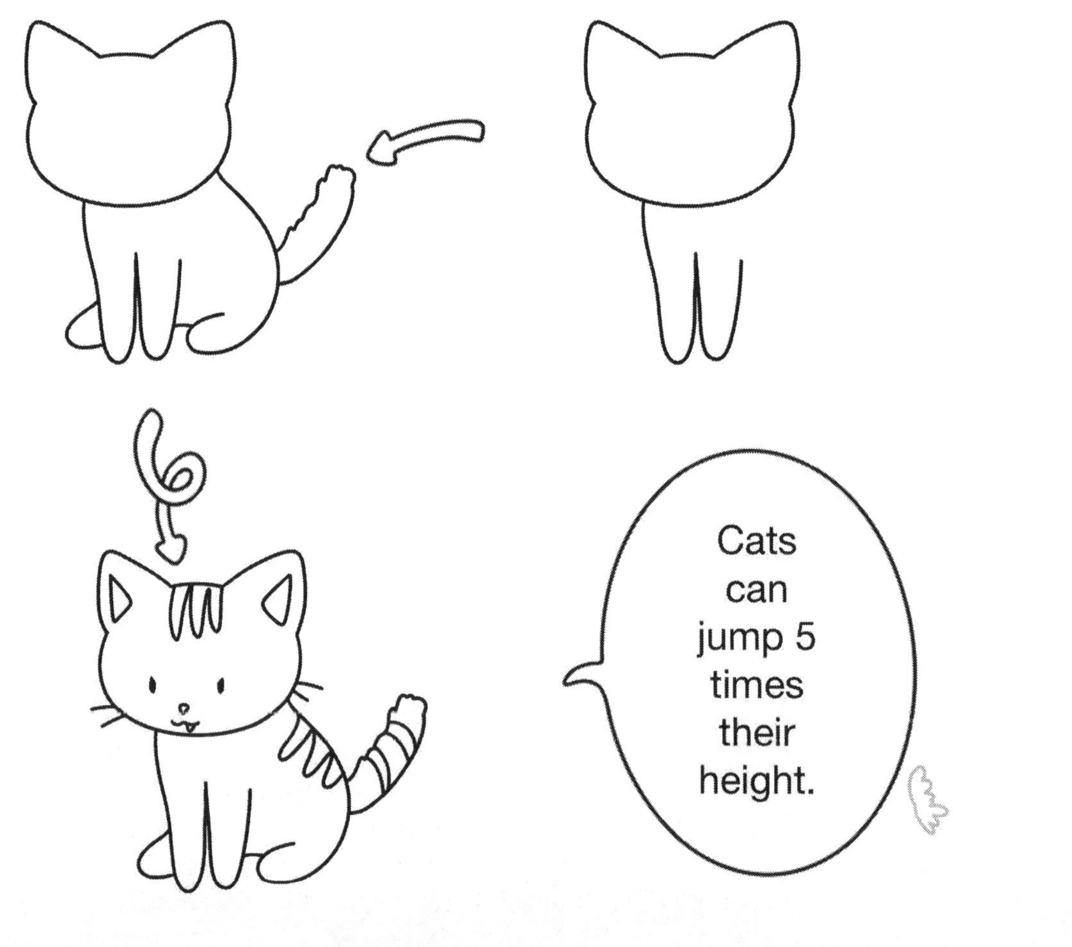

Chick

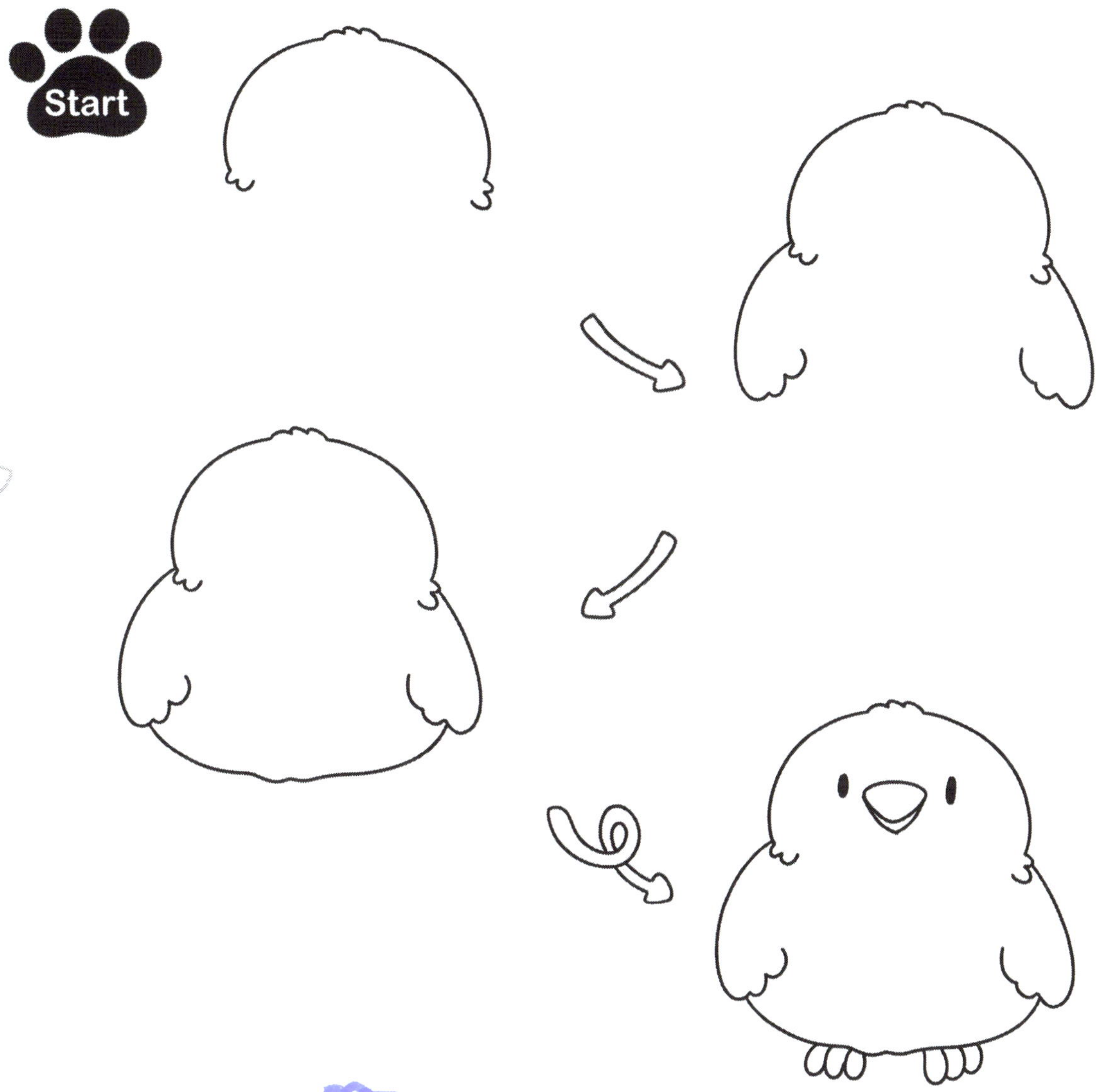

Chicken can recognize over 100 faces.

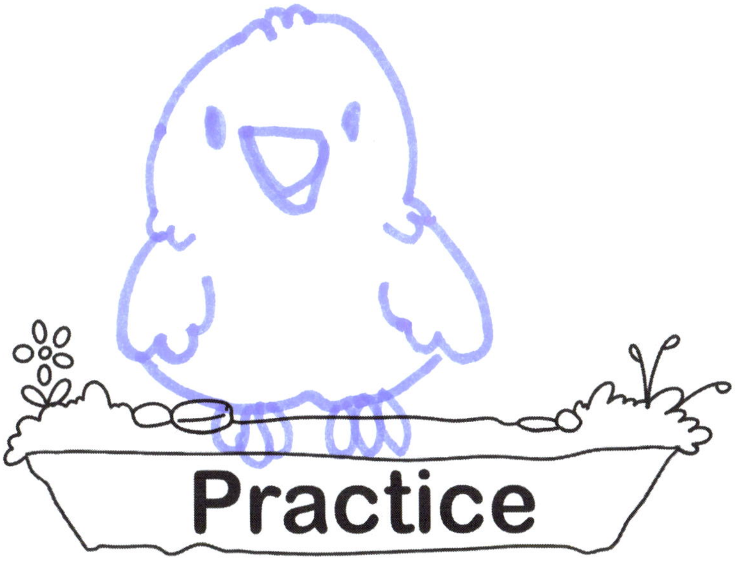

Panda

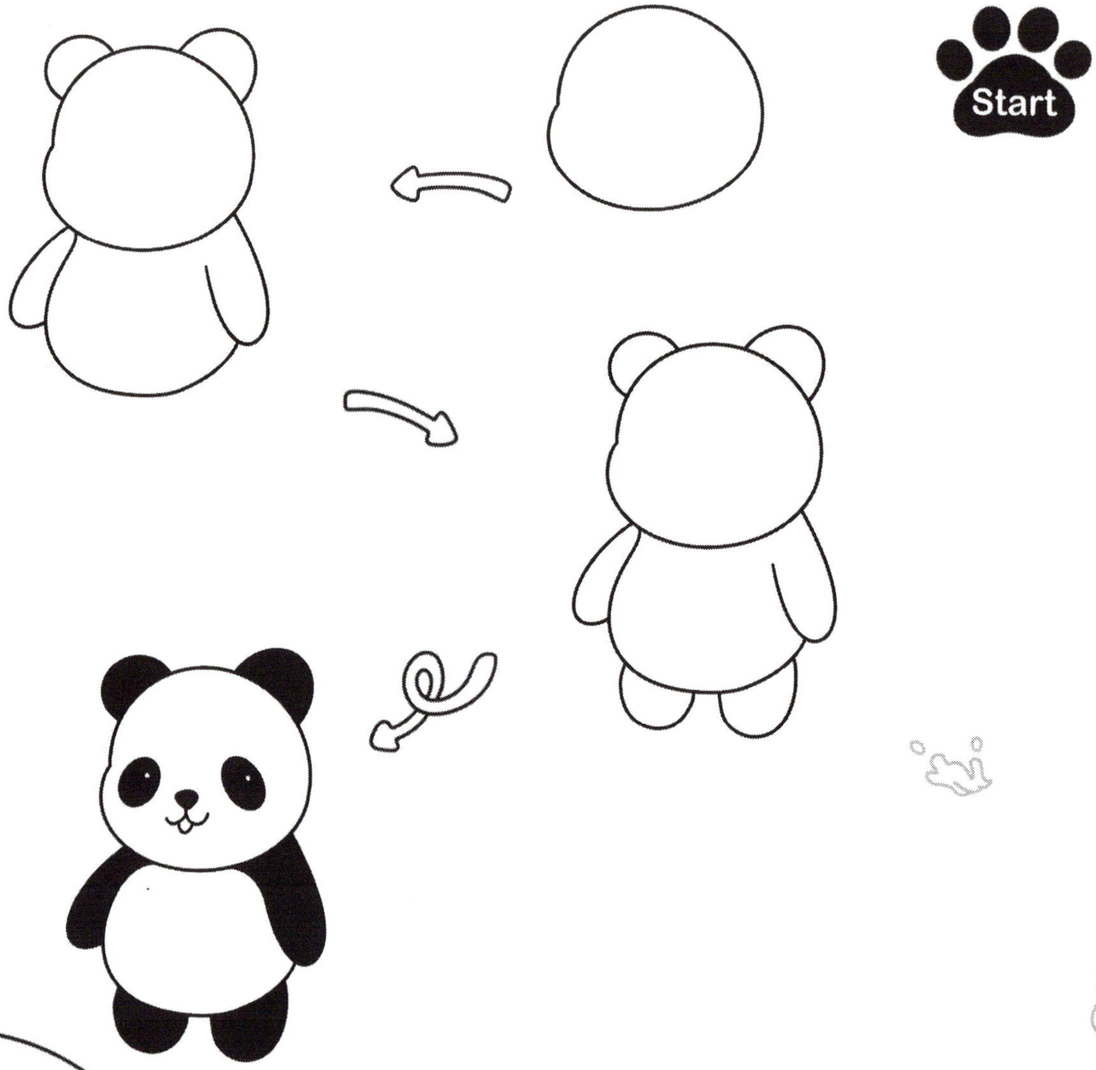

Pandas spend a lot of their day eating.

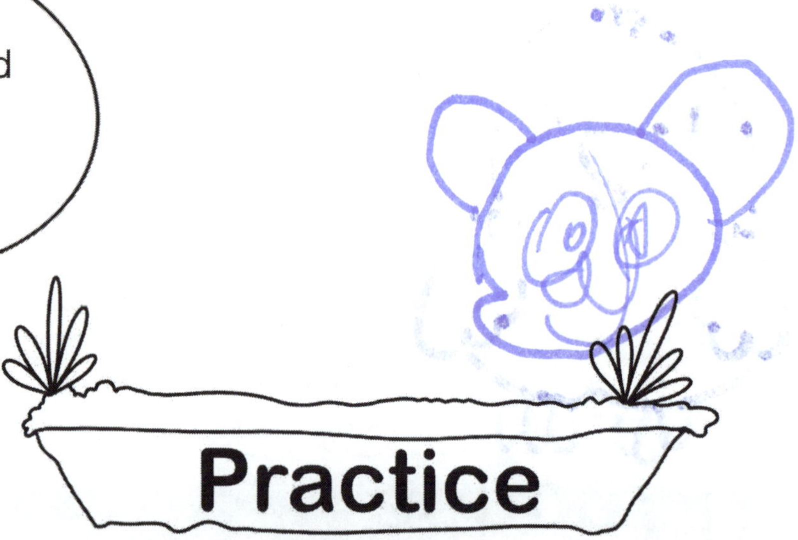

Starfish

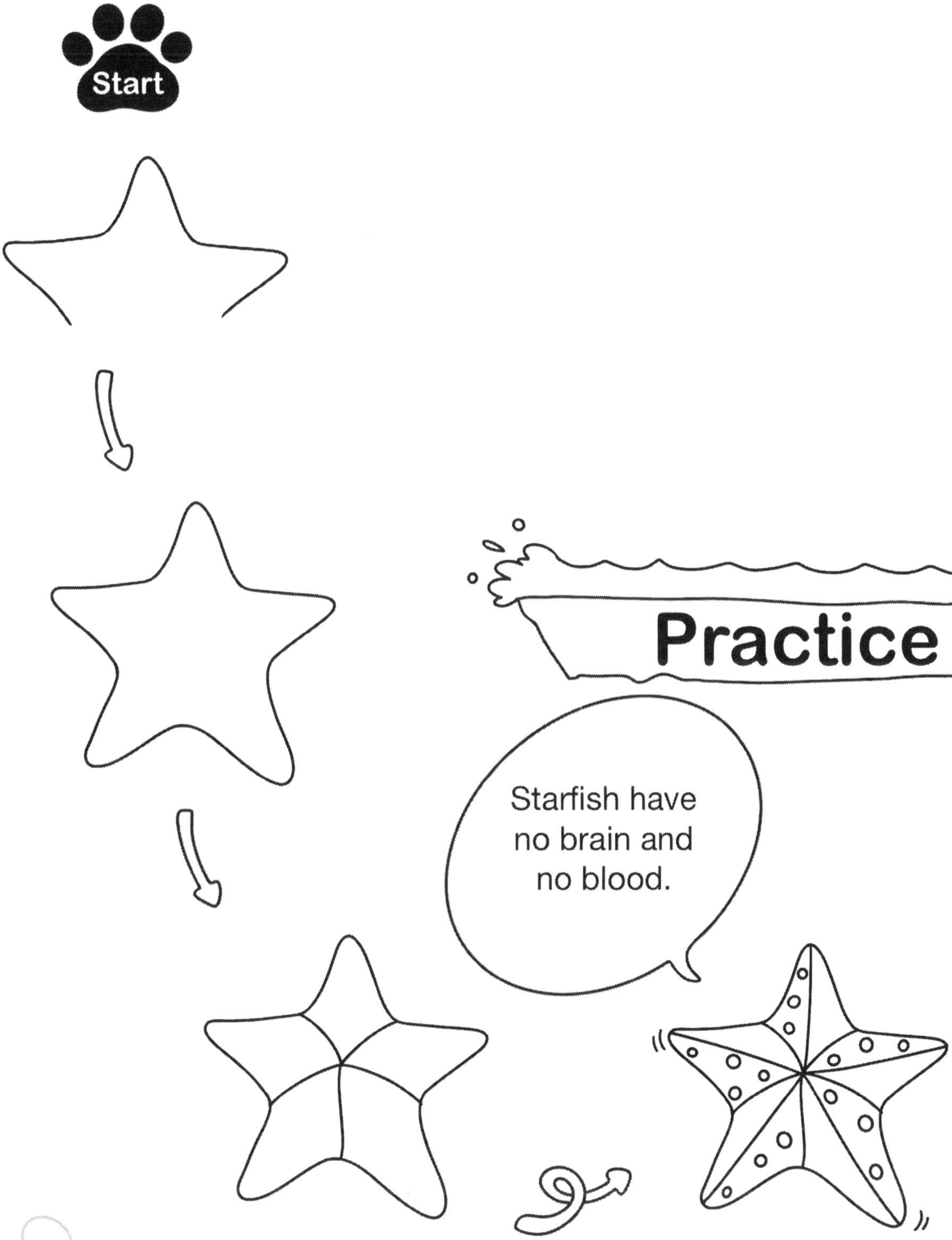

Practice

Snake

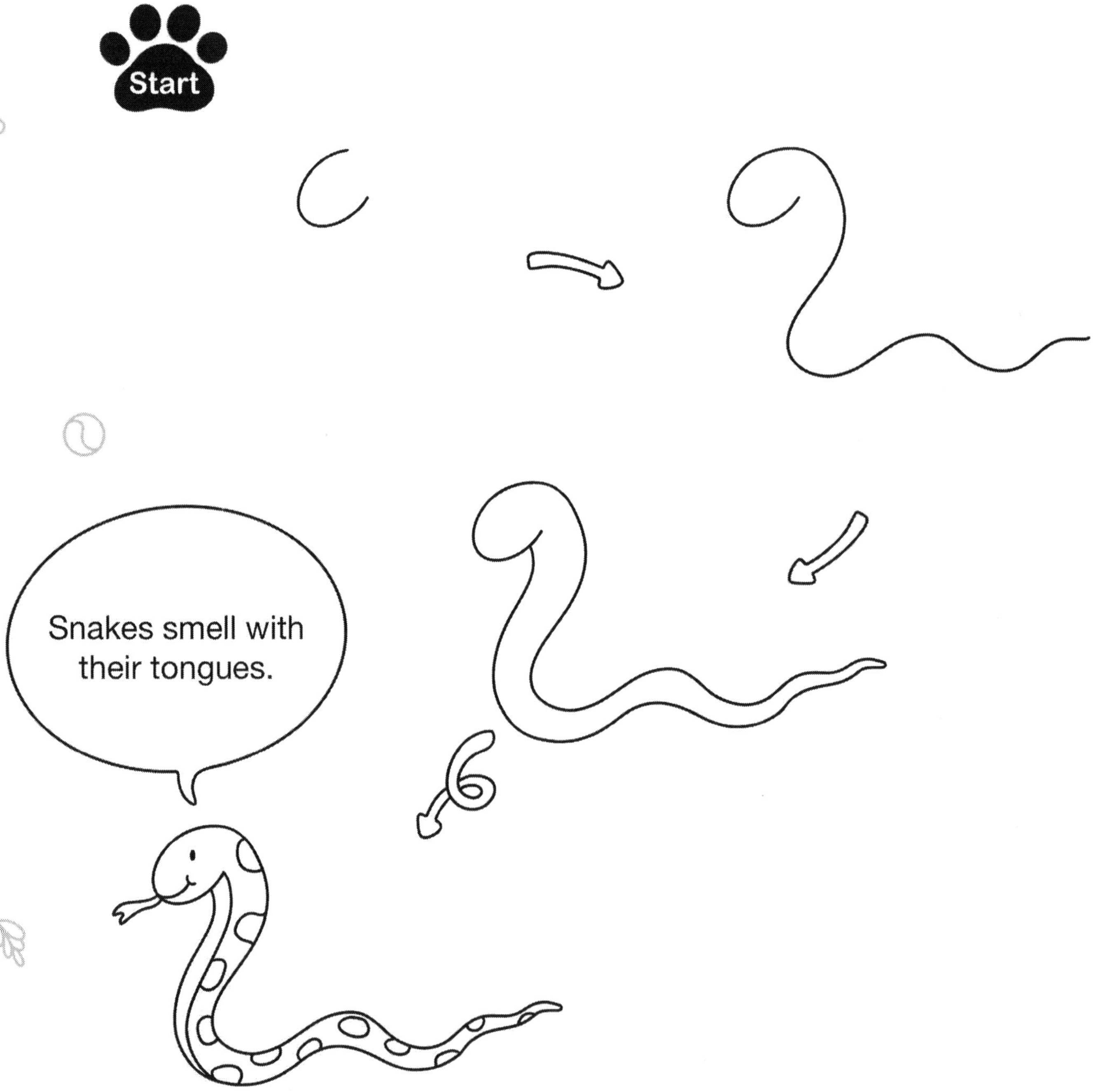

Practice

Squirrel

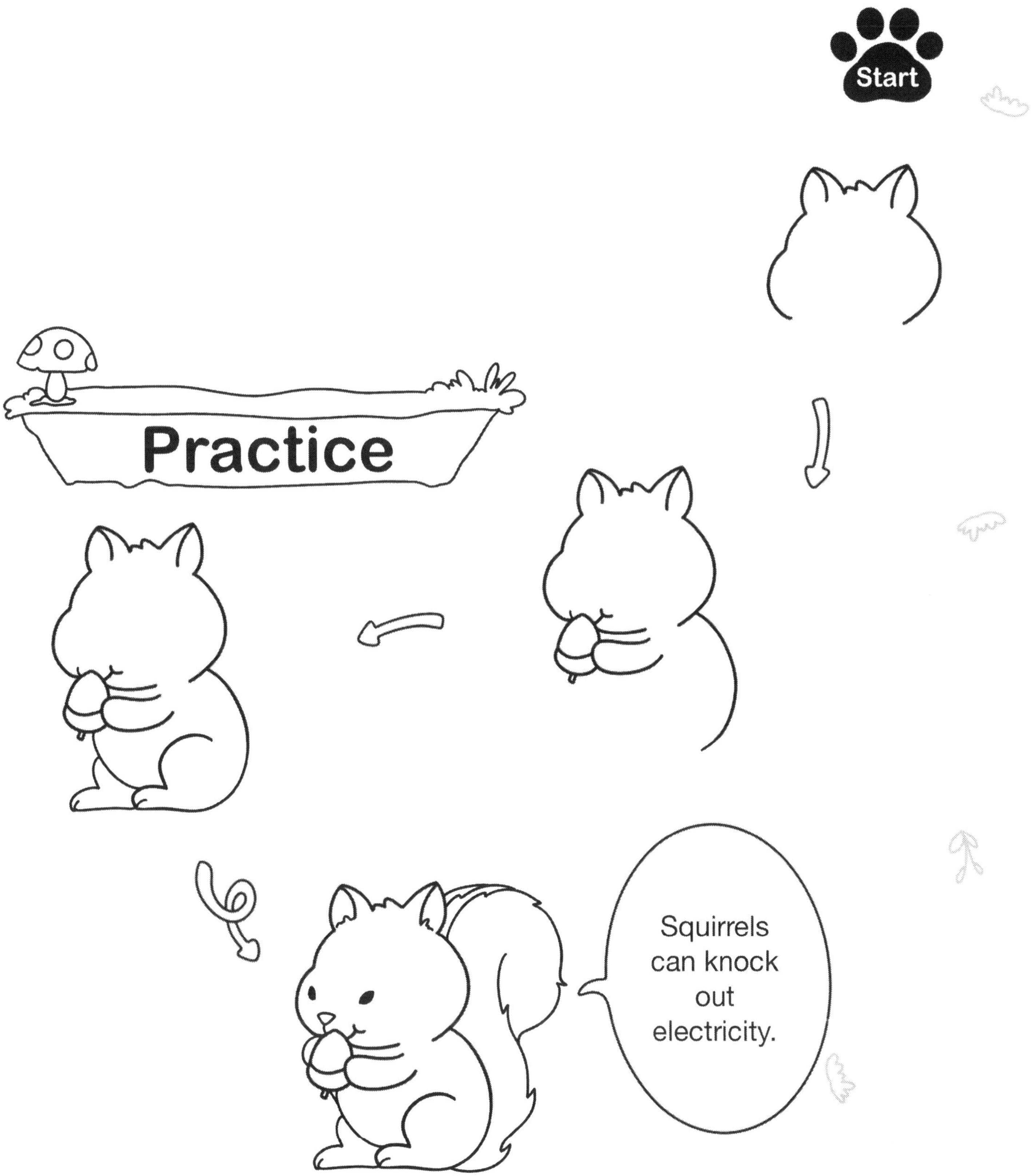

Giraffe

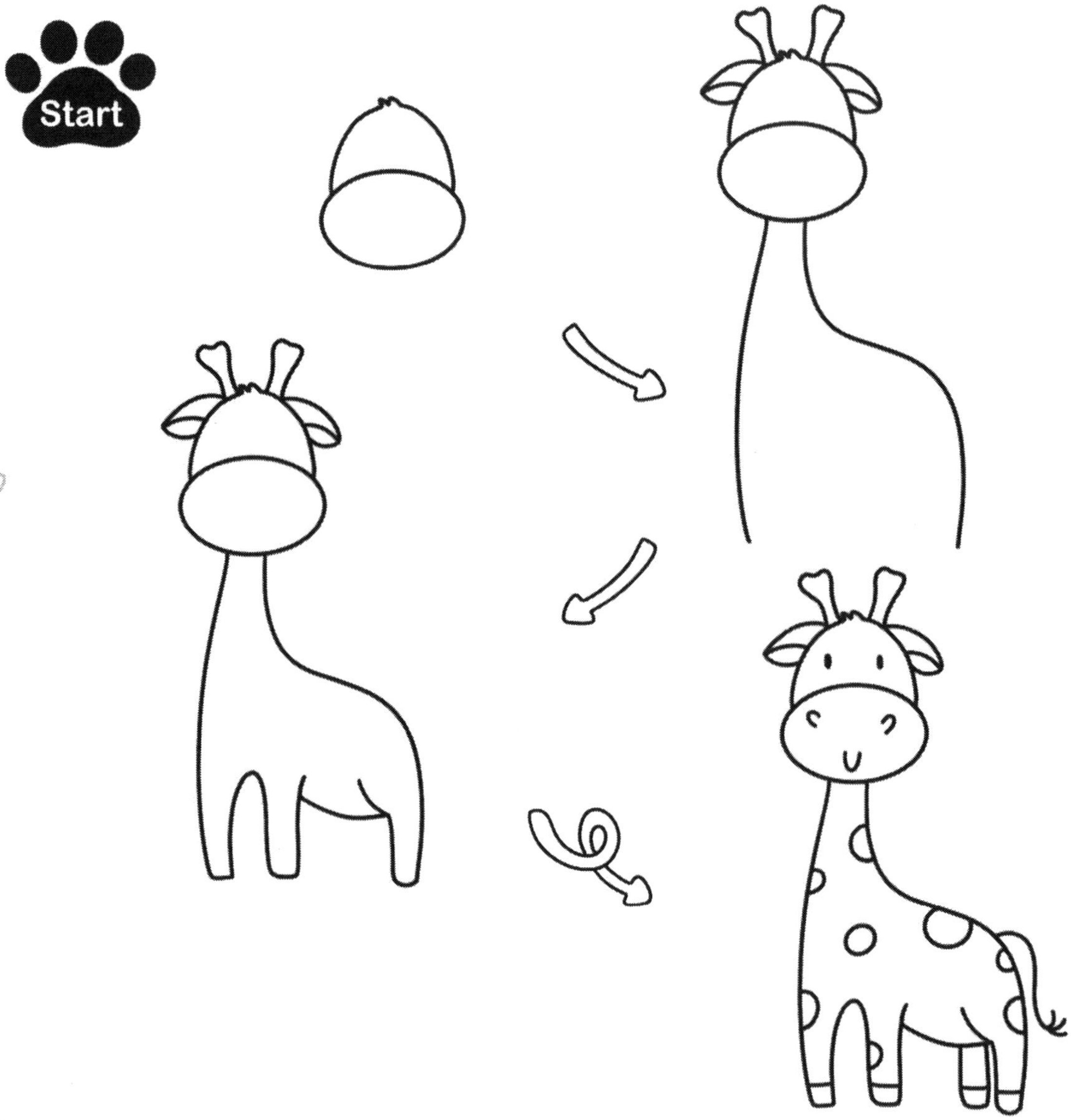

Giraffes have hearts that are 2 feet long.

Practice

Llama

Start

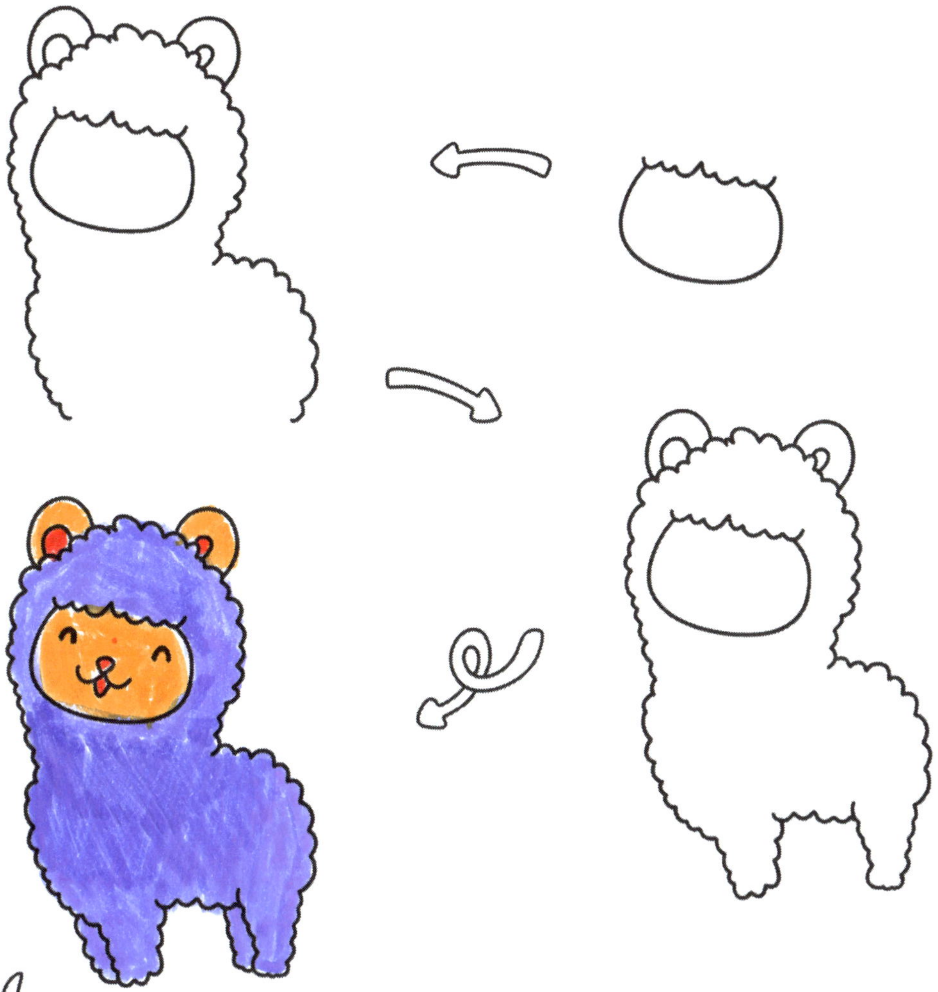

Llamas can run at a pace of up to 35 miles per hour.

Practice

Jellyfish

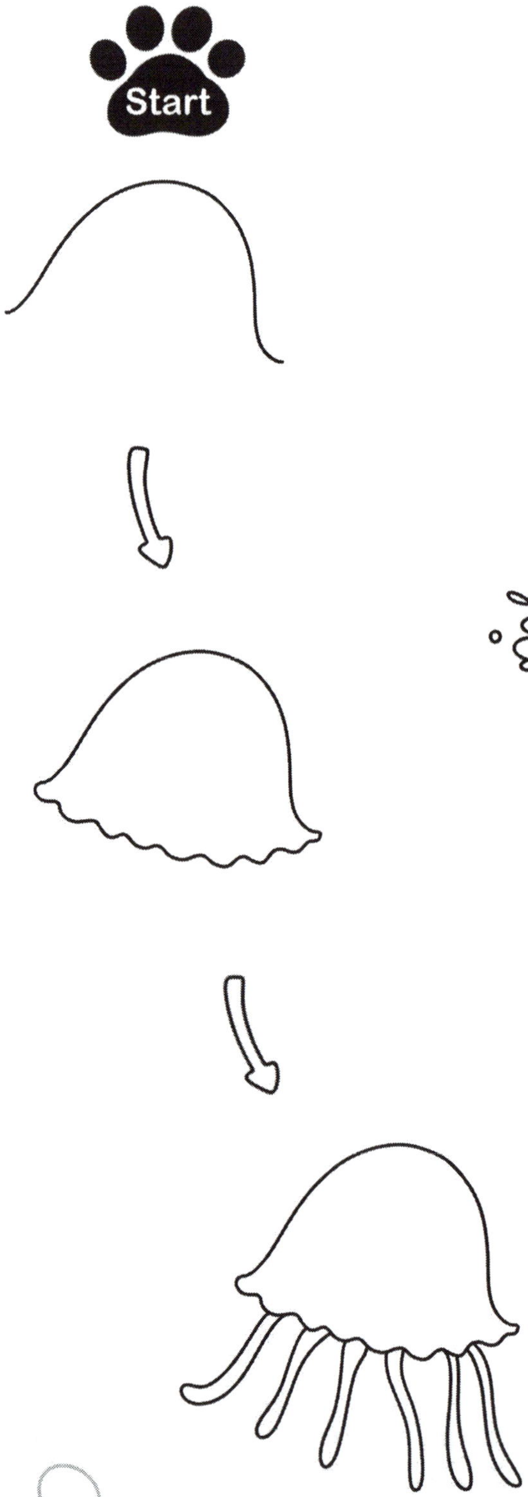

Practice

Jellyfish can glow in the dark.

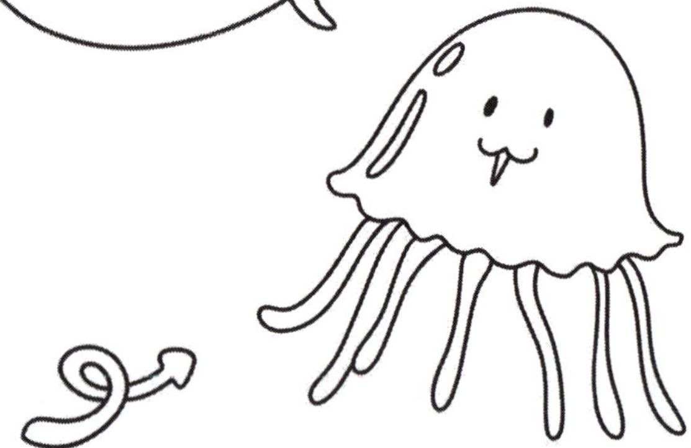

Bear

Start

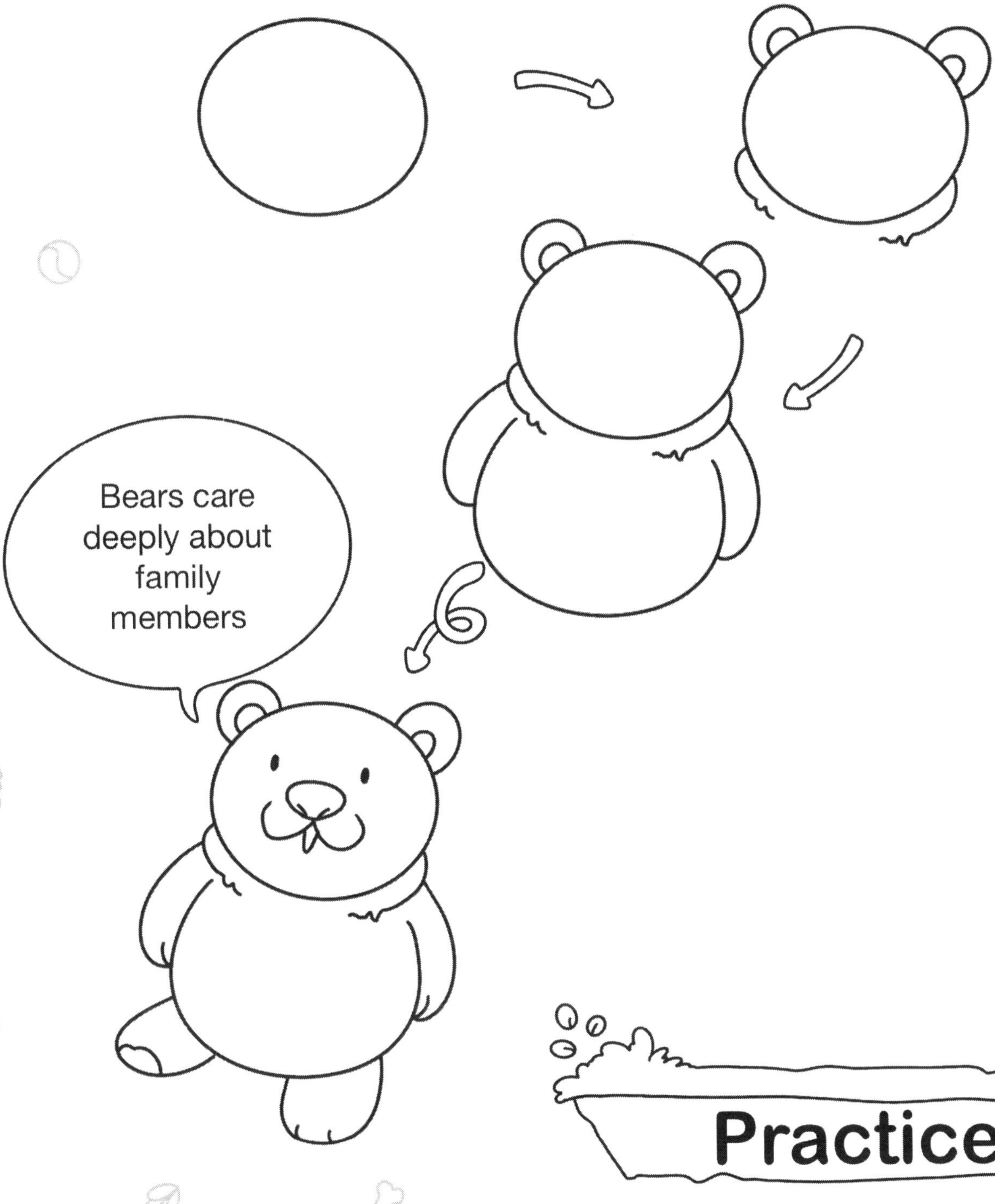

Practice

Camel

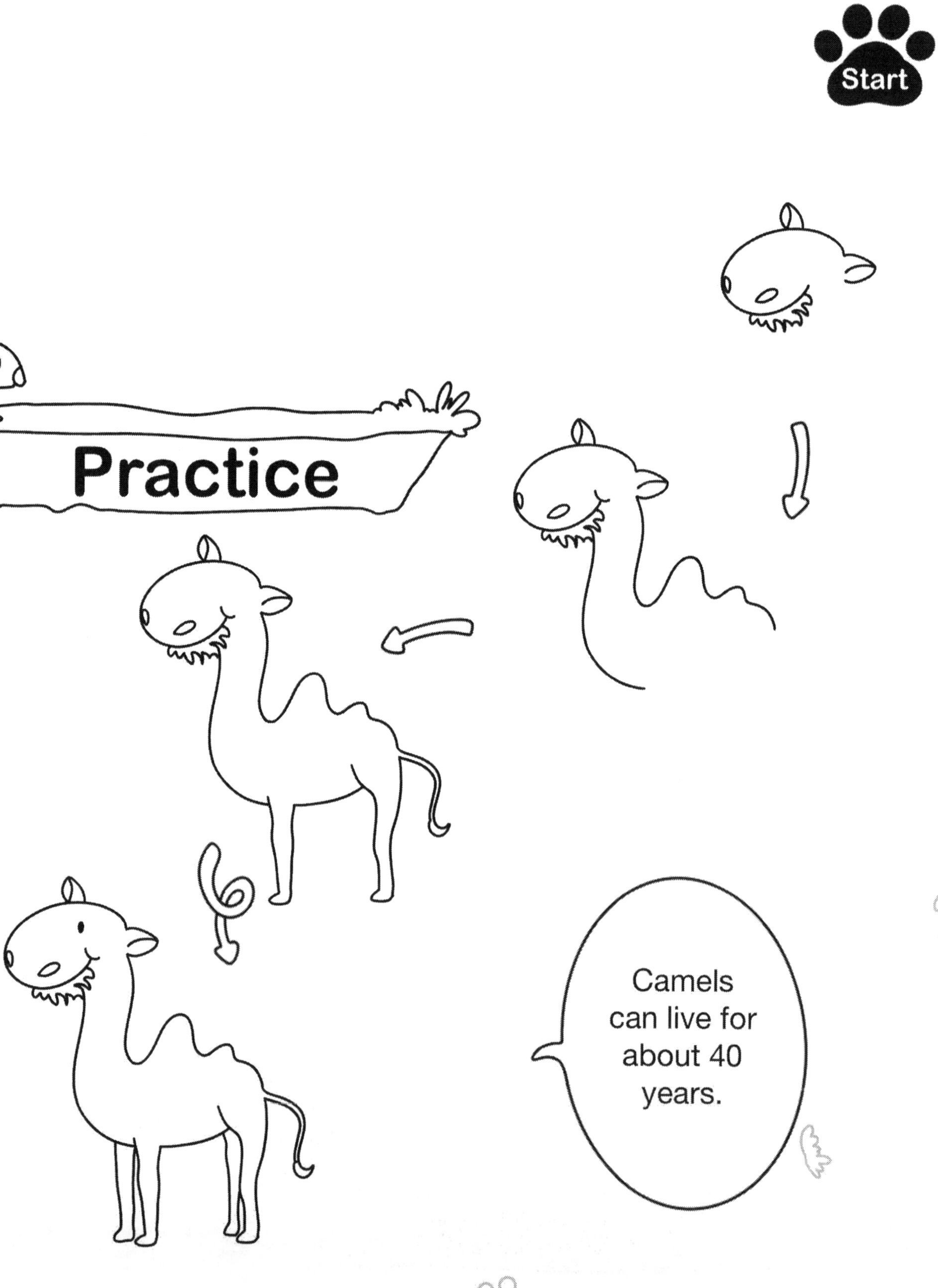

Practice

Camels can live for about 40 years.

Pig

Start

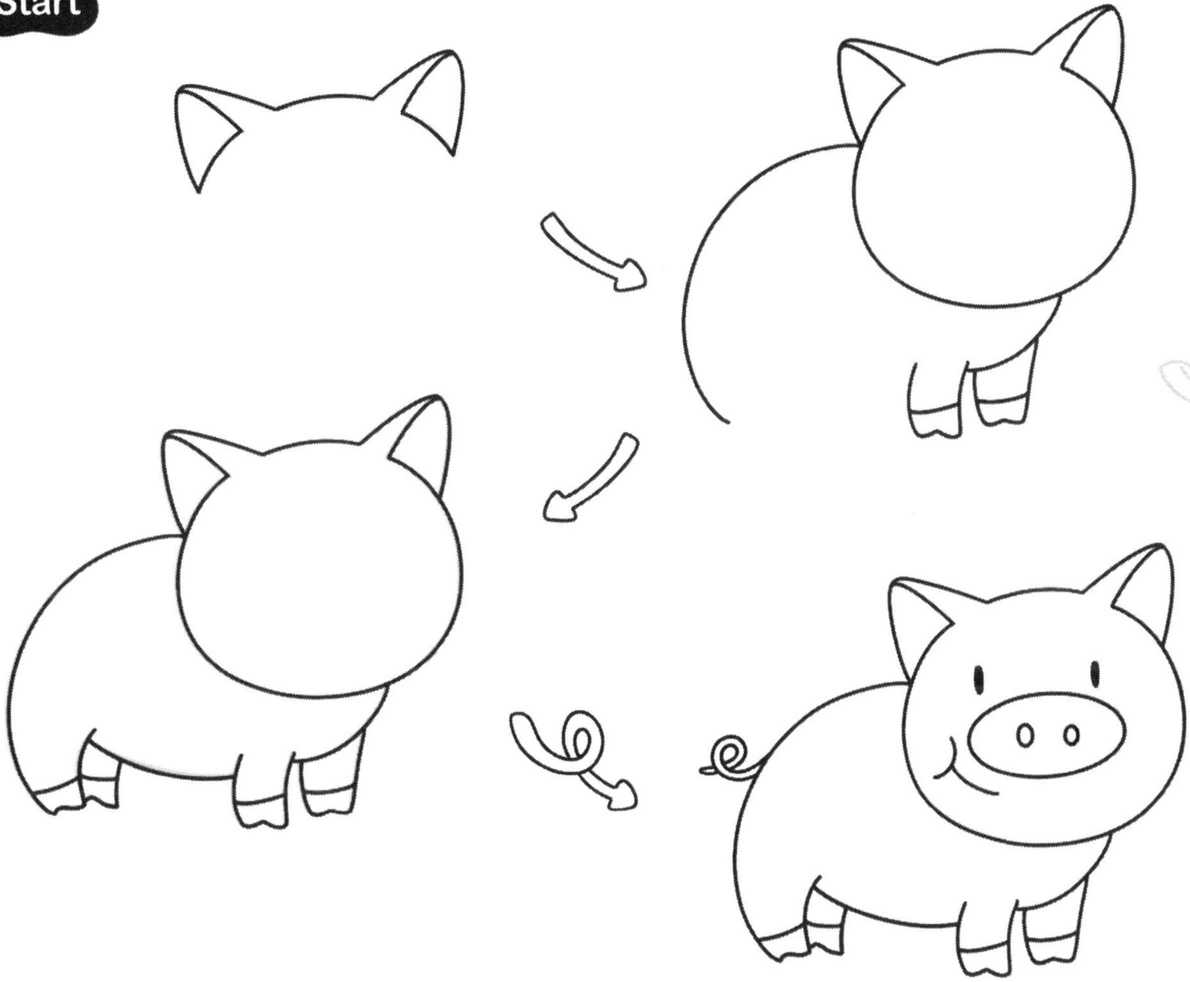

Pigs are very clean animals.

Practice

Dove

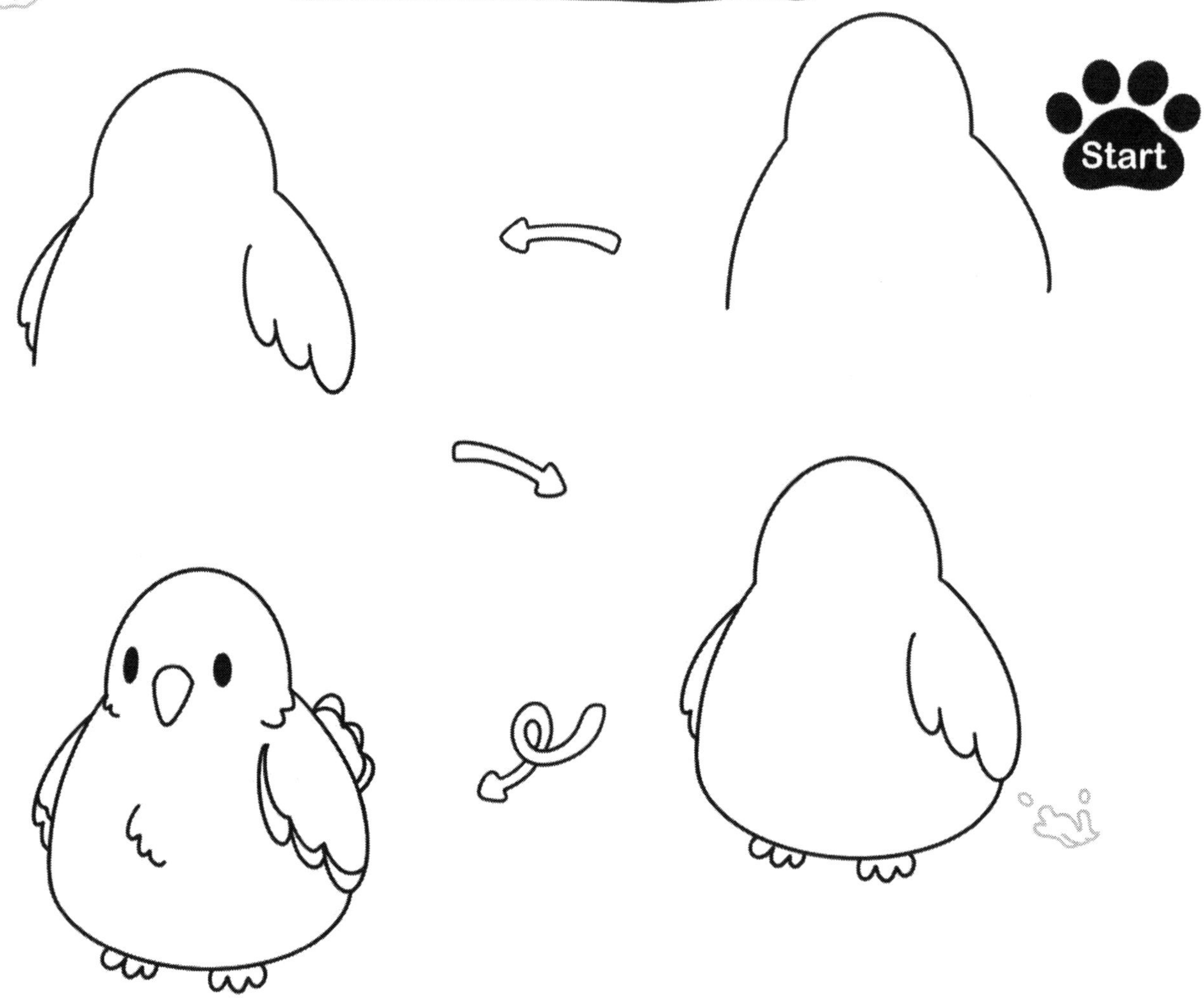

Doves are slightly smaller than pigeons.

Practice

Dolphin

Start

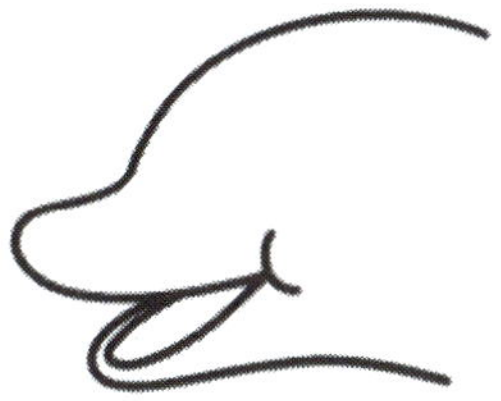

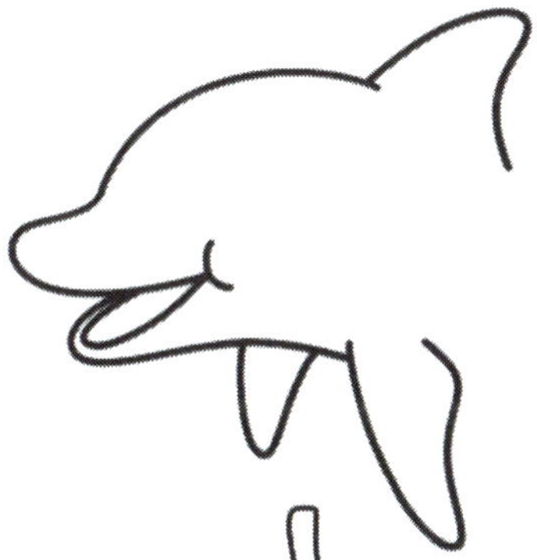

Practice

Dolphins have conical-shaped teeth.

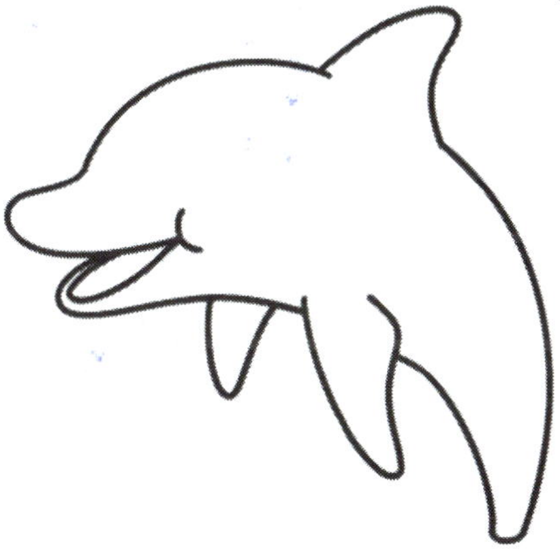

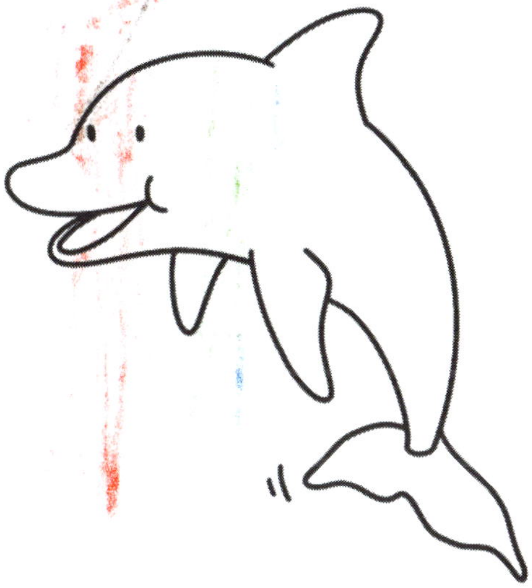

Fox

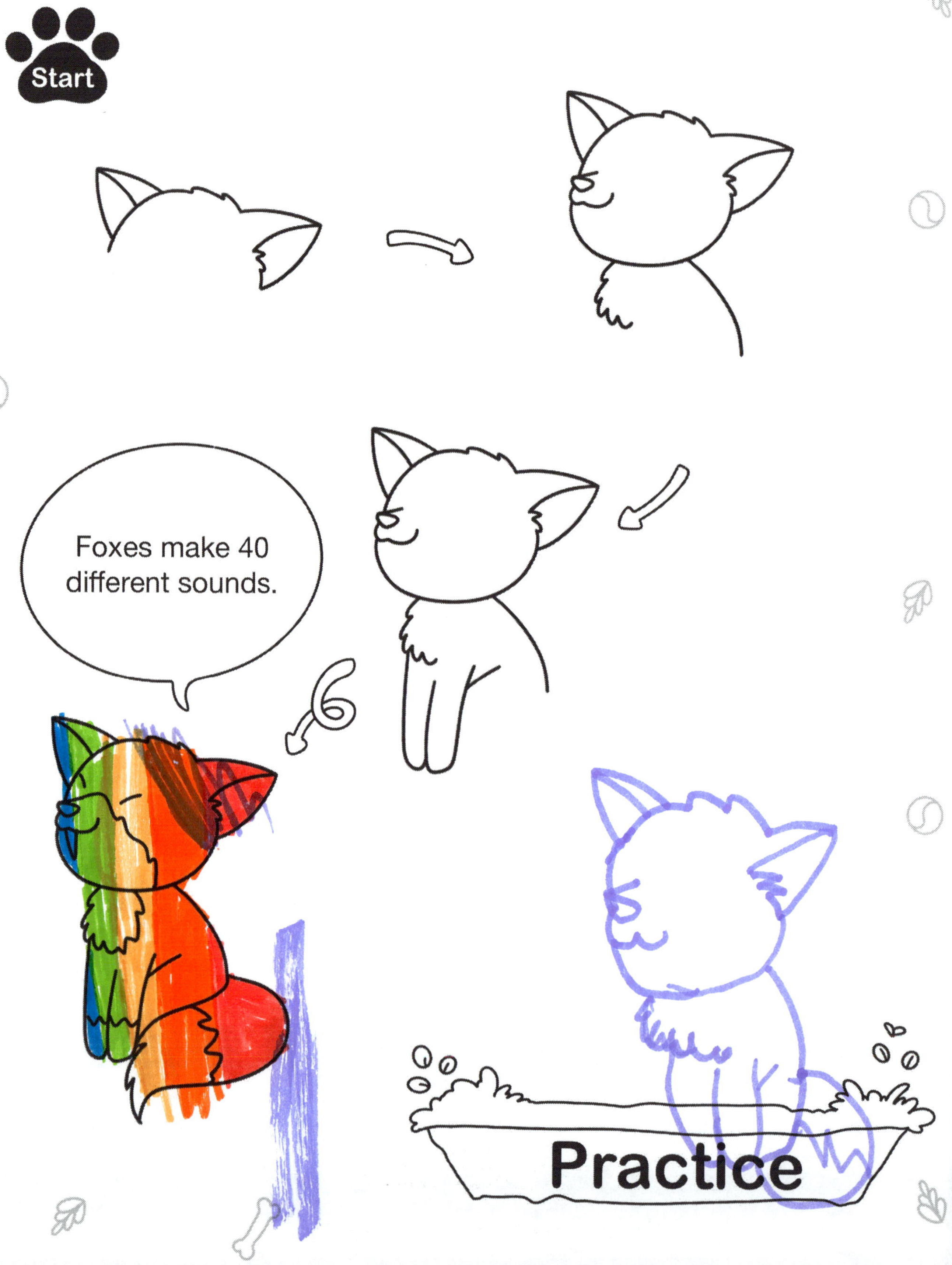

Cow

Start

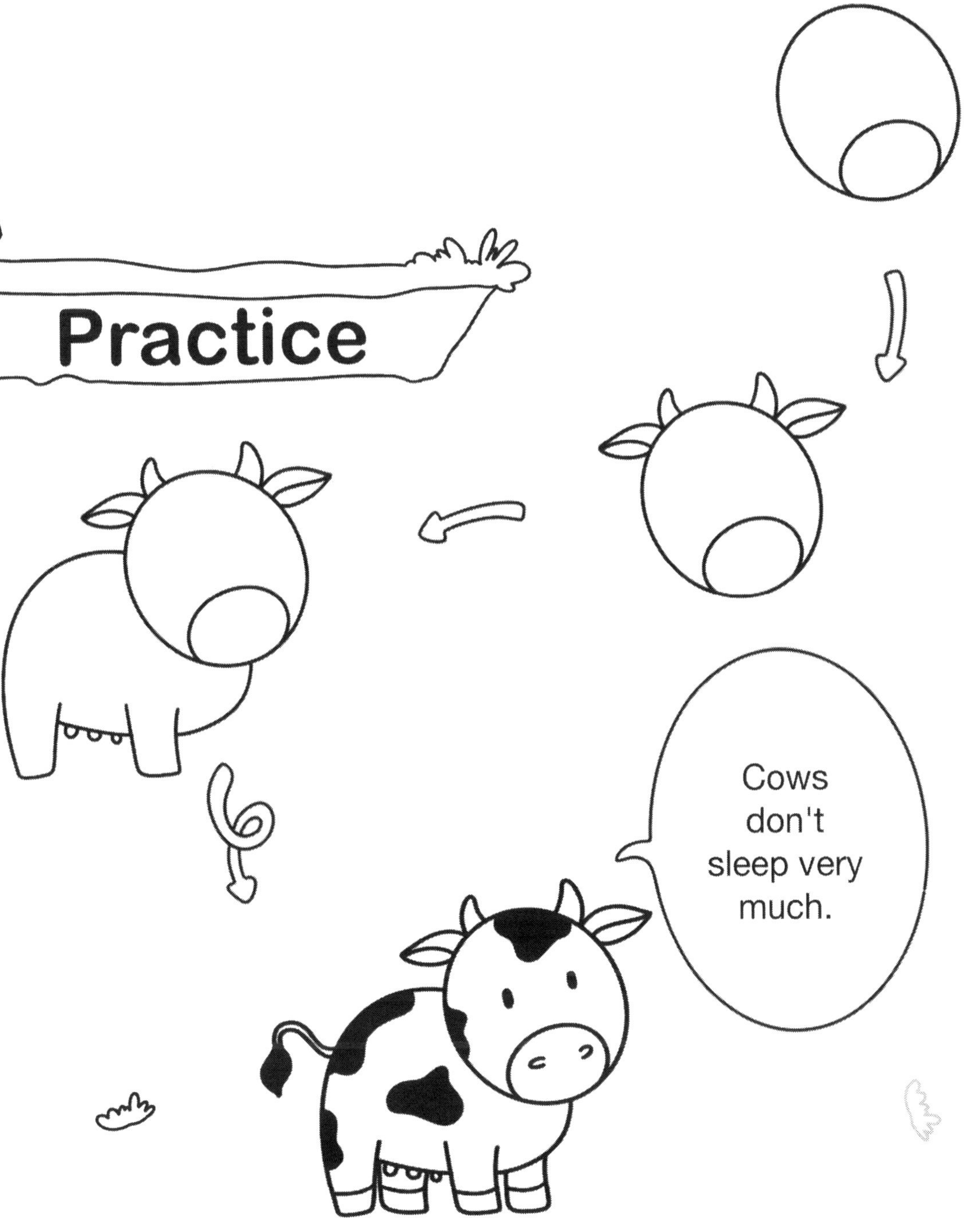

Practice

Lion

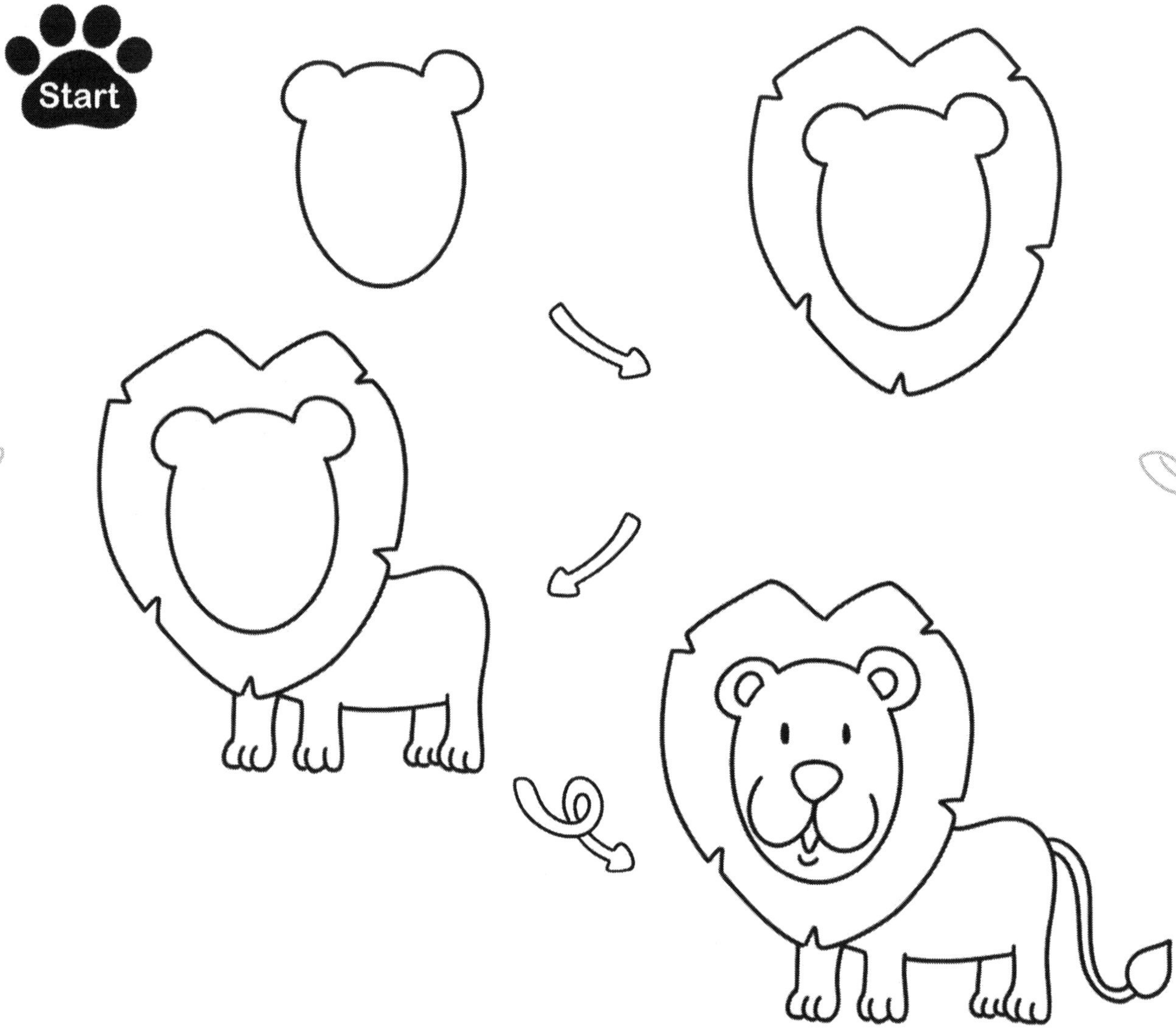

Lions can weigh up to 420 pounds.

Practice

Elephant

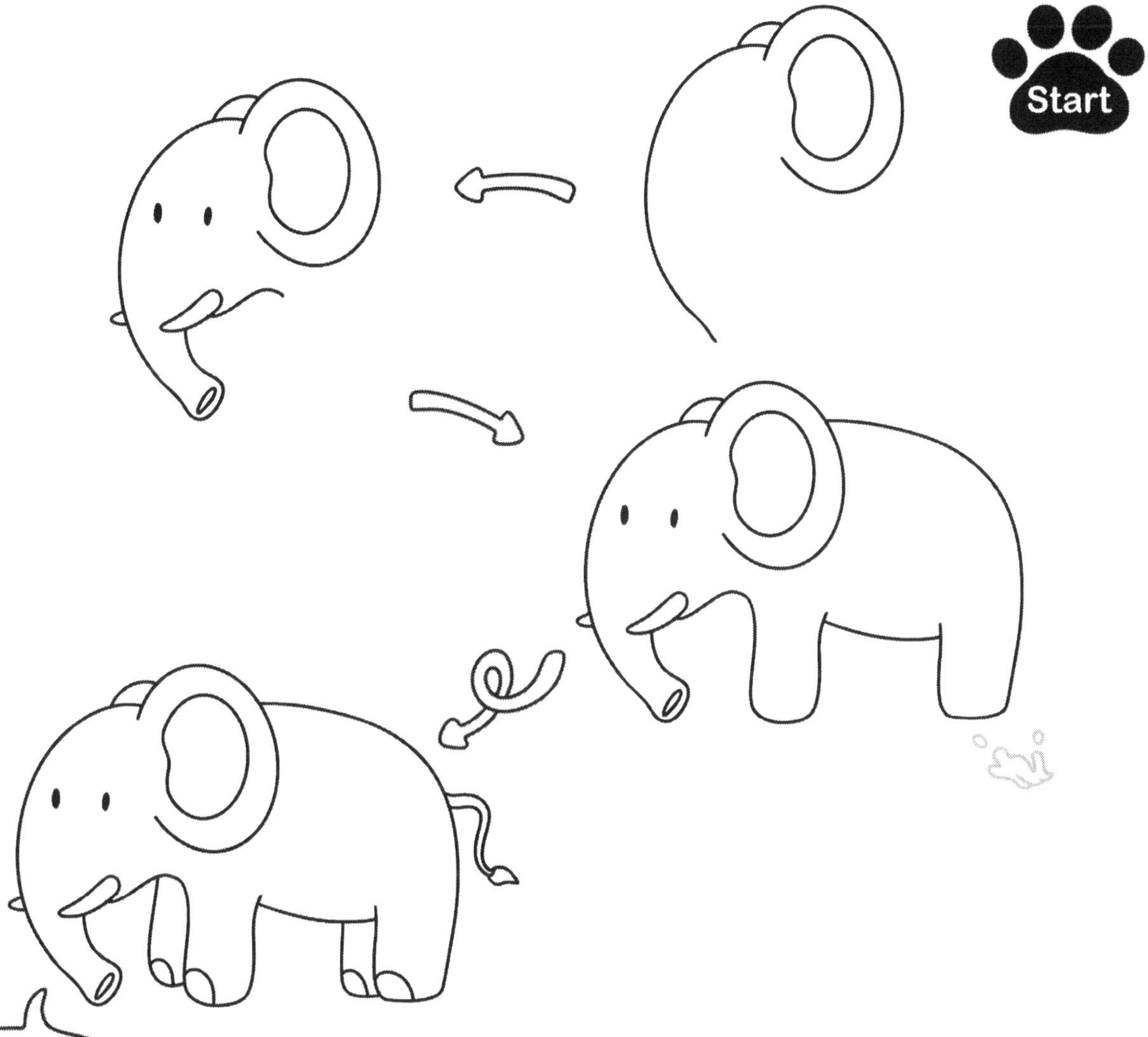

Elephants can constantly eat.

Practice

Shark

Start

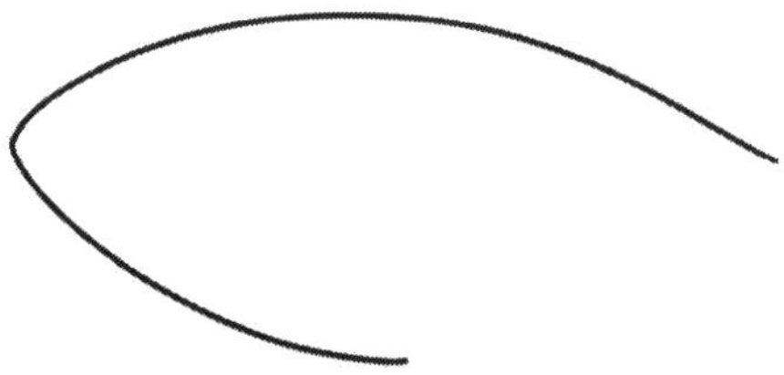

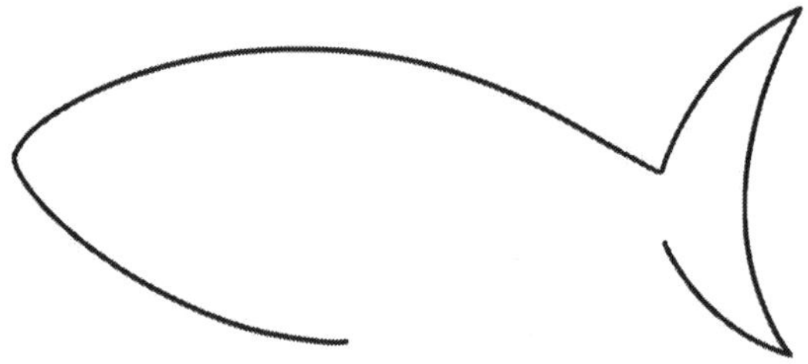

Practice

Sharks do not have bones

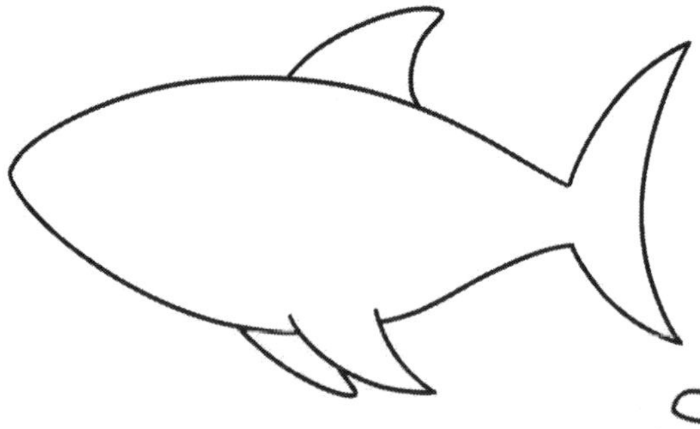

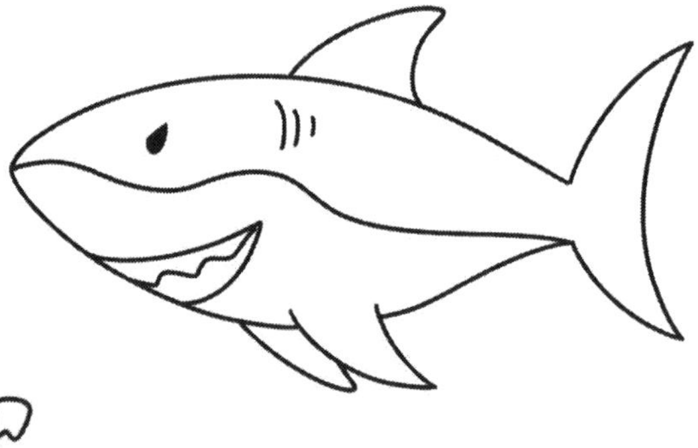

Donkey

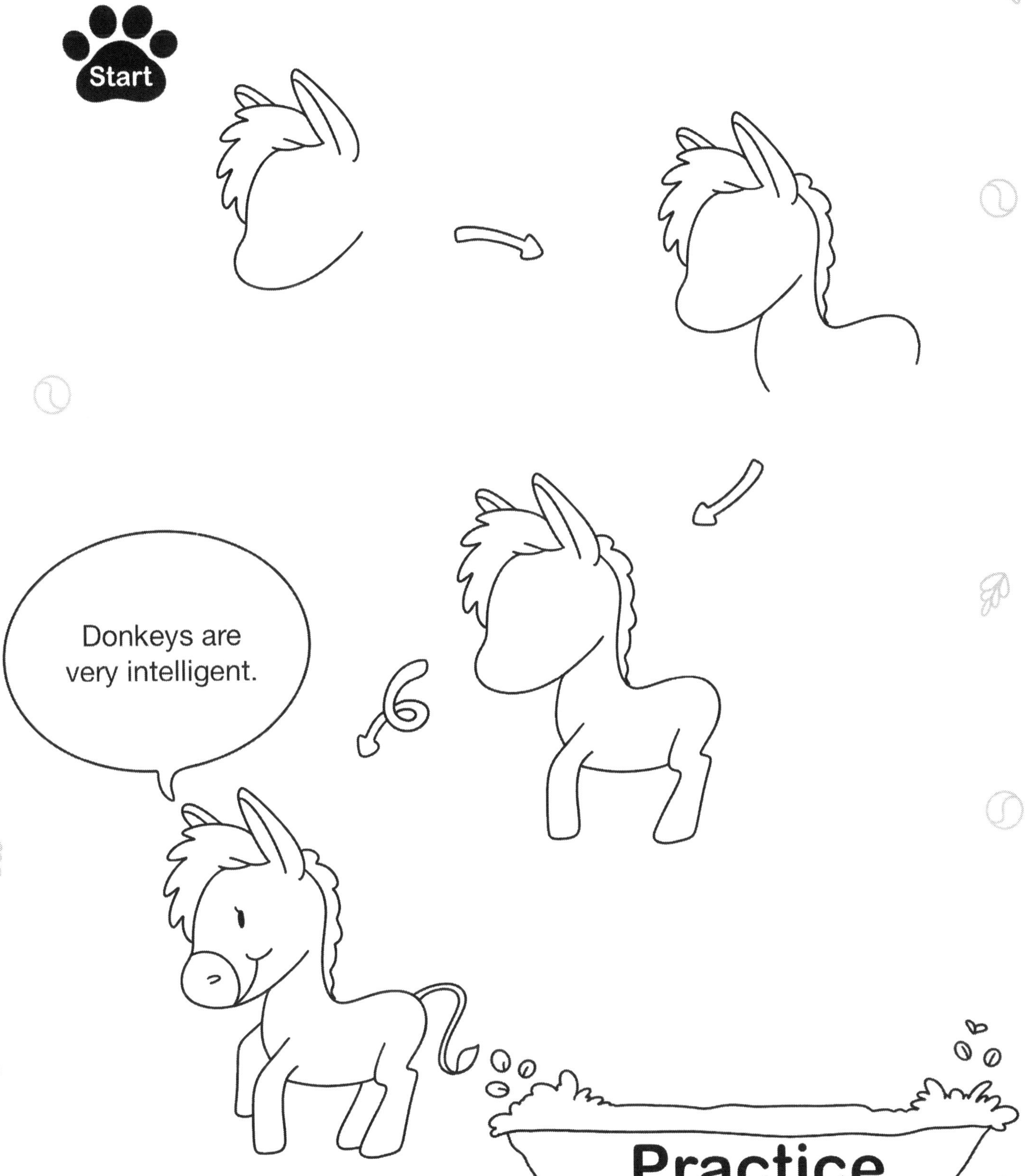

Practice

Zebra

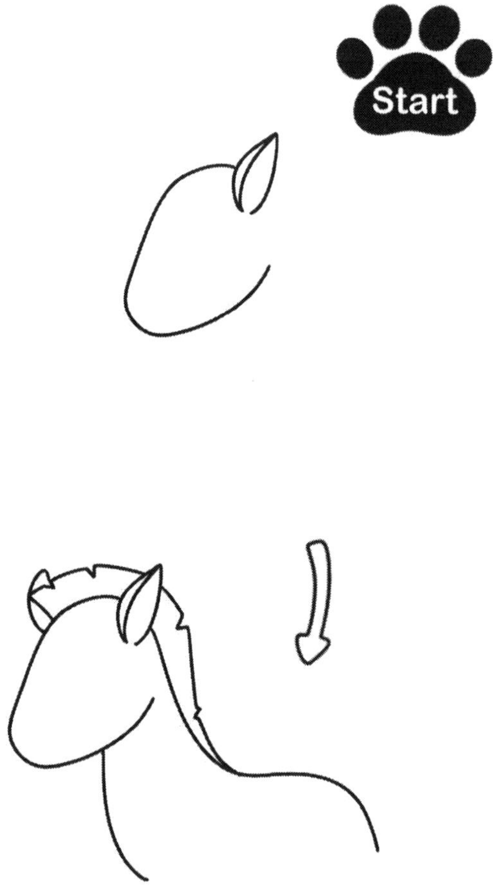

Practice

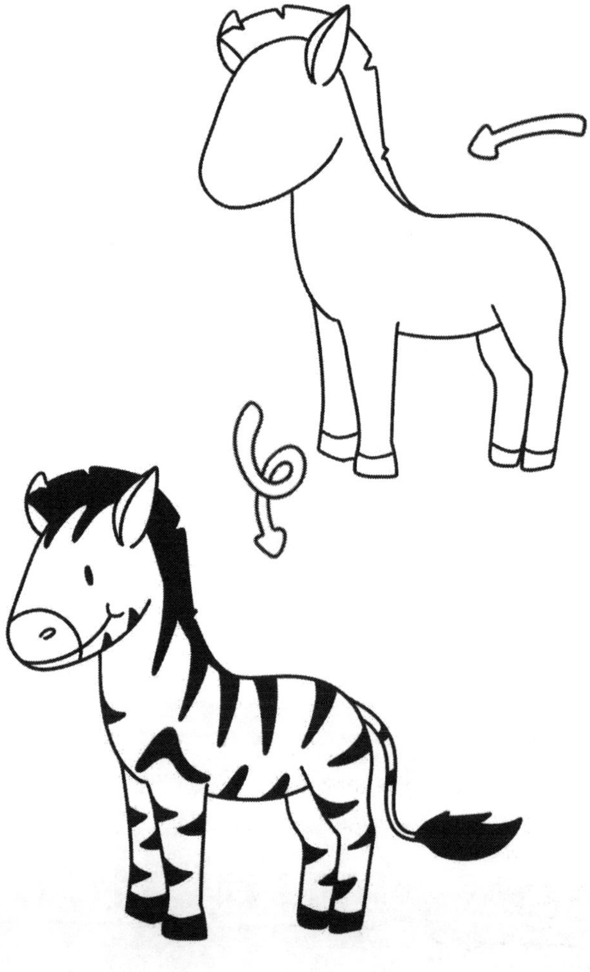

Zebras can run up to 40 miles per hour.

Porcupine

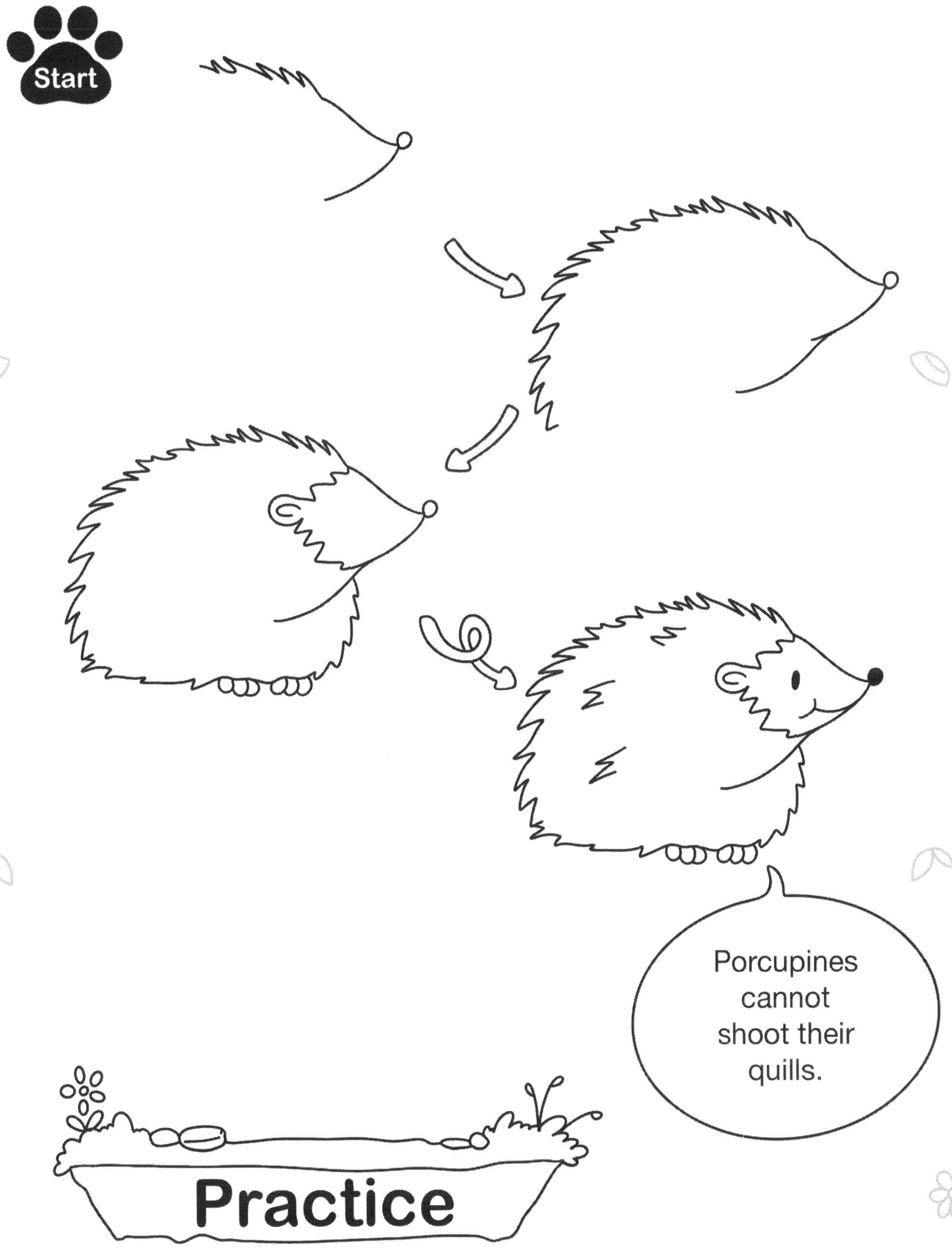

Practice

Bat

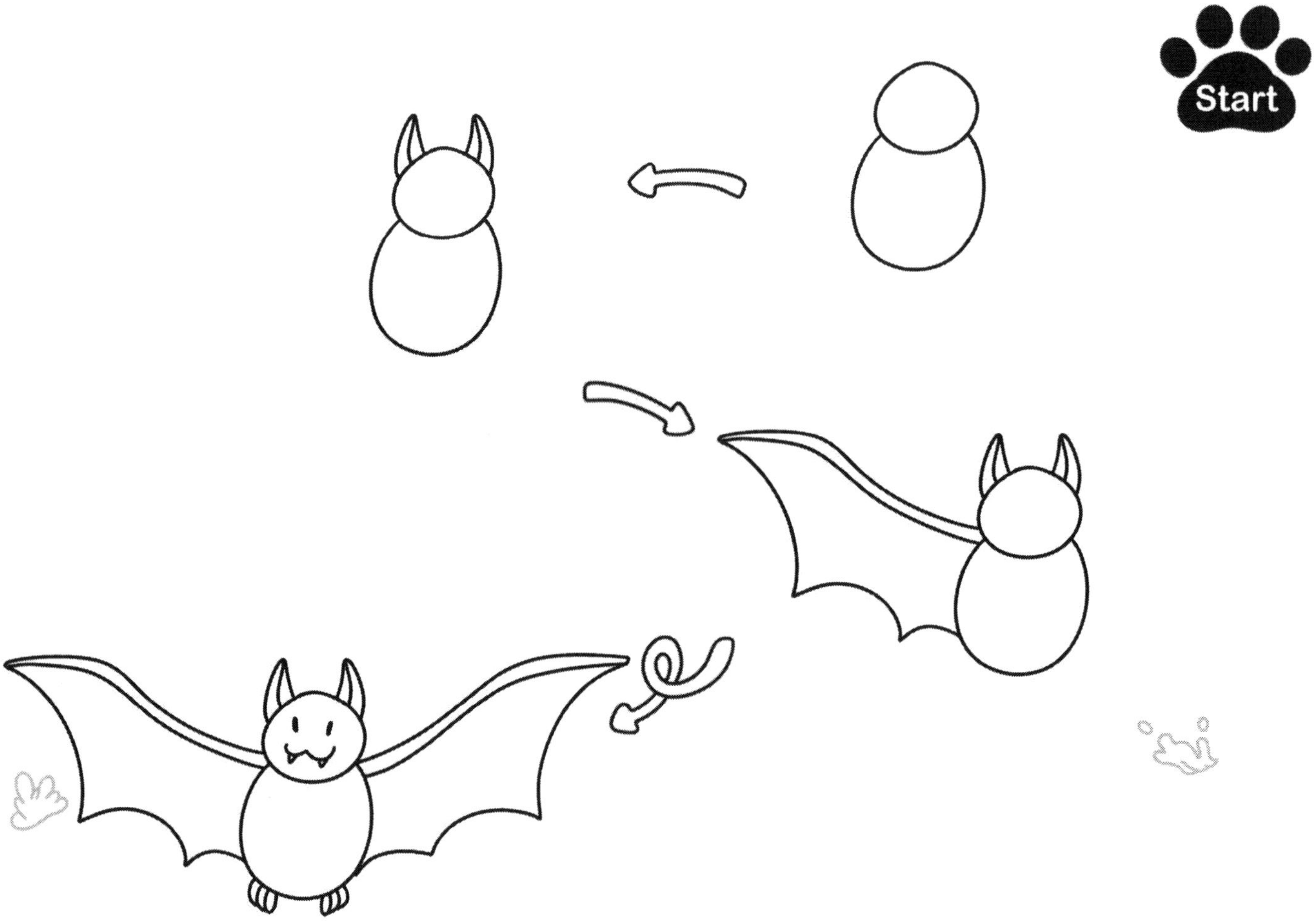

Bats can
eat up to
1,200
mosquitoes
an hour.

Practice

Alligator

Start

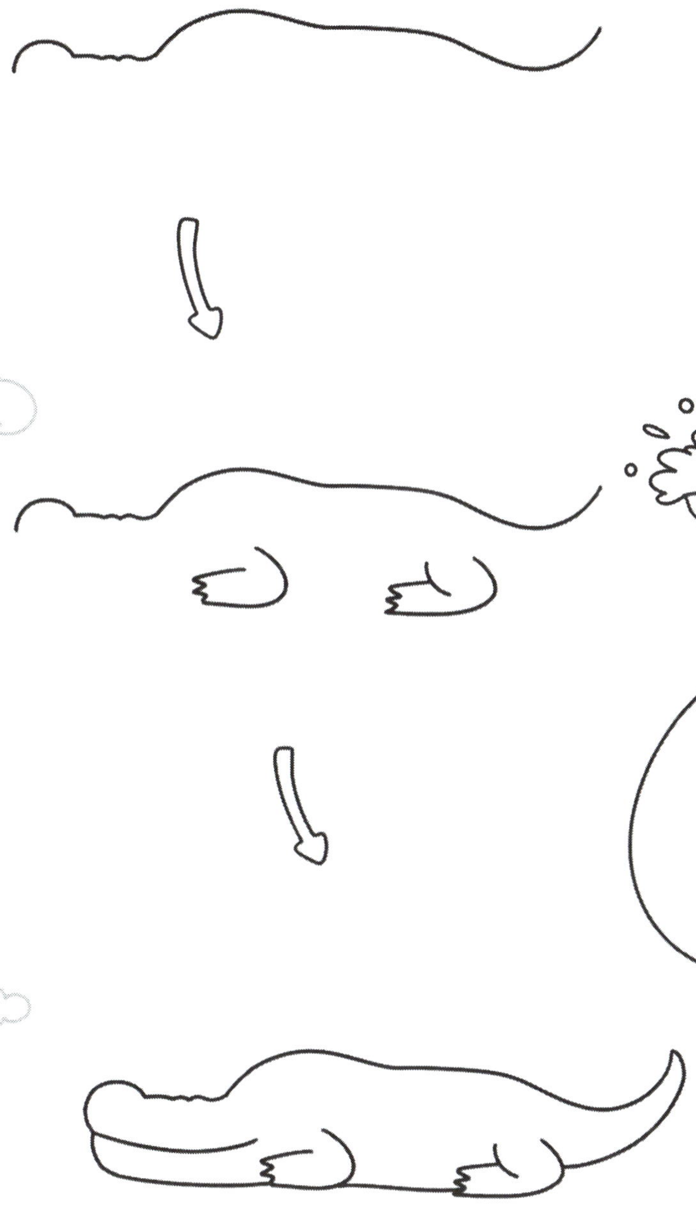

Practice

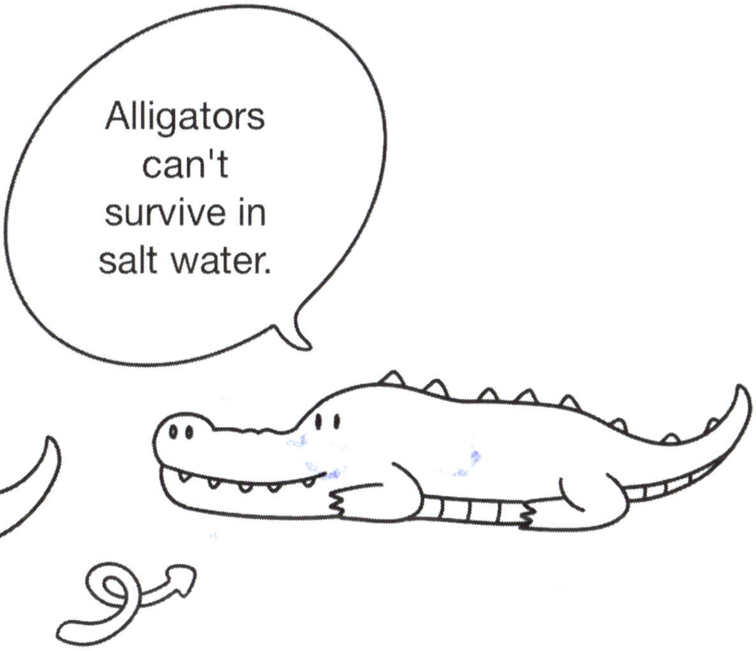

Owl

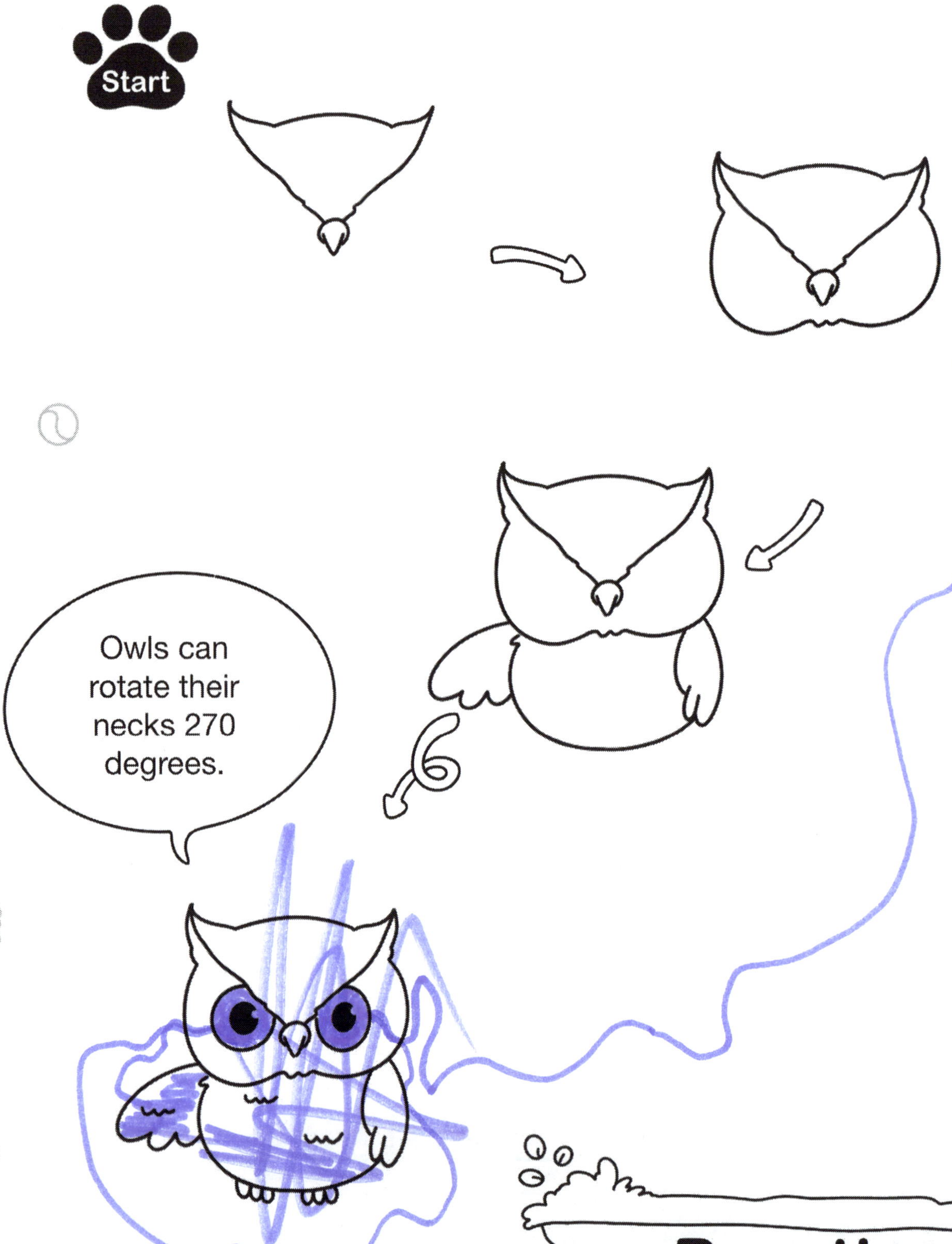

Practice

Frog

Start

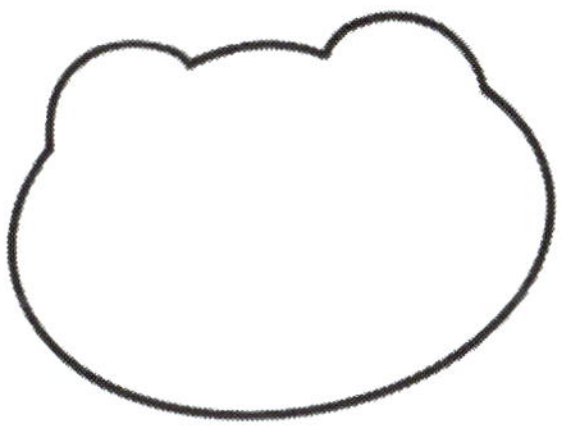

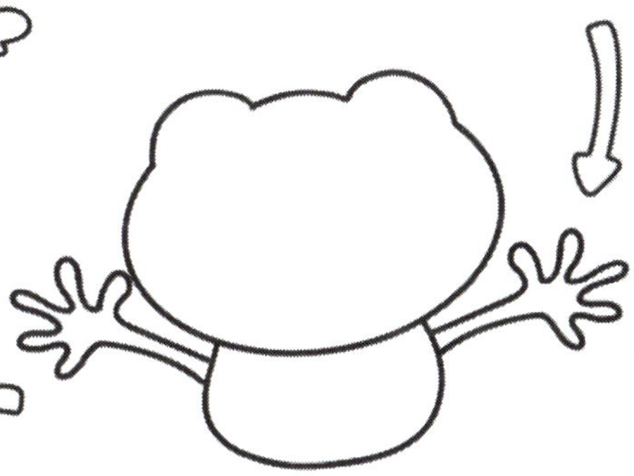

Practice

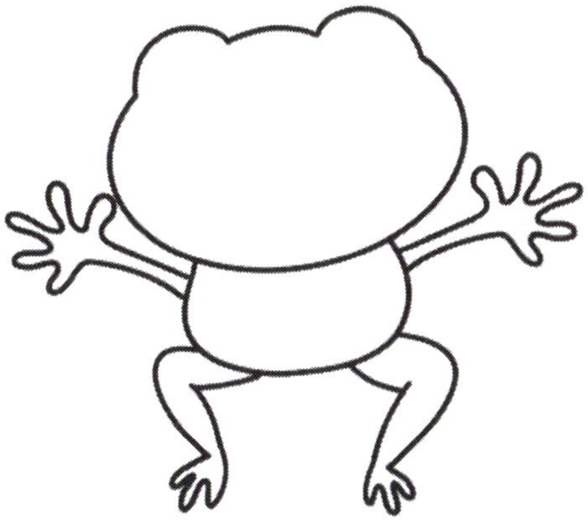

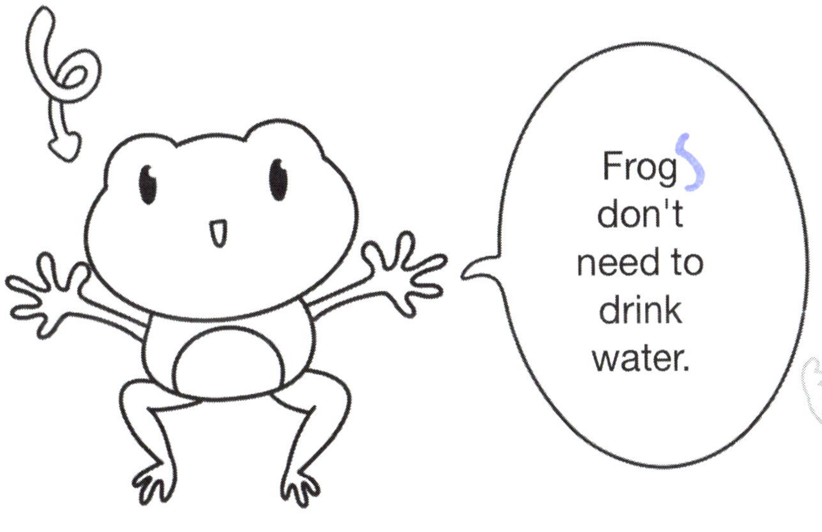

Horse

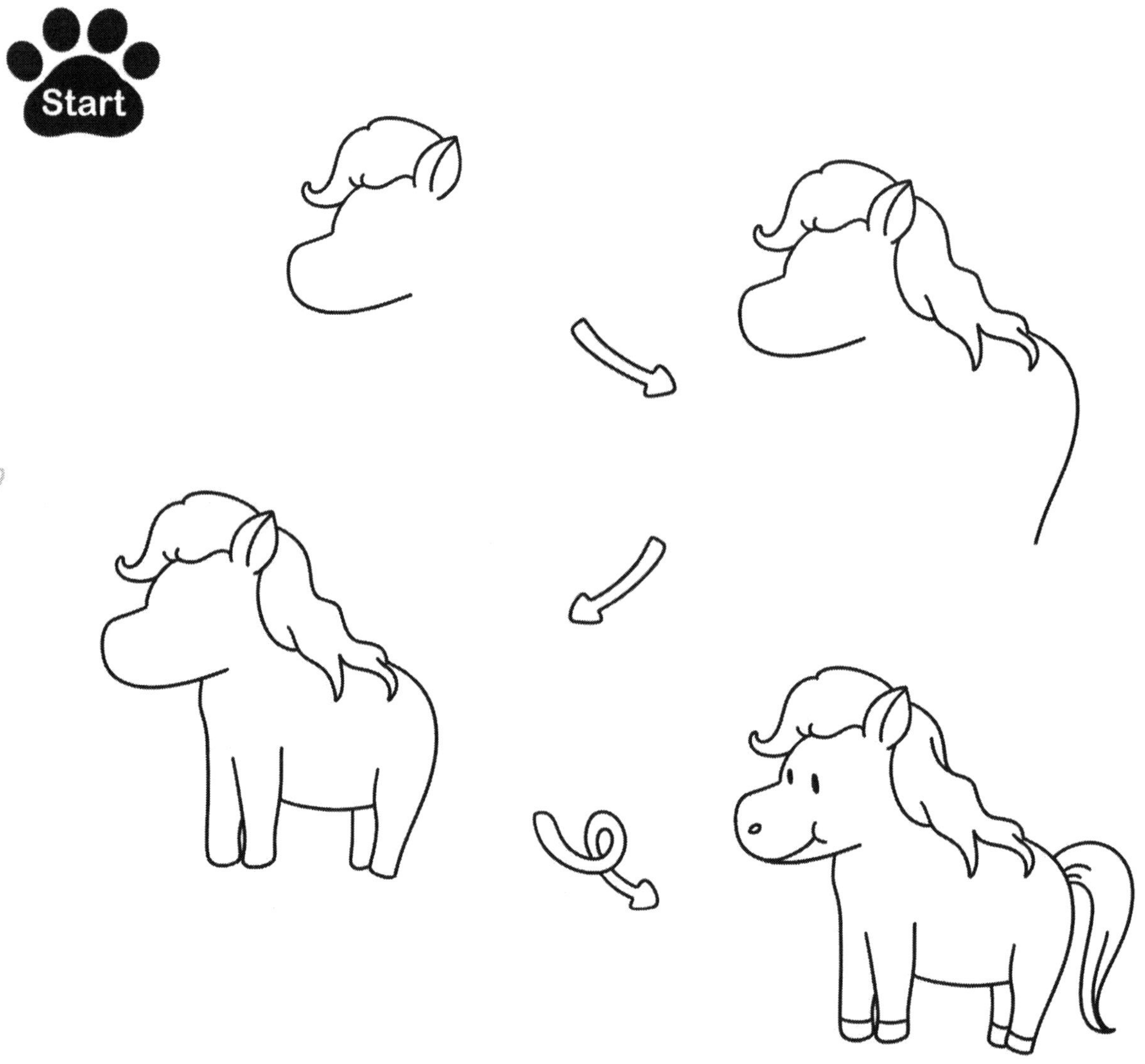

Horses can't breathe through their mouths.

Practice

Duck

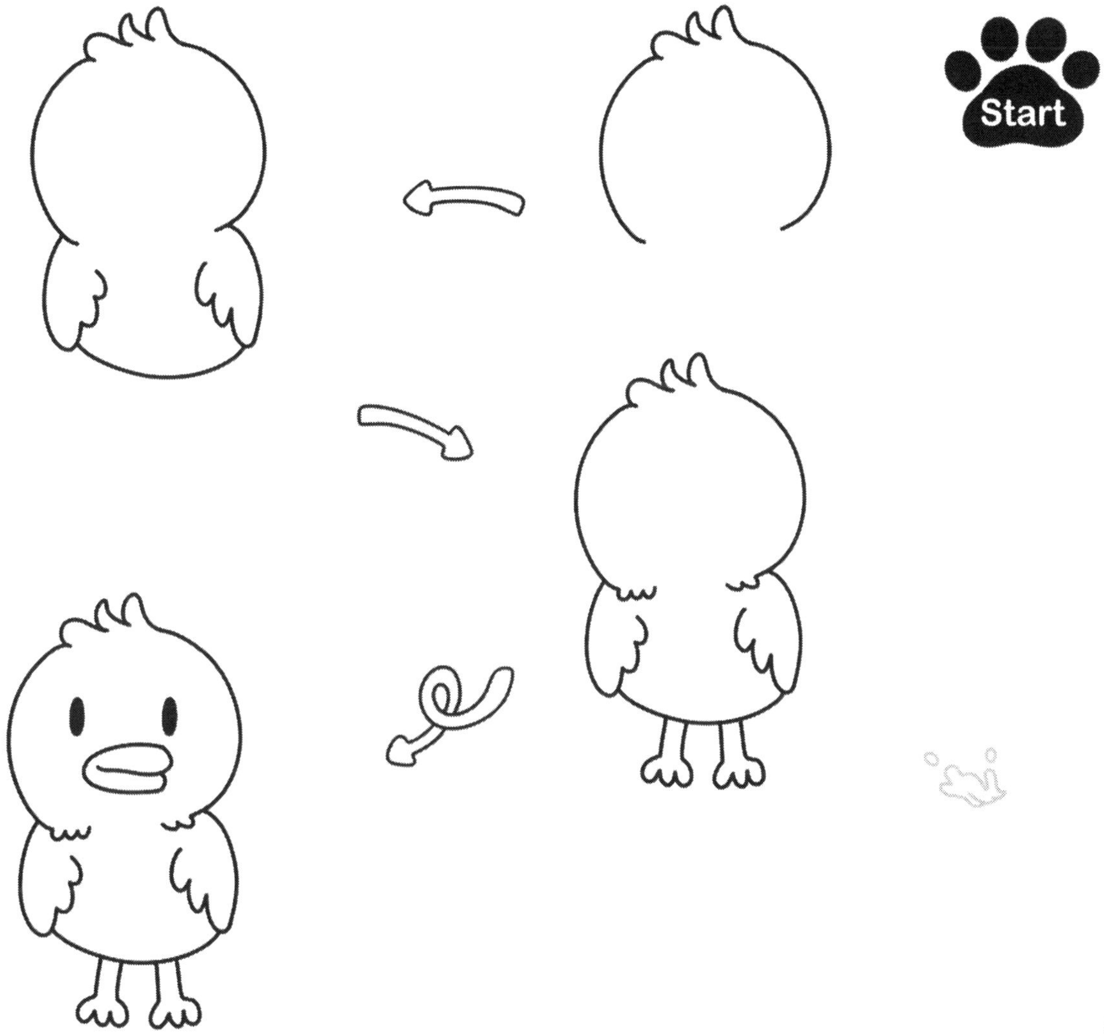

Ducks are birds in the family Anatidae.

Practice

Octopus

Start

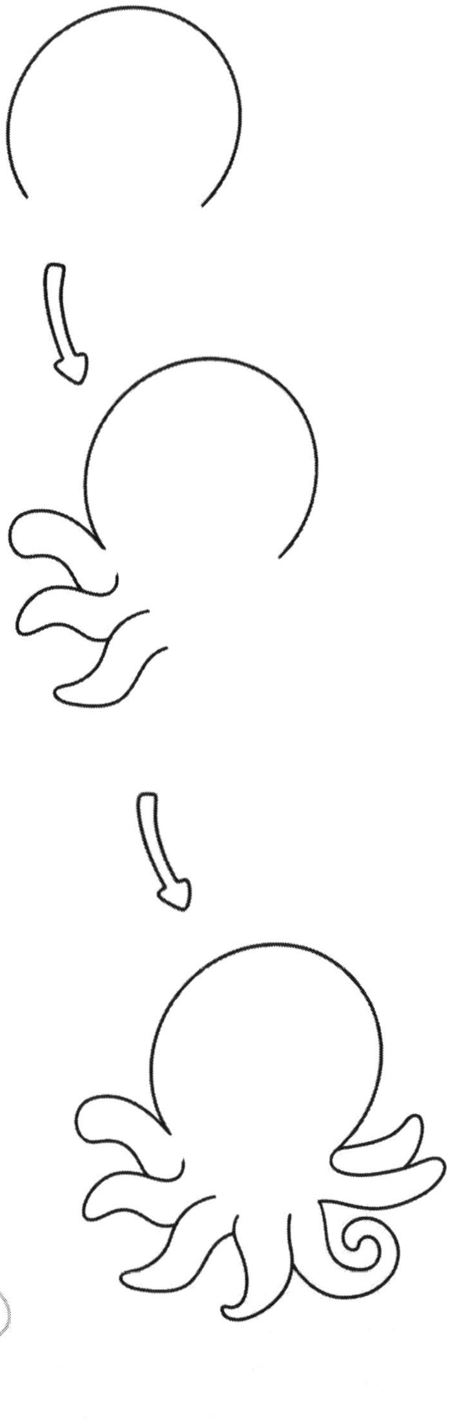

Practice

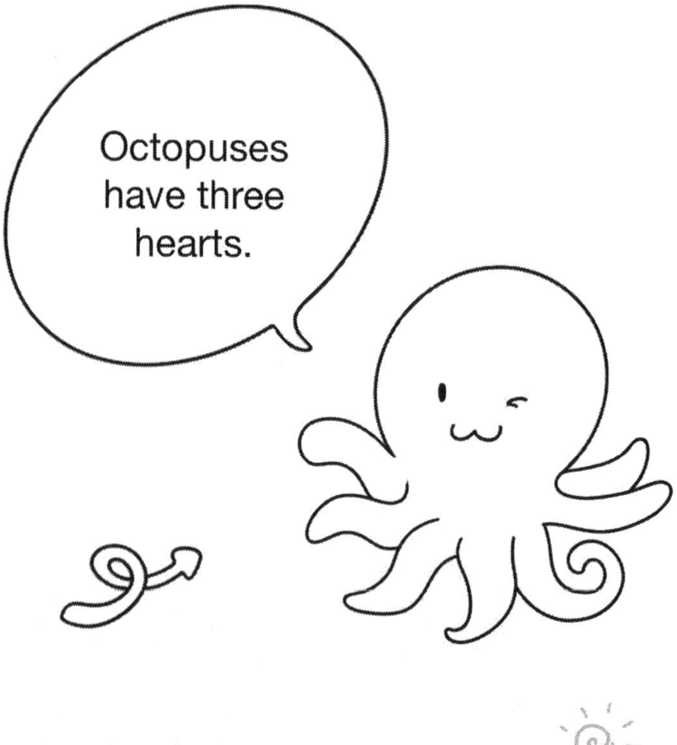

Kangaroo

Start

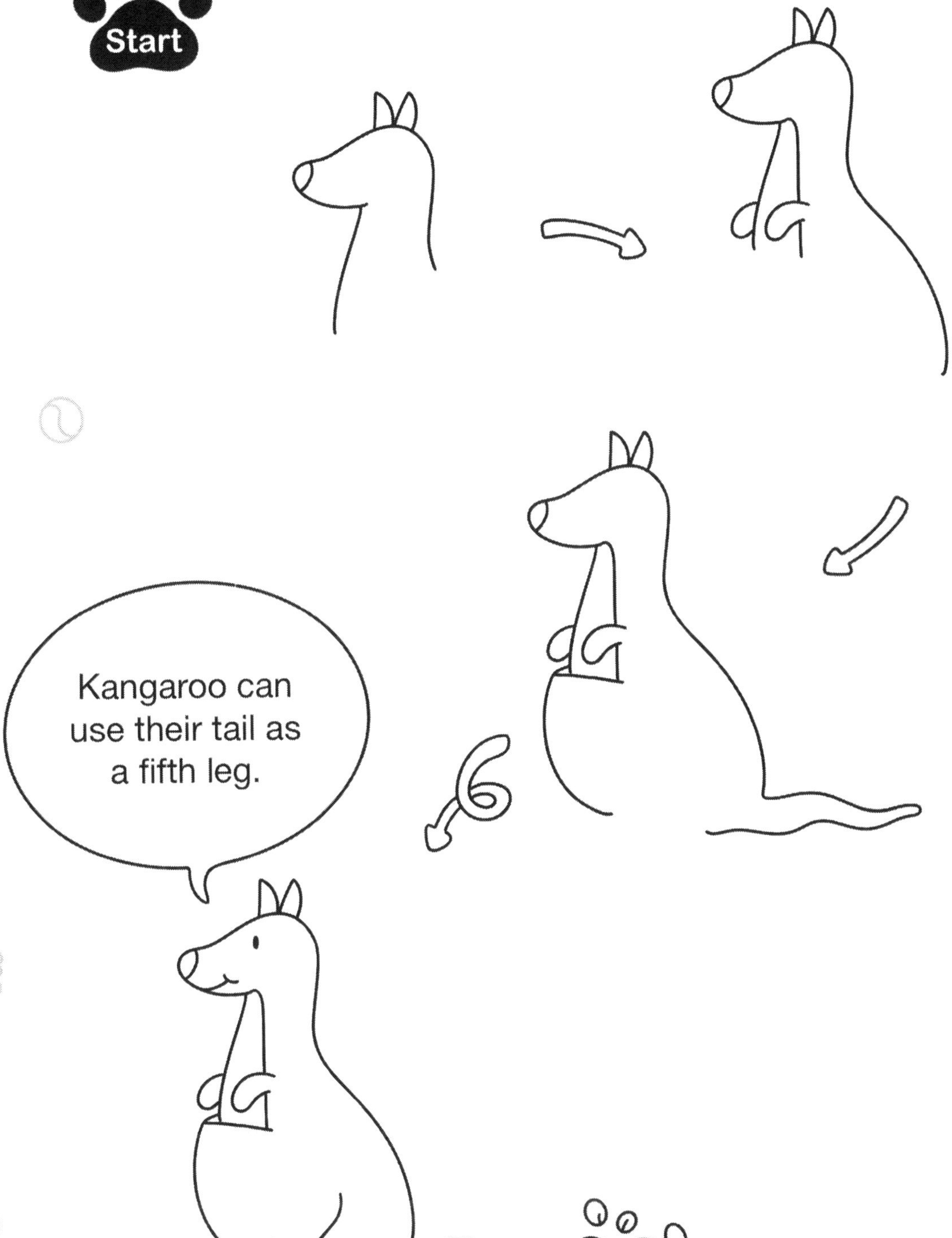

Practice

Koala Bear

Practice

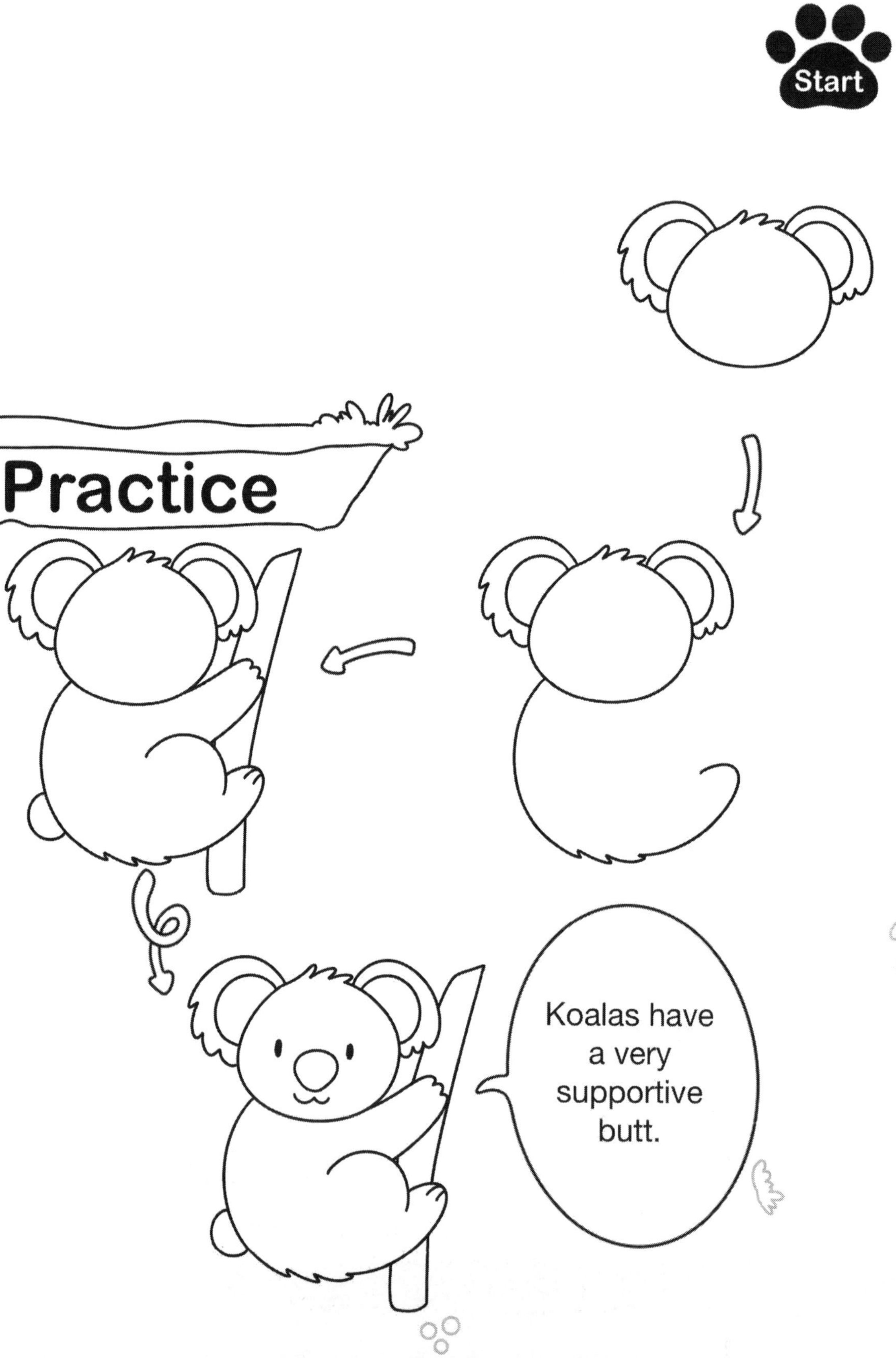

Ladybug

Start

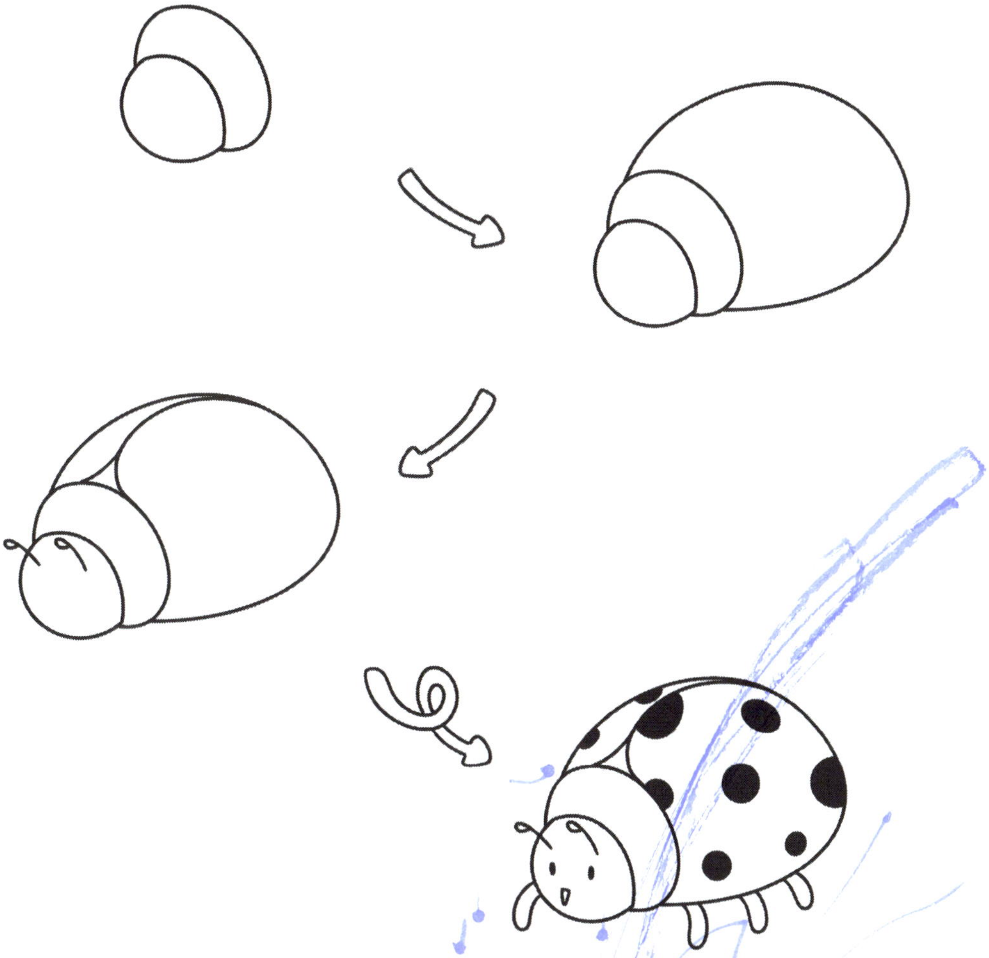

Ladybugs smell with their feet.

Practice

Dinosaur

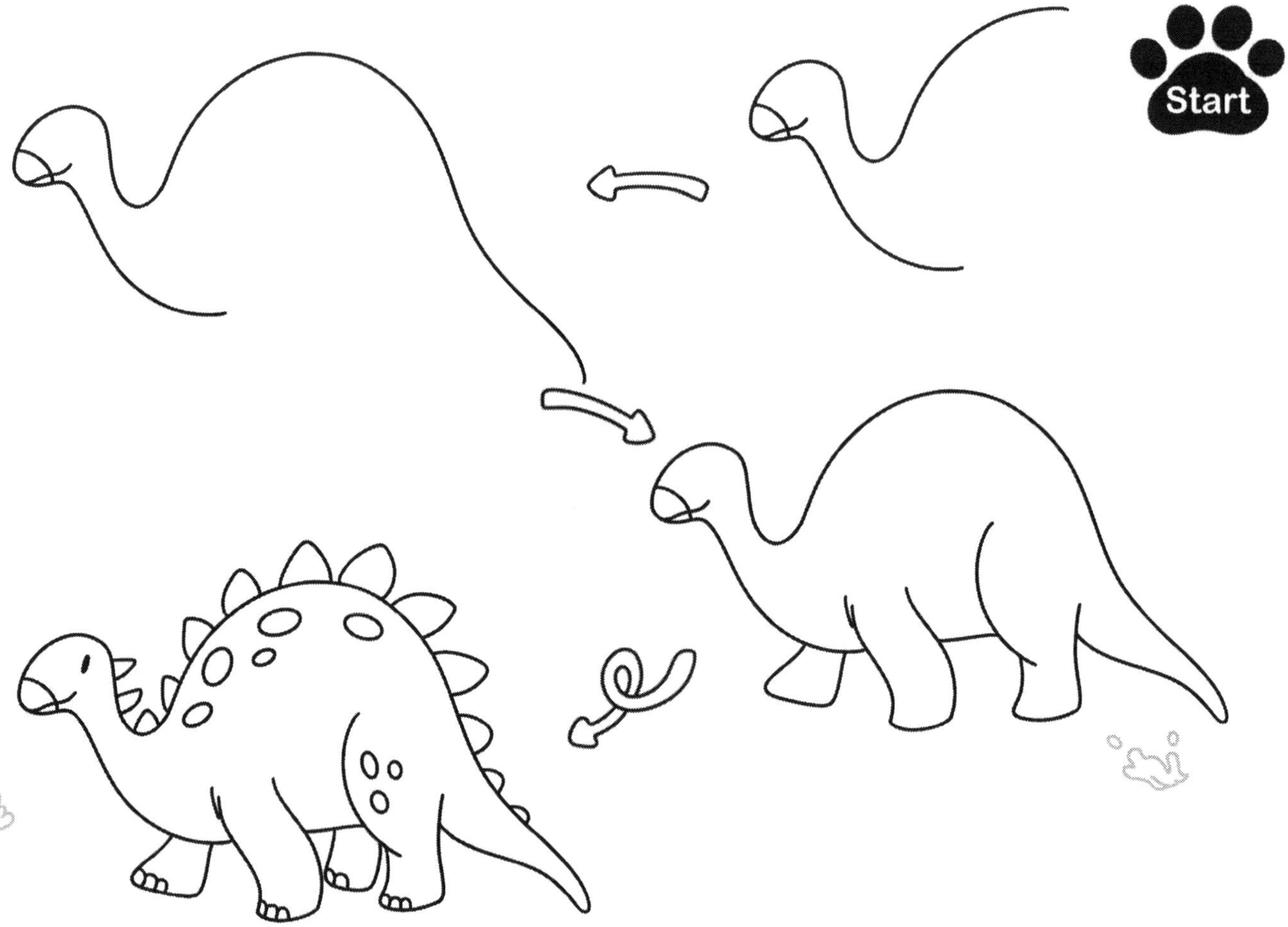

Dinosaurs were around millions of years ago!

Practice

Turtle

Start

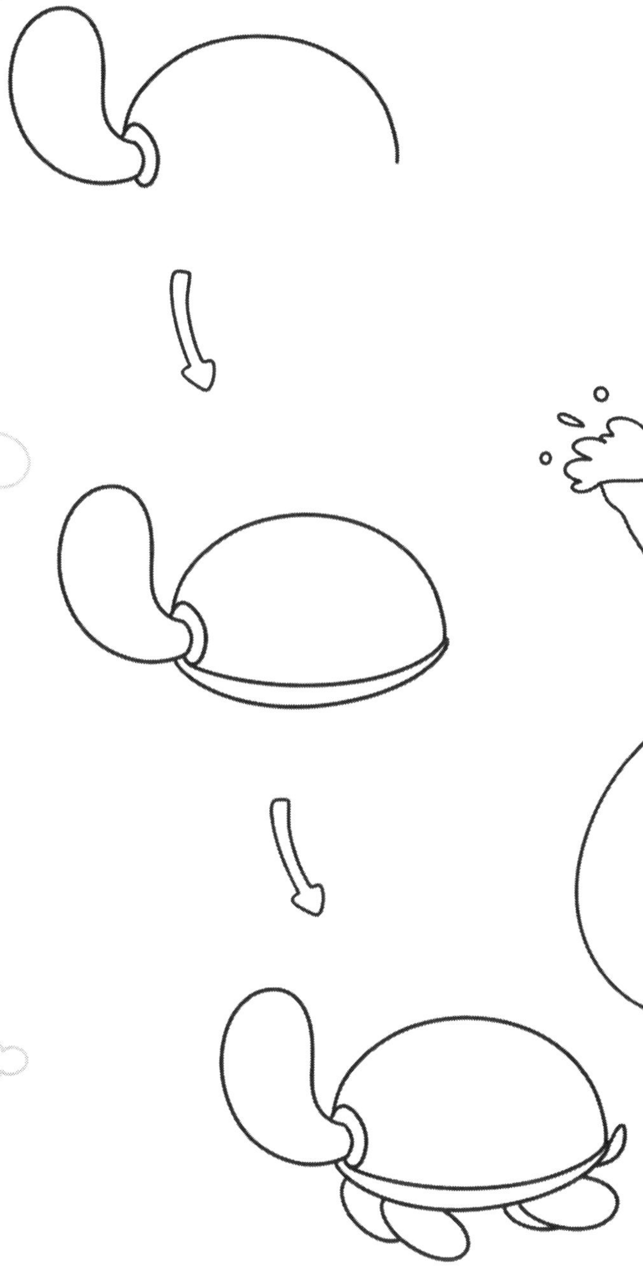

Practice

Turtles have a second shell.

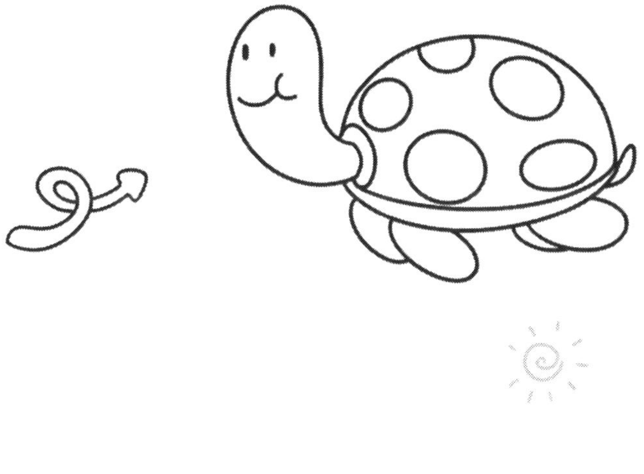

Dragon

Start

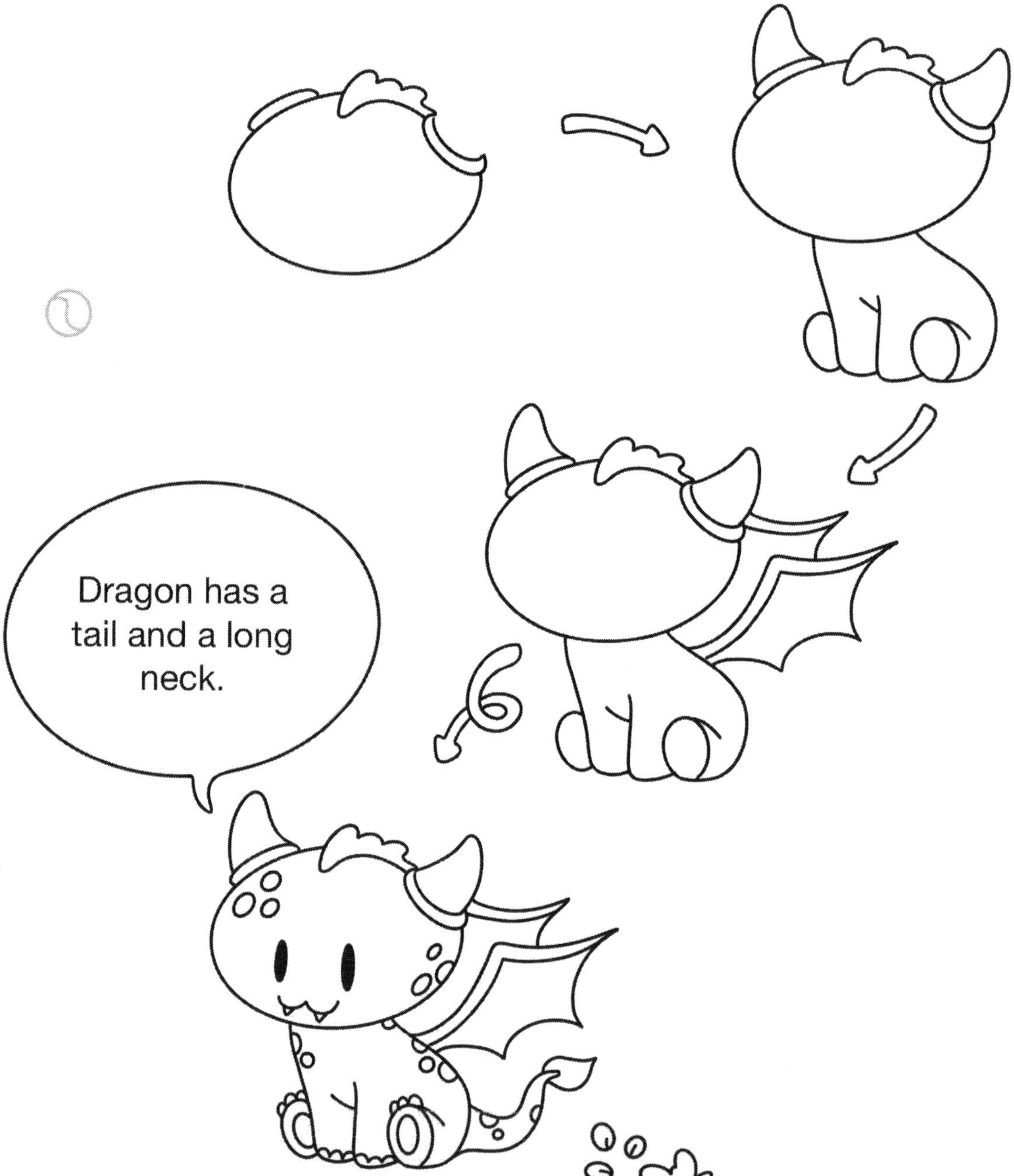

Practice

Snail

Start

Practice

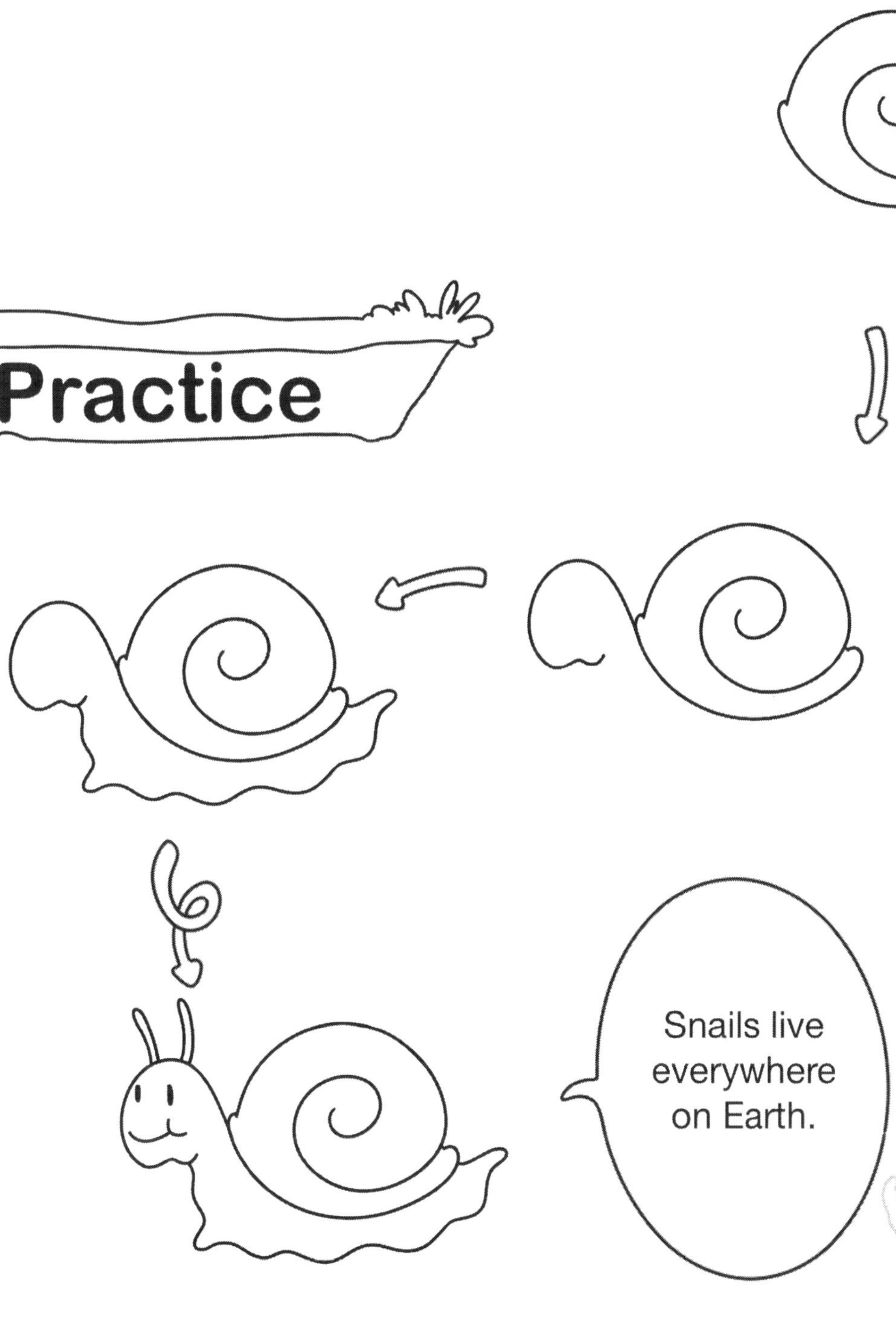

Eagle

Start

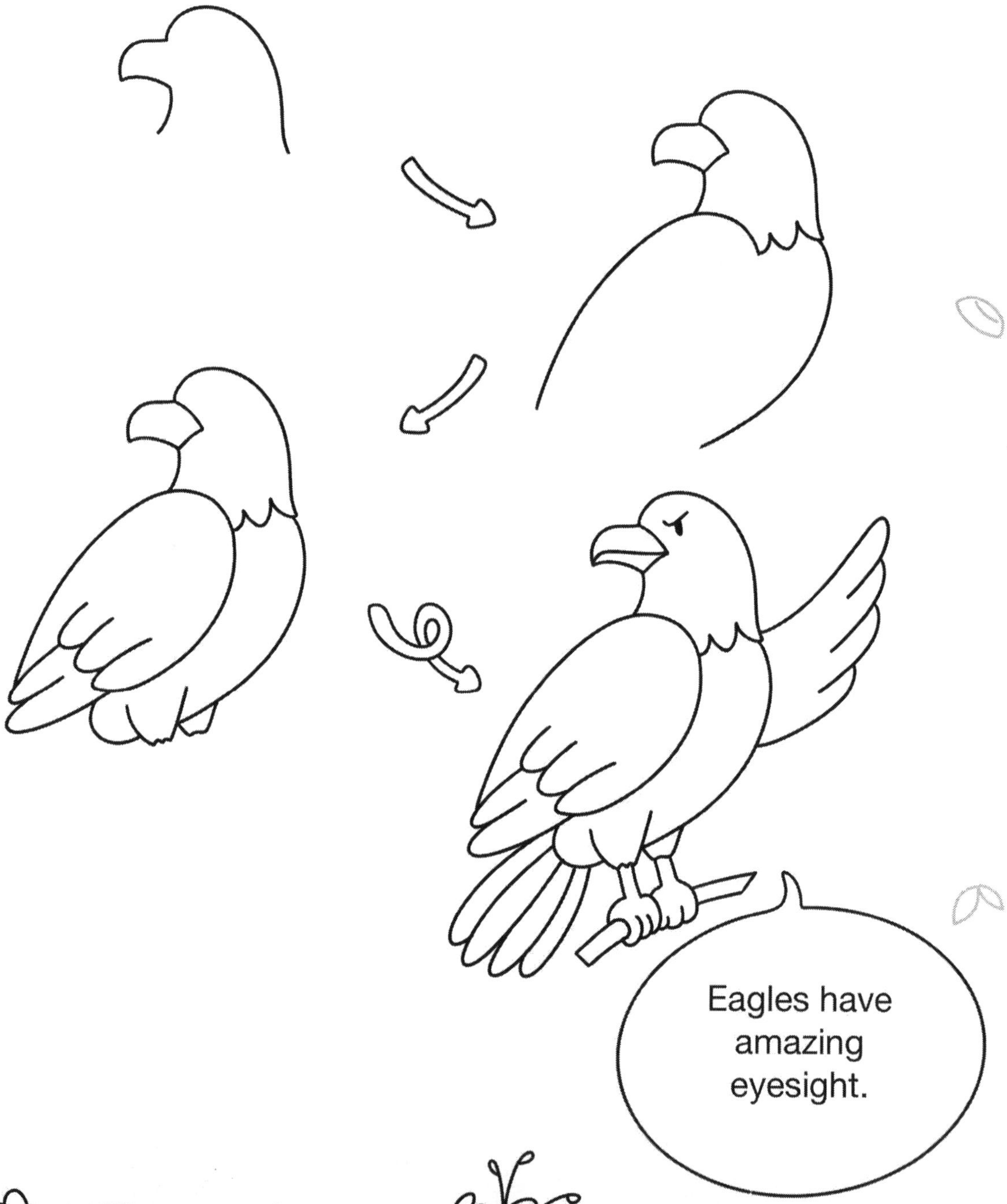

Practice

Puma

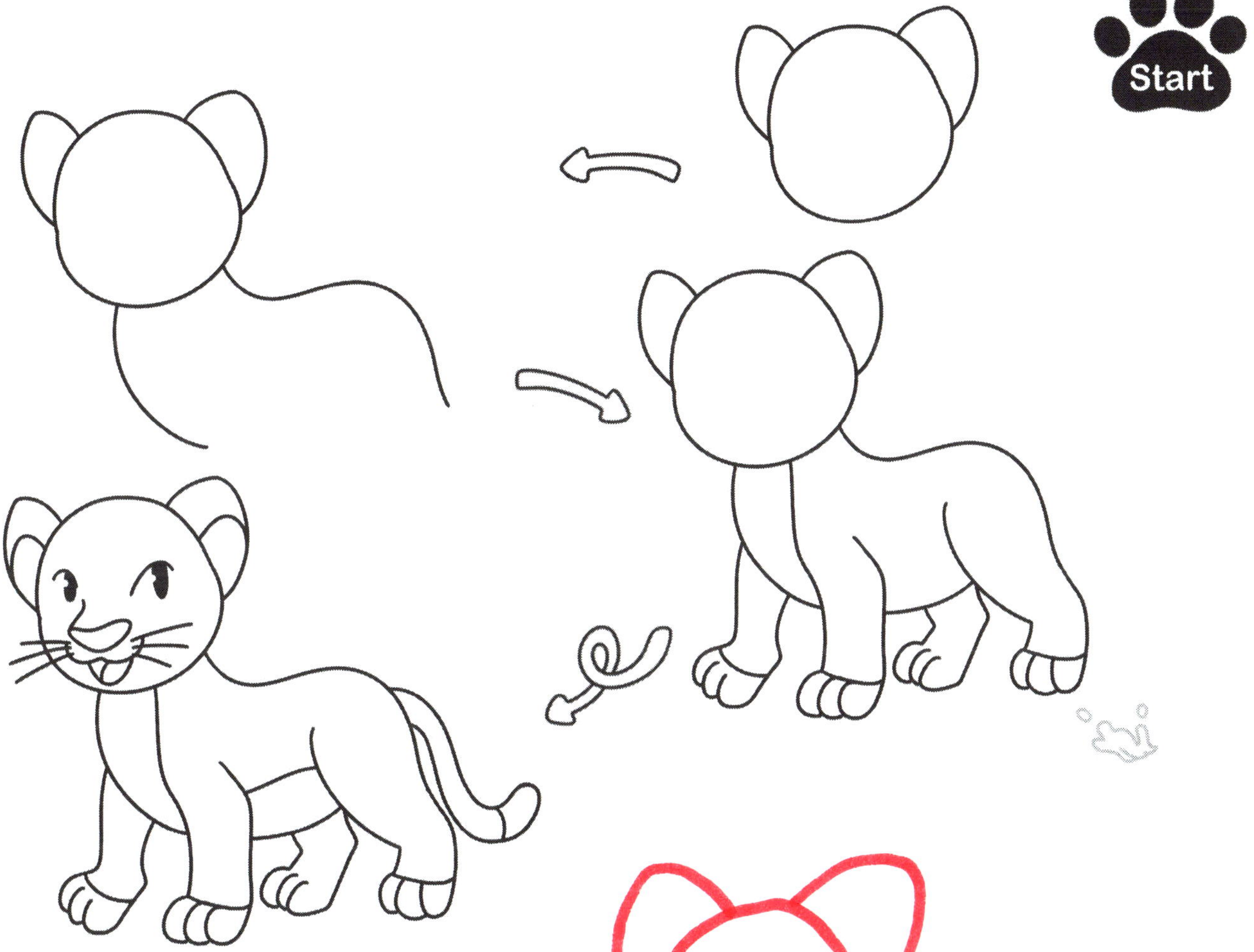

Puma is the world's fourth largest cat.

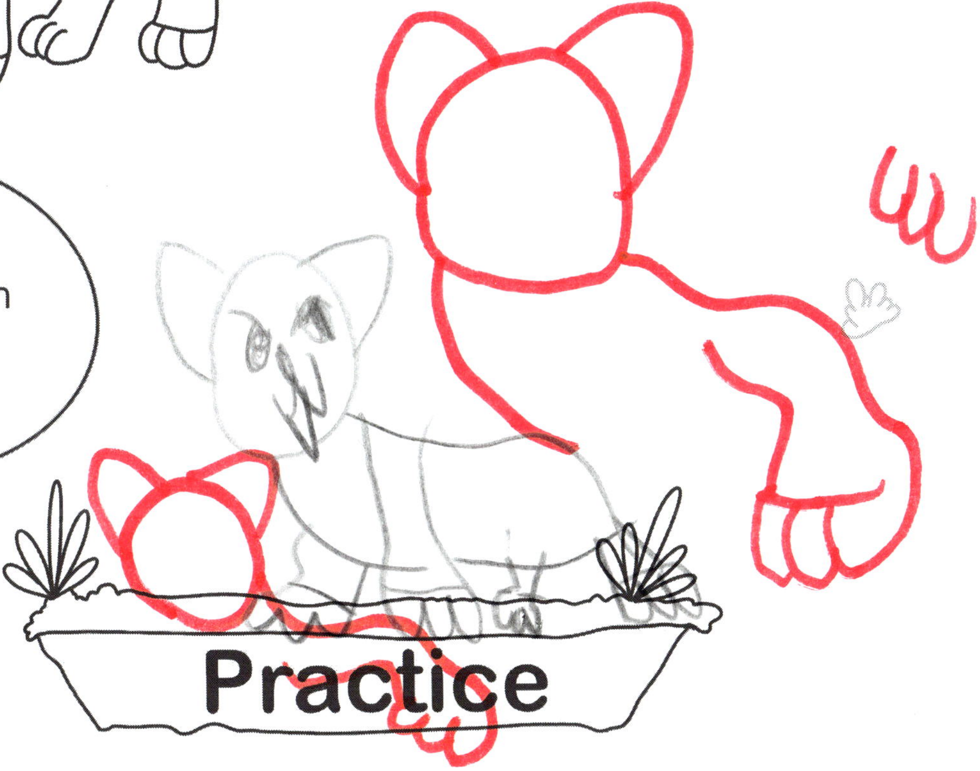

Eel

Start

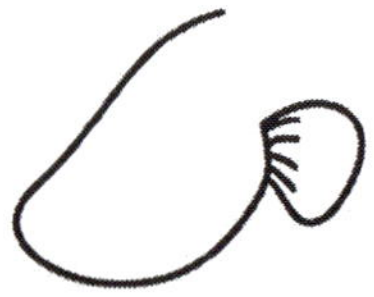

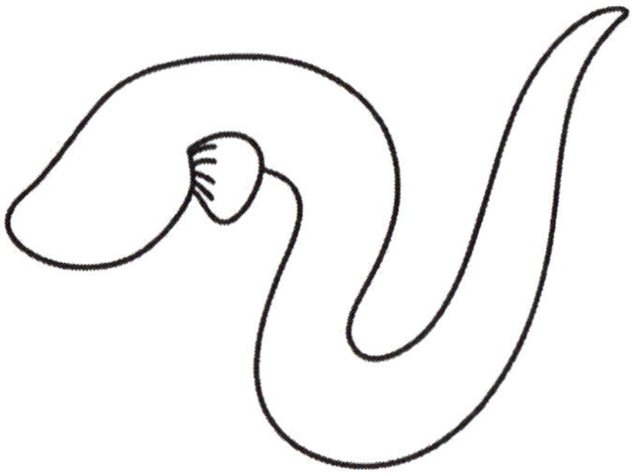

Practice

Eel have gills and very sharp teeth.

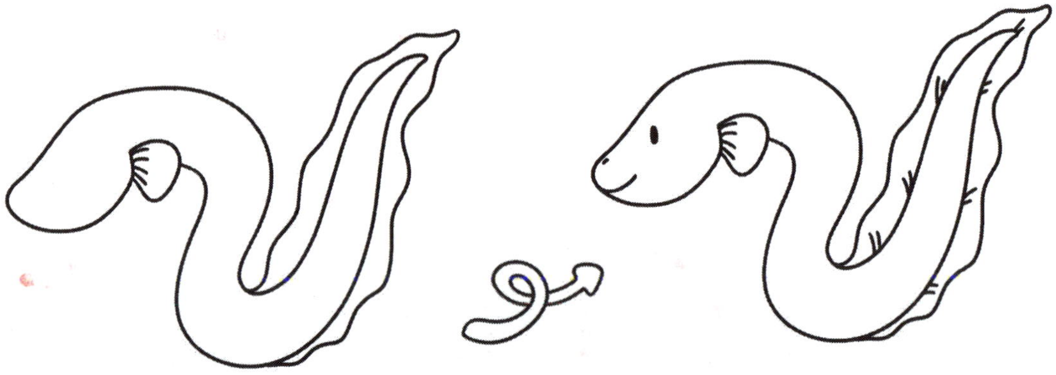

Parrot

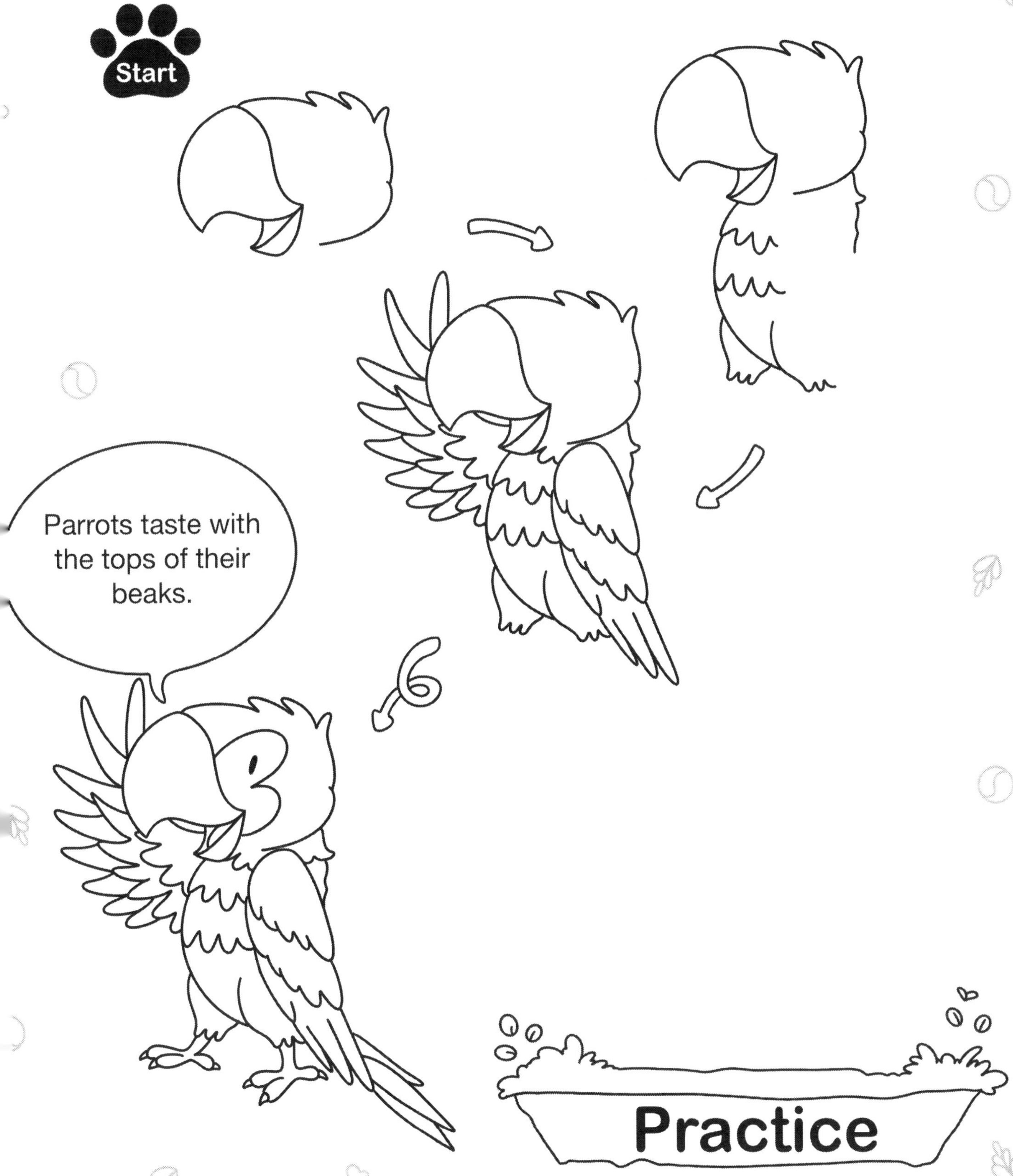

Mouse

Start

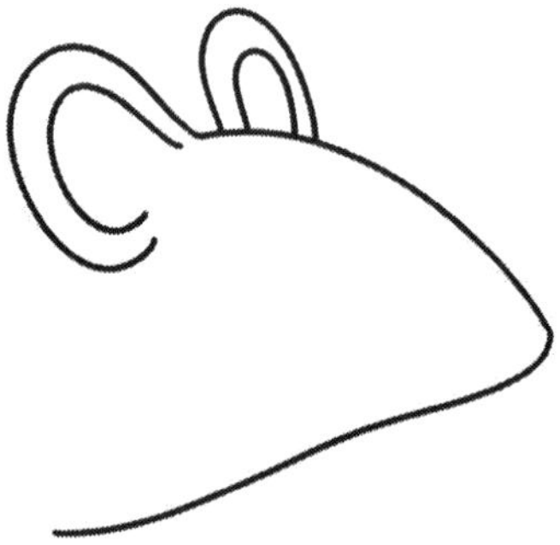

Practice

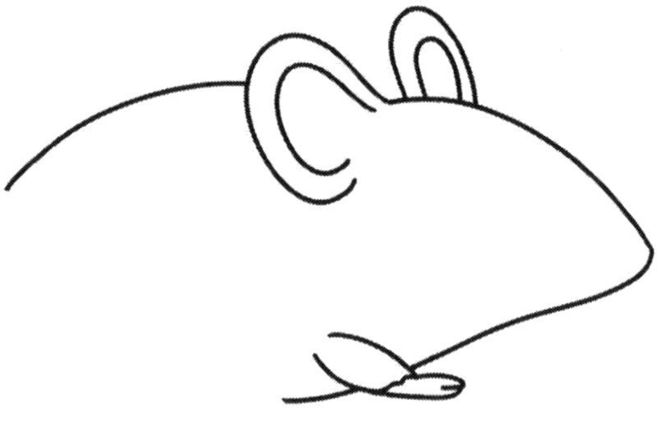

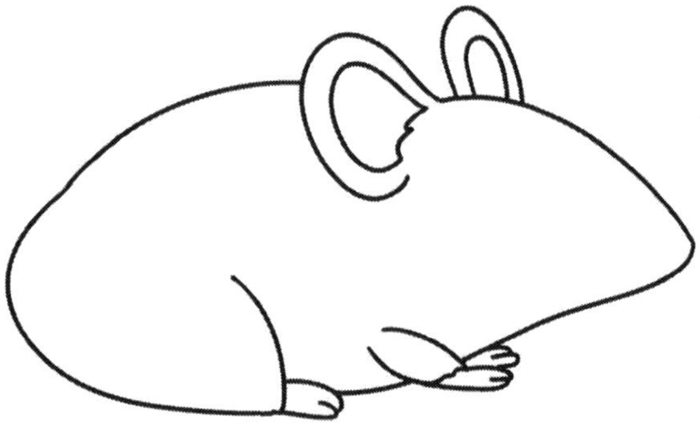

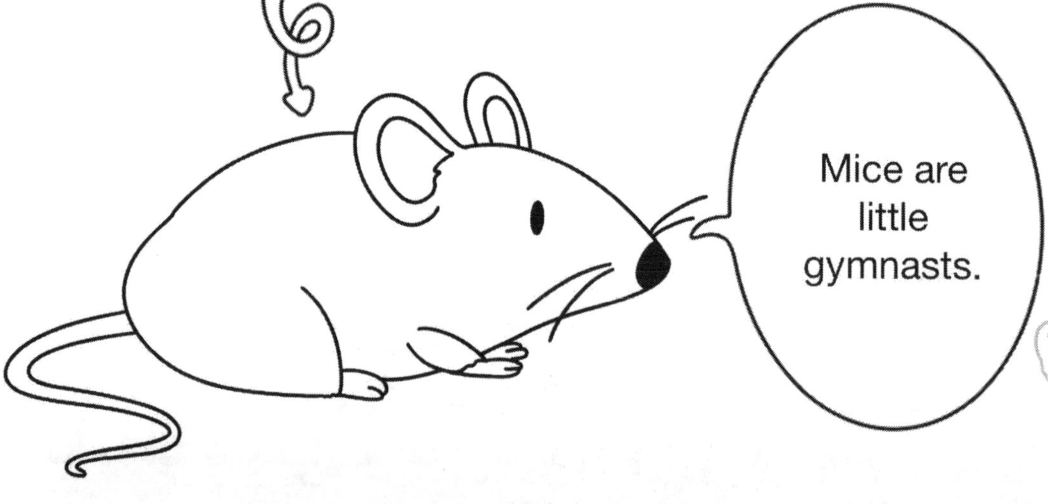

Beaver

Start

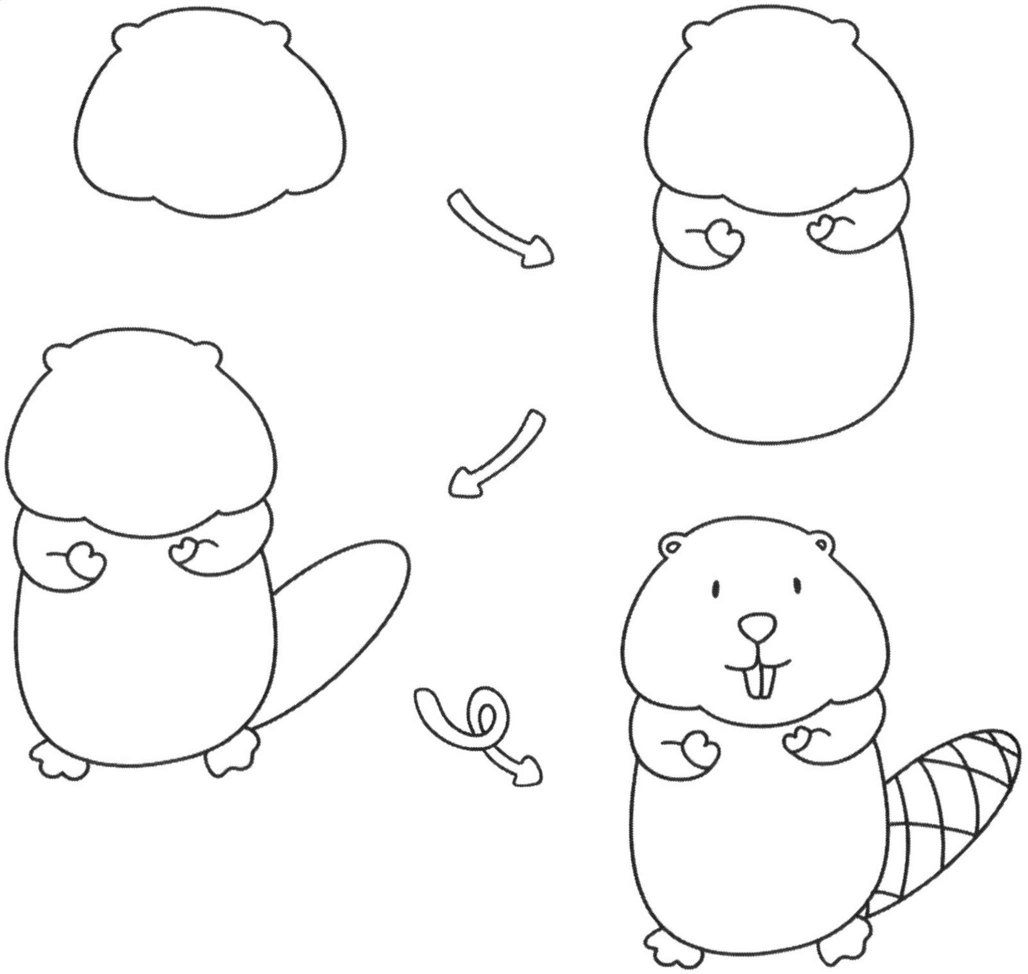

Beavers eat wood!

Practice

Mosquito

Start

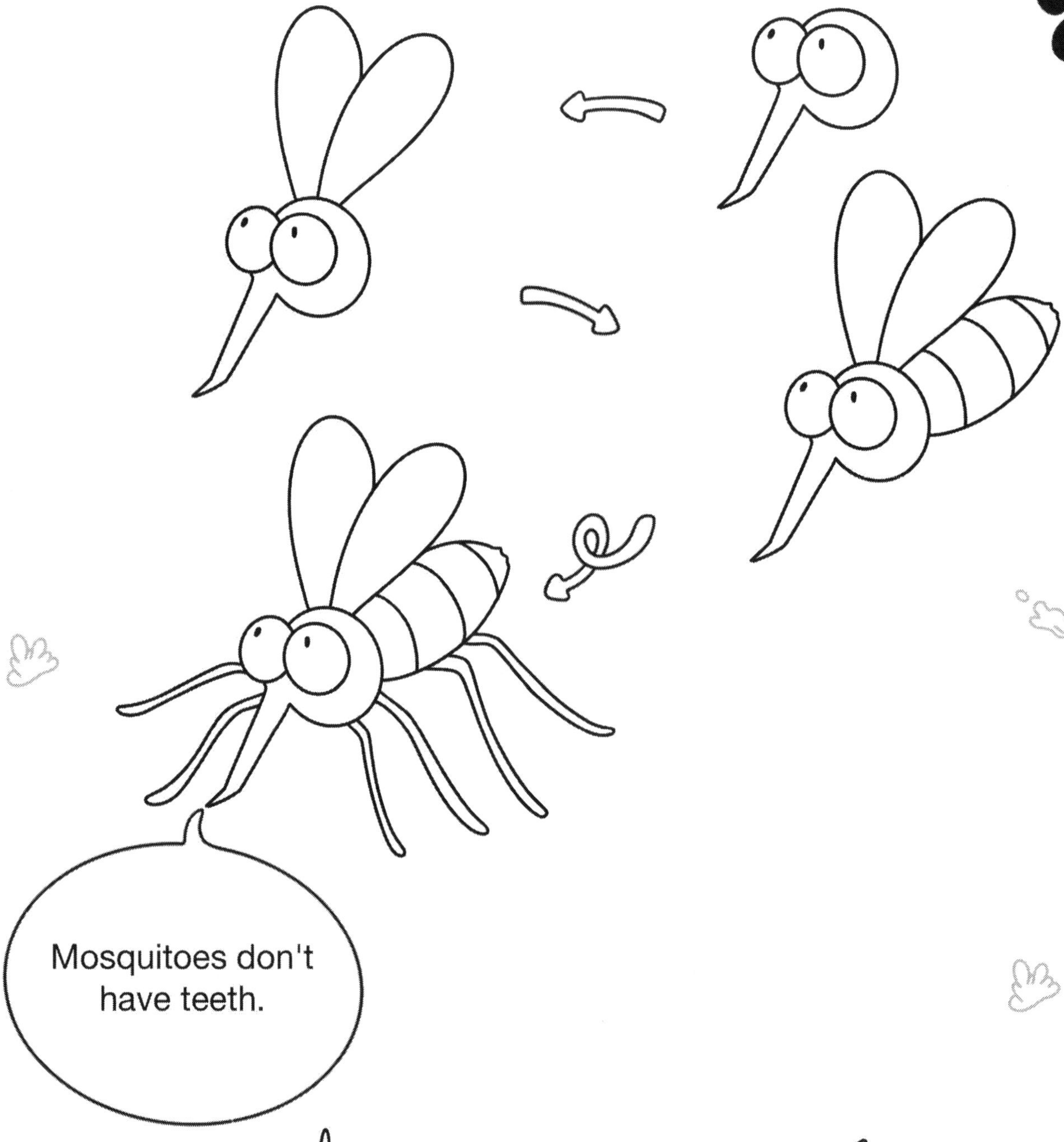

Practice

Crab

Start

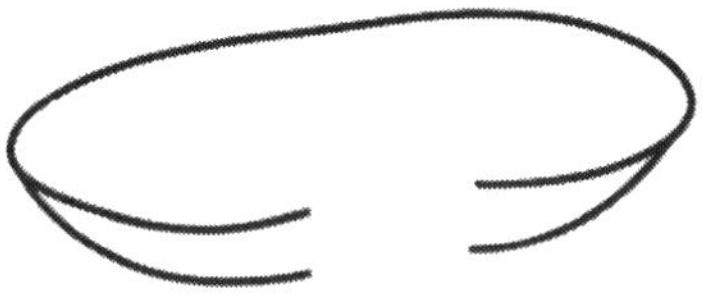

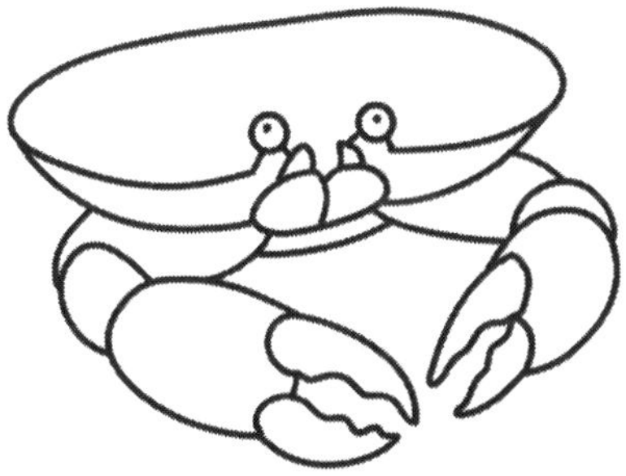

Practice

Crabs are super old!

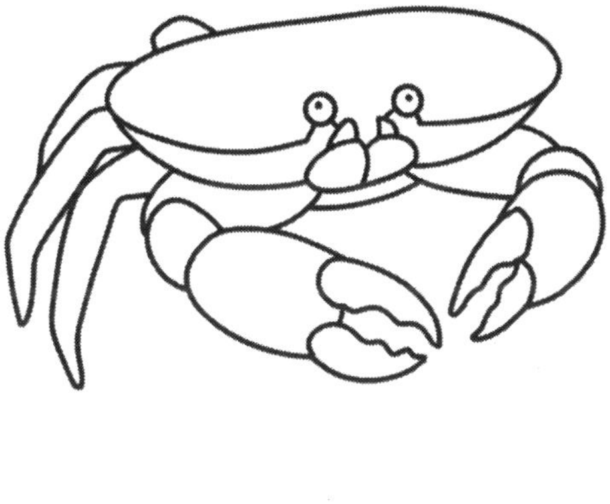

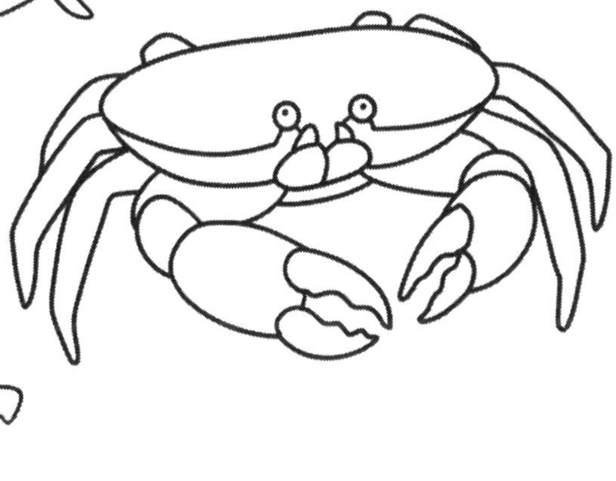

Buffalo

Start

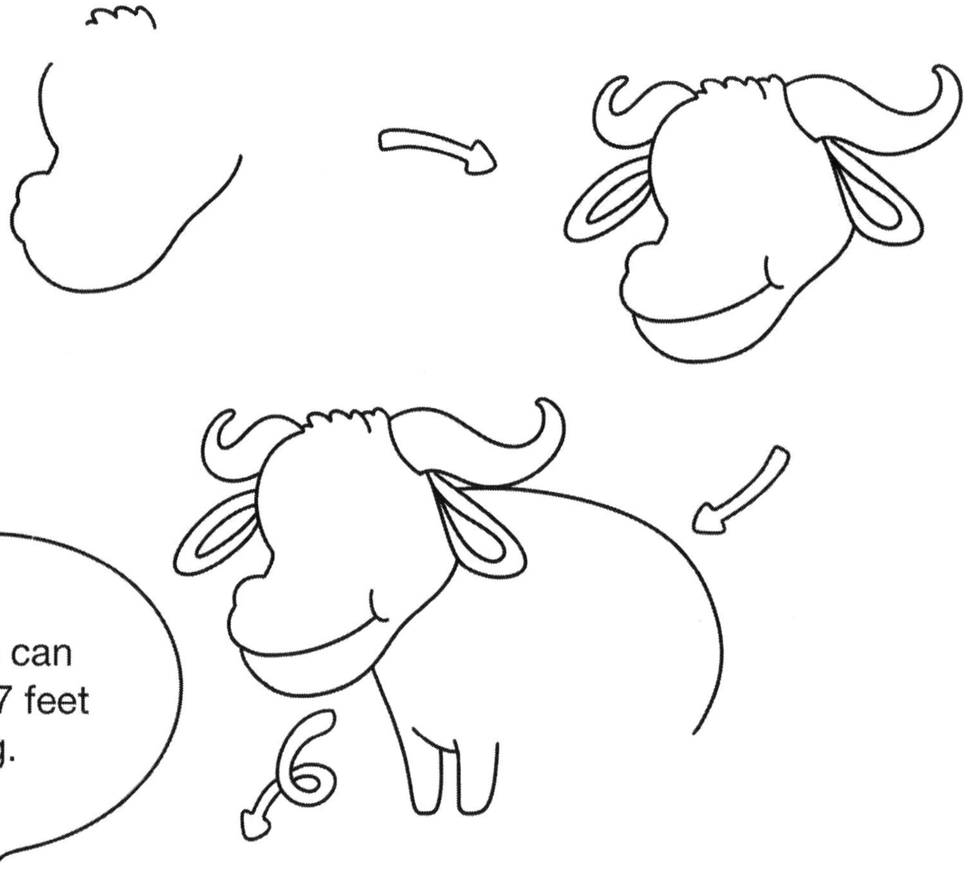

Buffalo can be 6 to 7 feet long.

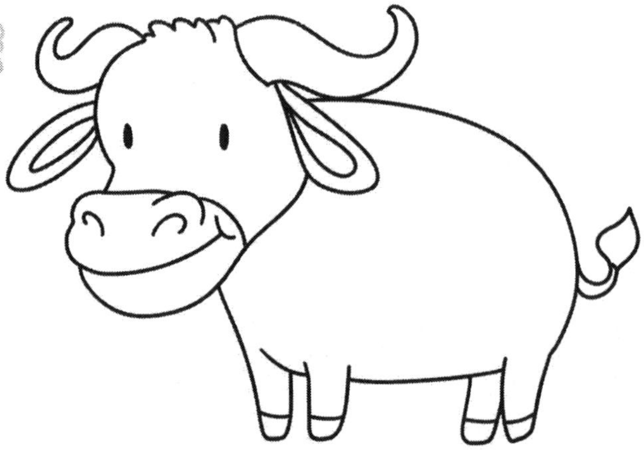

Practice

Lizard

Start

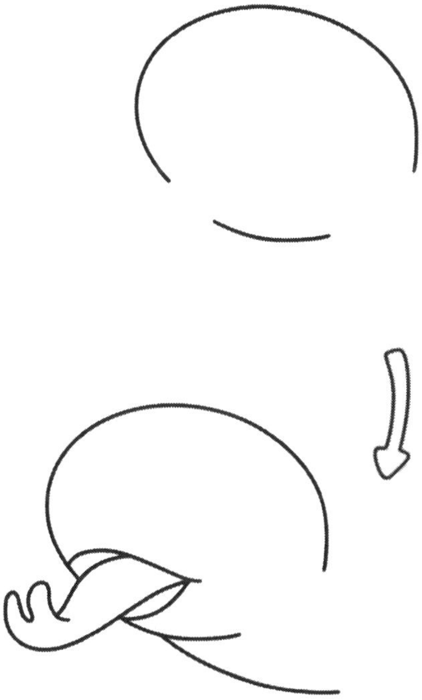

Practice

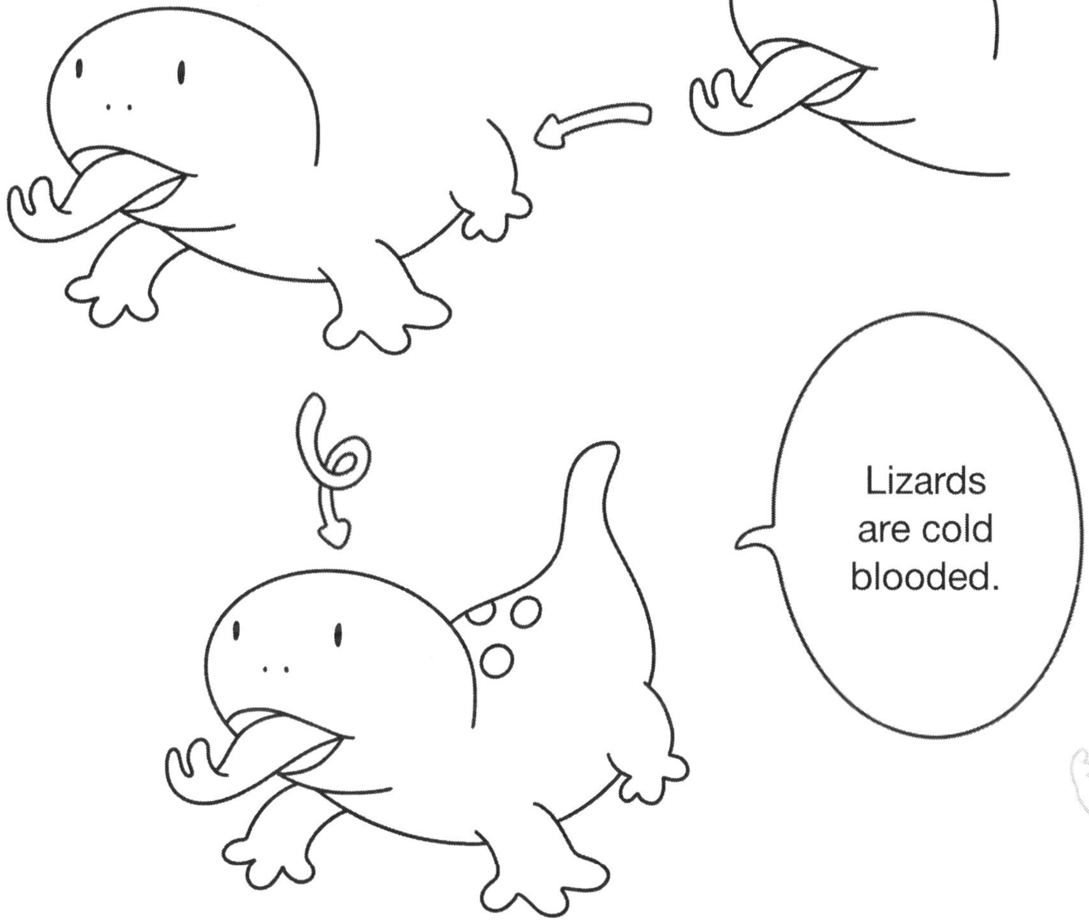

Wolf

Start

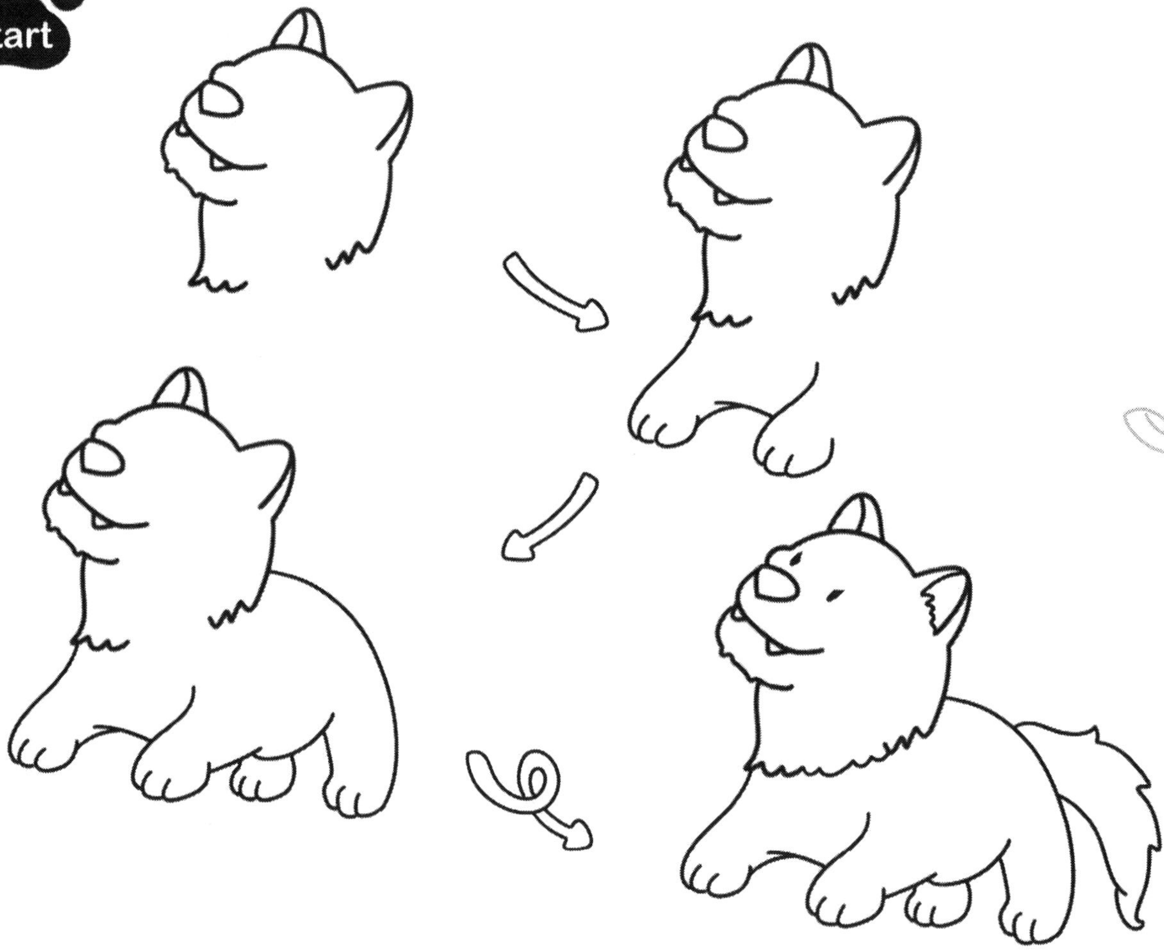

Wolves will die for each other.

Practice

Sloth

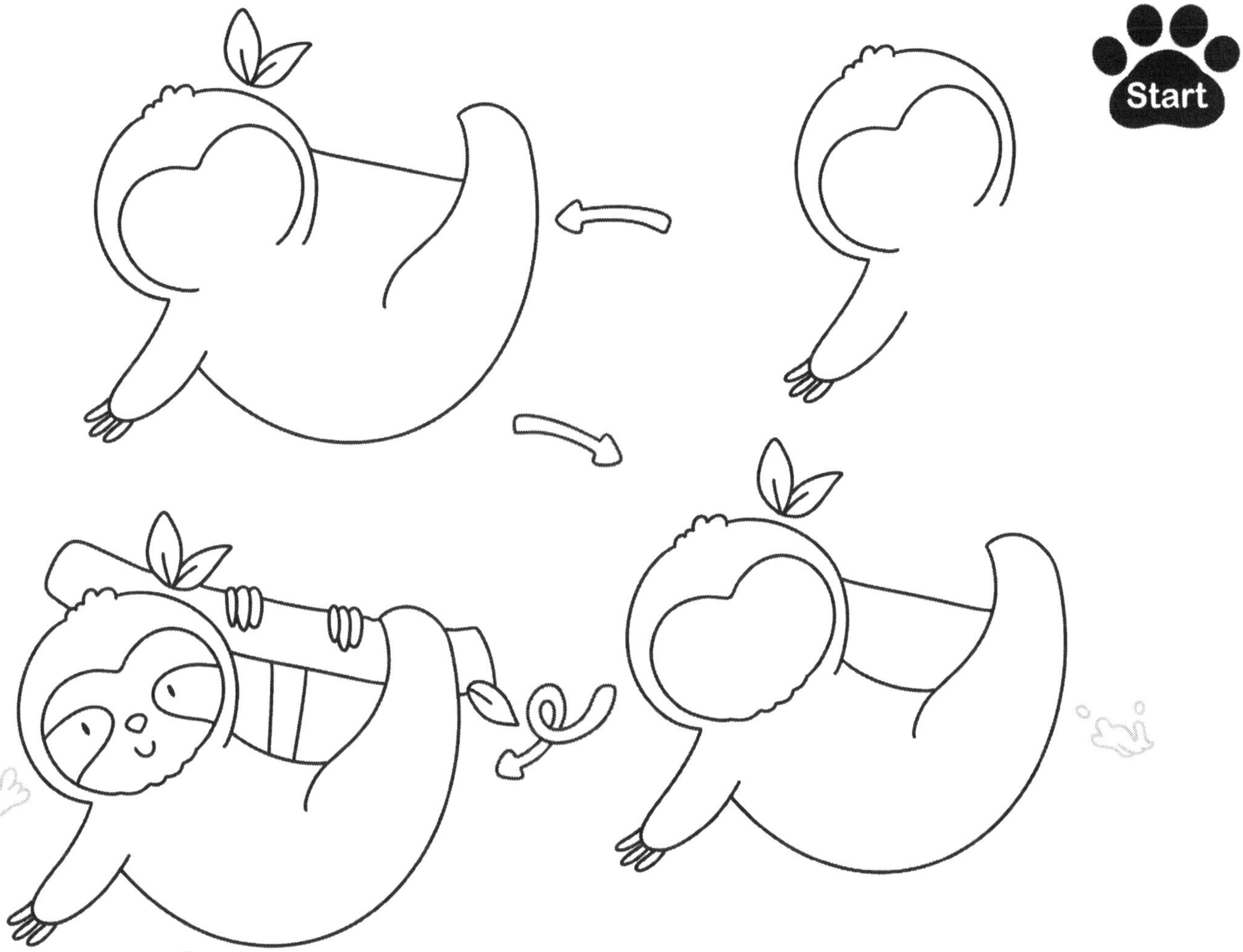

Sloths are blind in bright daylight.

Practice

Seahorse

Start

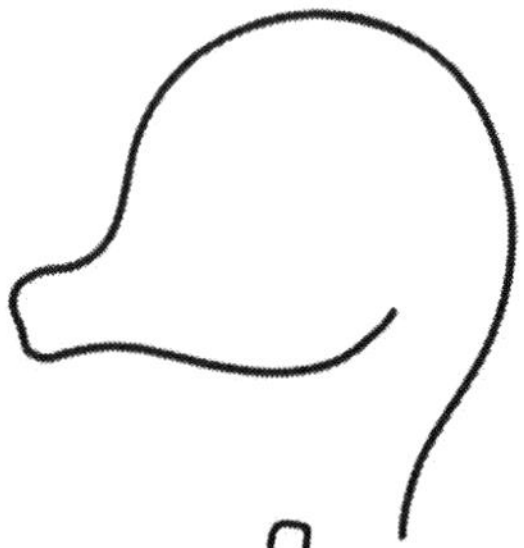

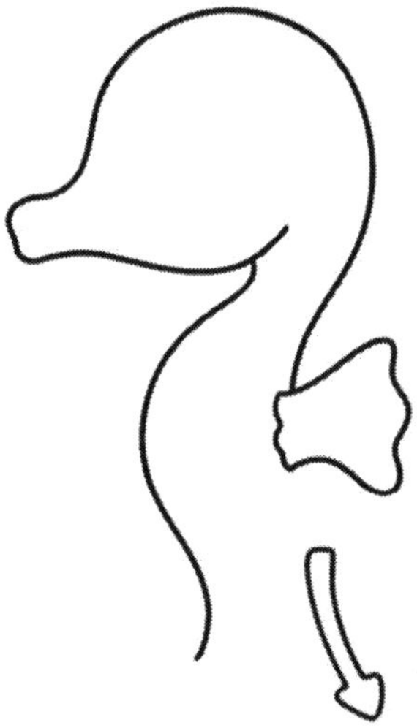

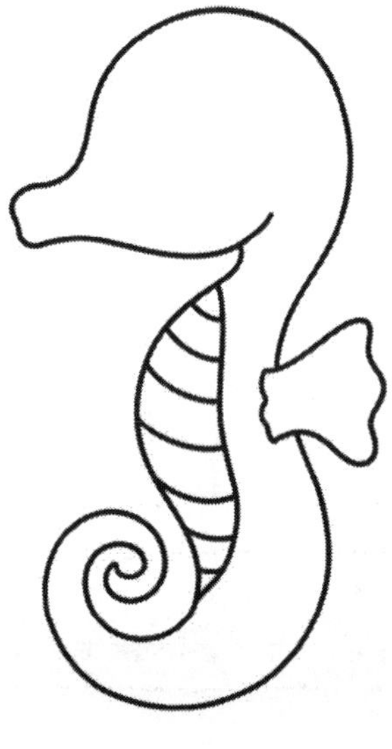

Practice

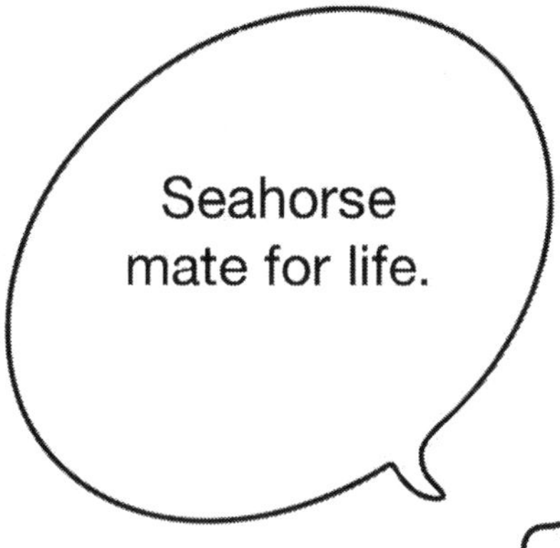

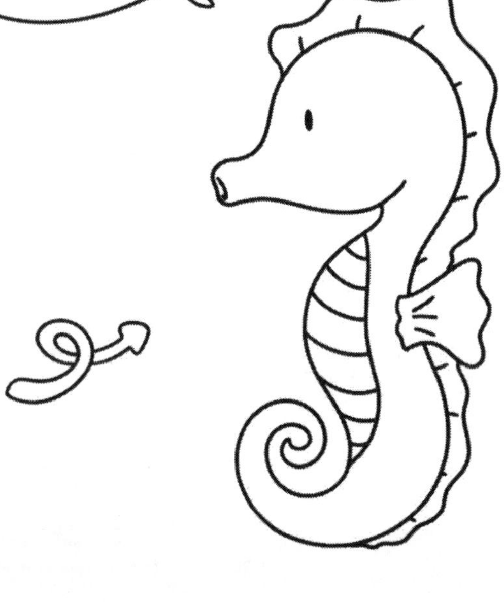

Lamb

Start

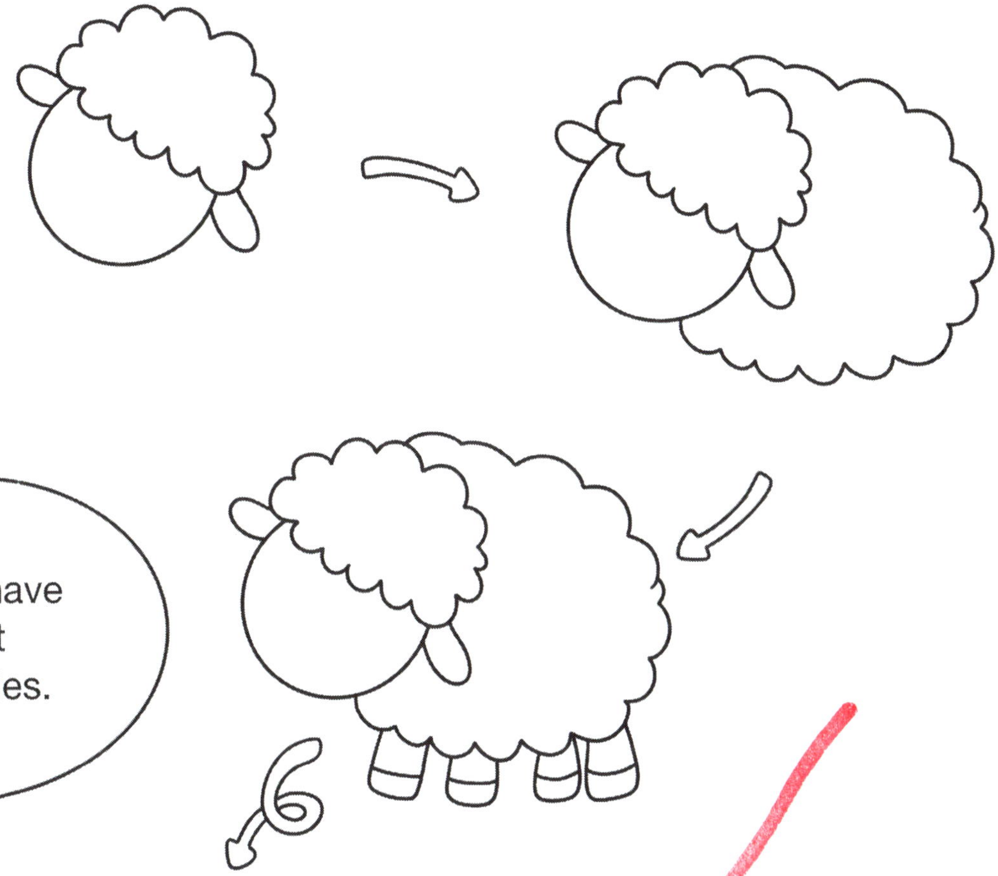

Sheep have great memories.

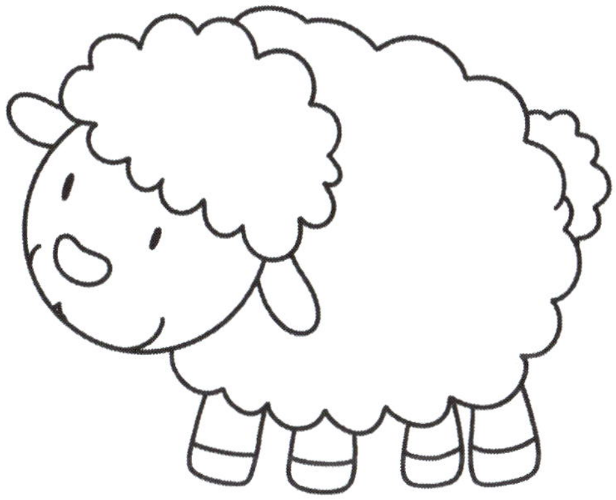

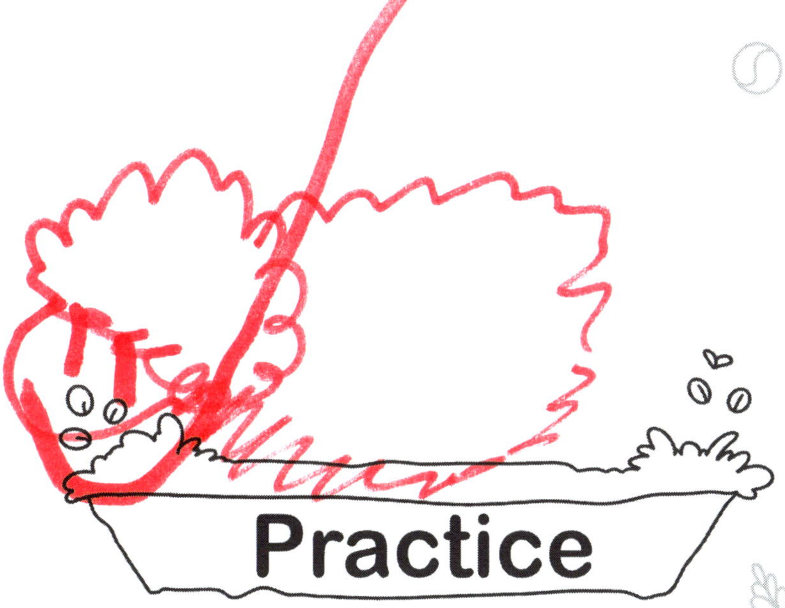

Raccoon

Start

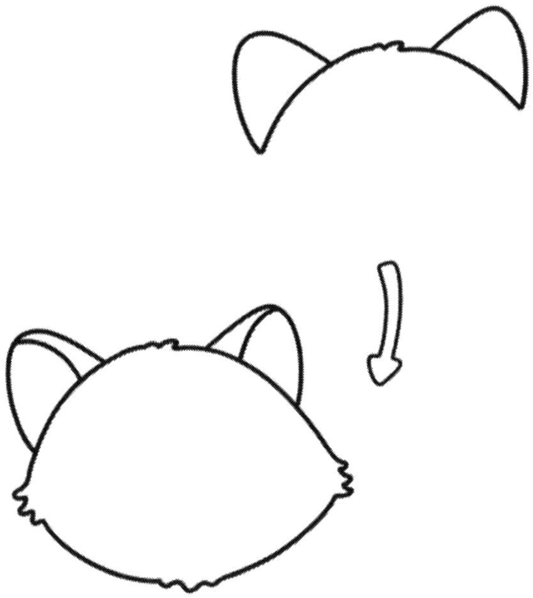

Practice

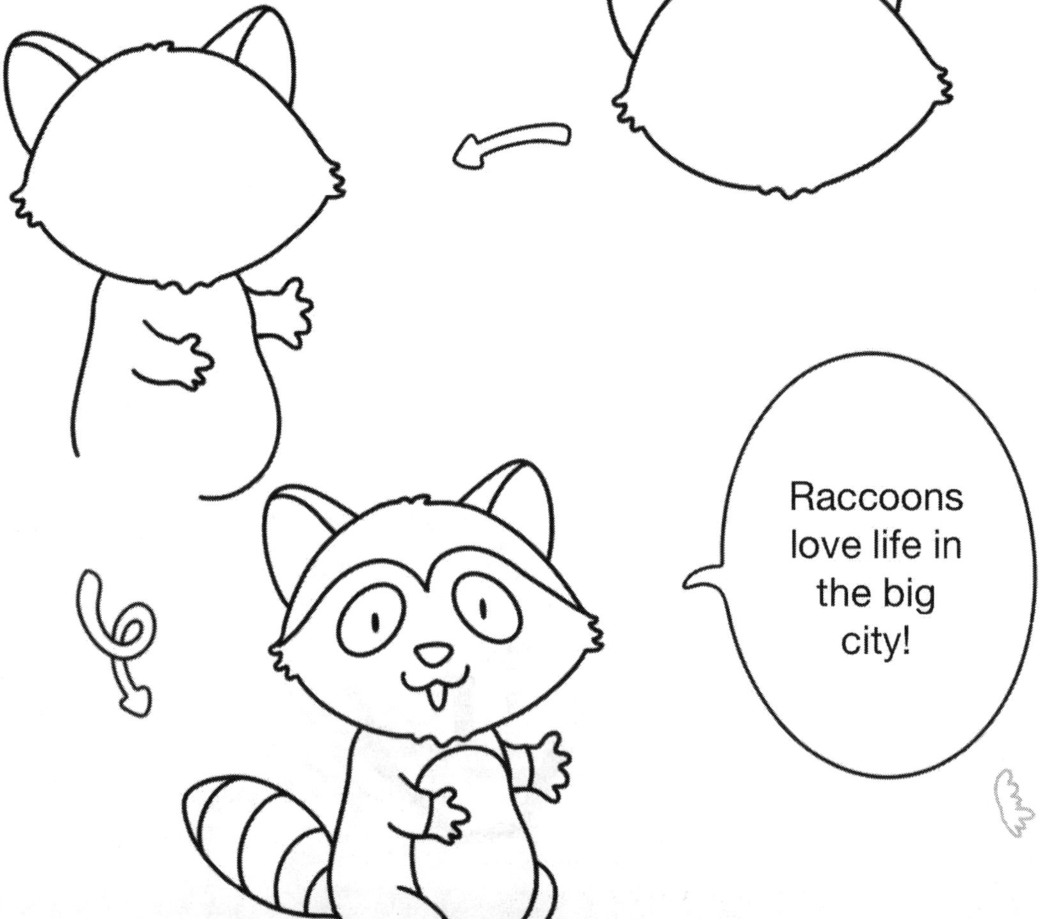

Rhinoceros

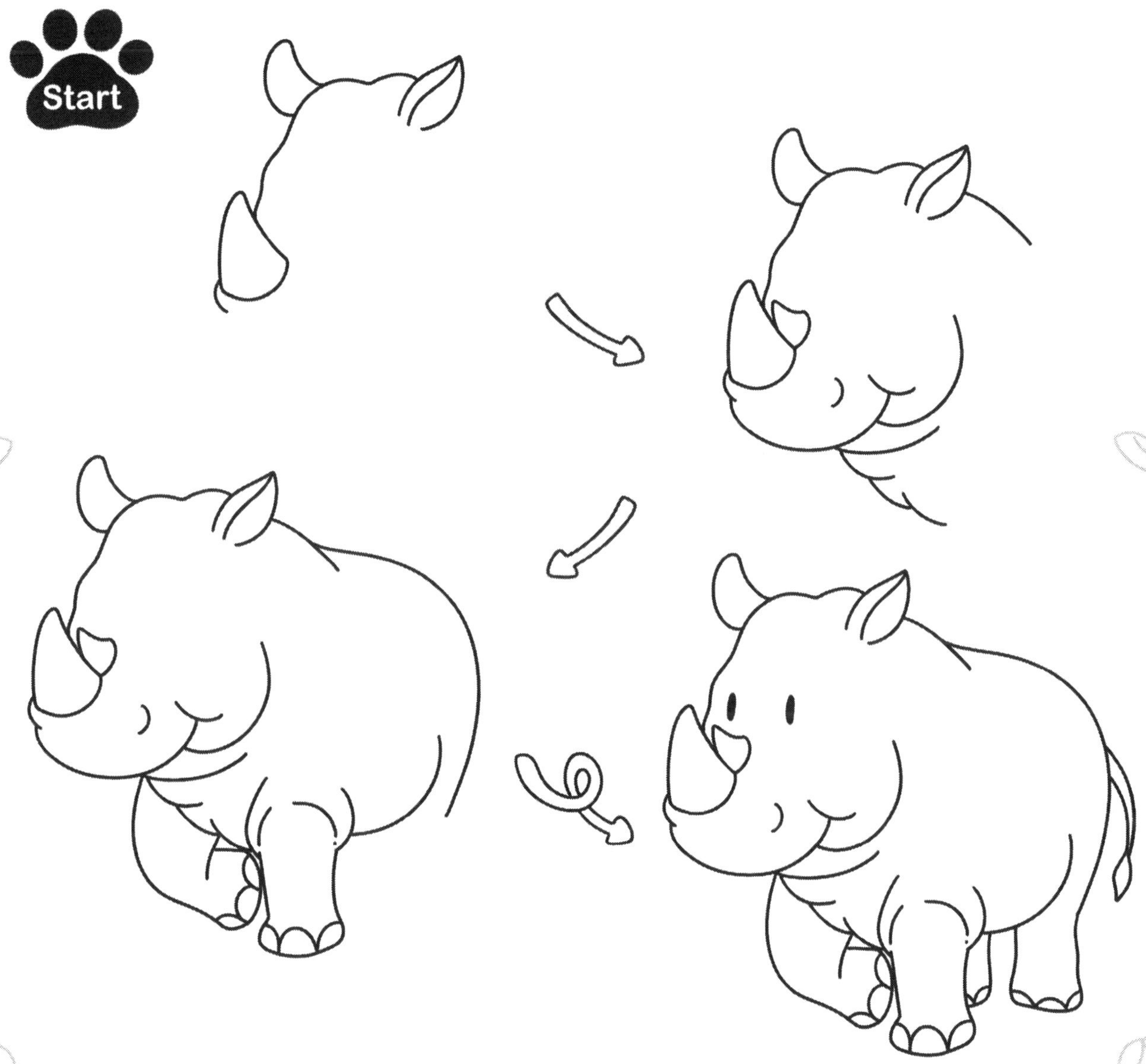

Rhinoceros have poor vision.

Practice

Ostrich

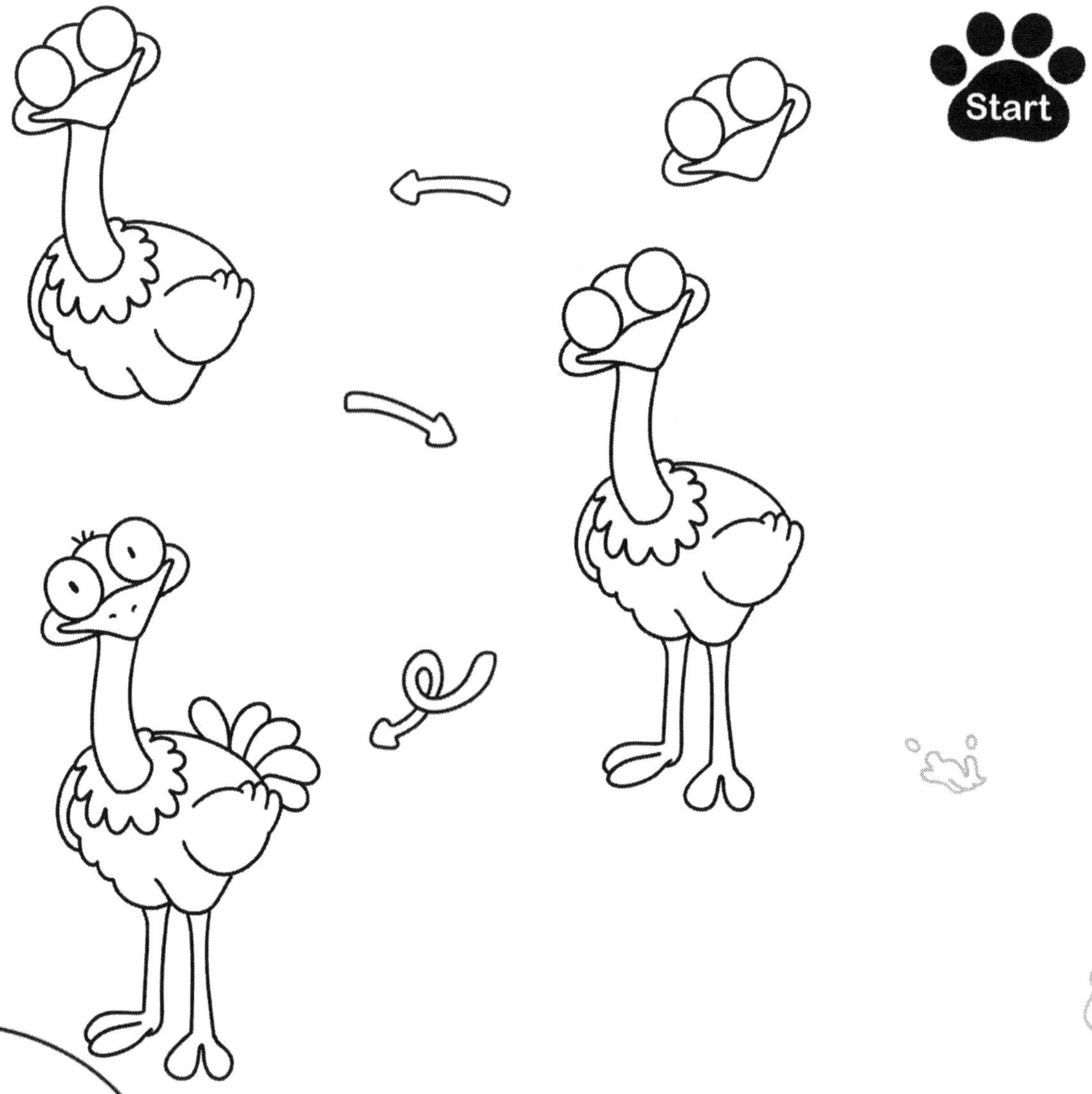

Ostrich have three stomachs.

Practice

Lobster

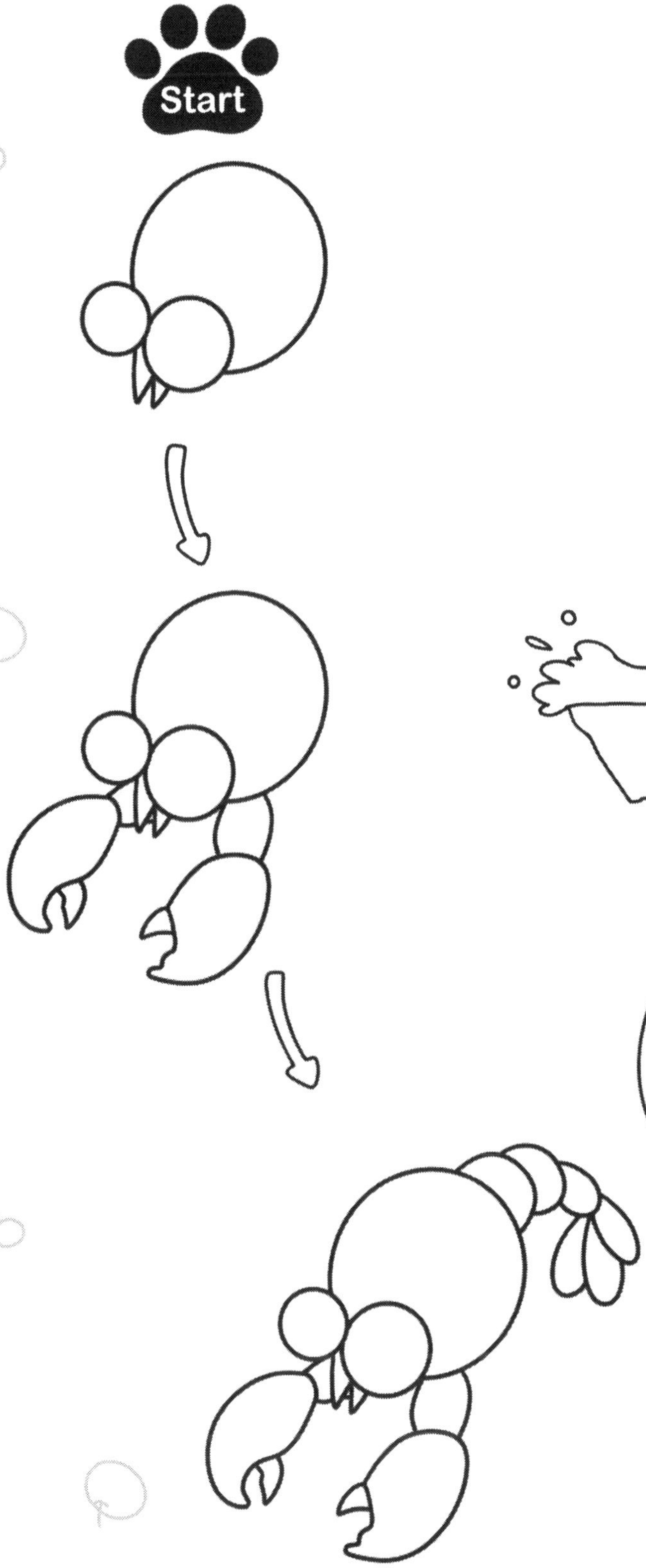

Practice

Lobster chew with their stomachs.

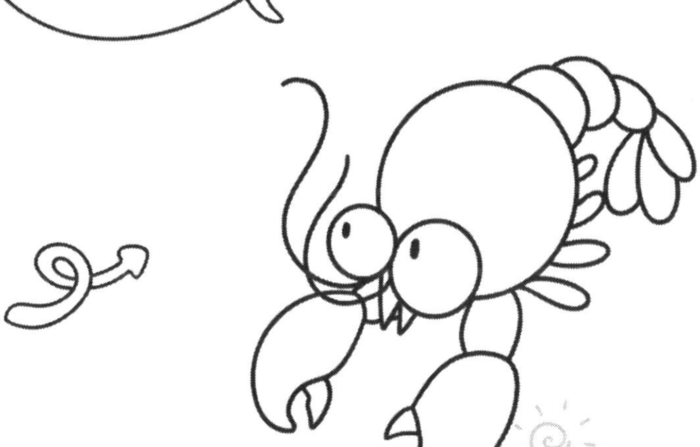

Cockroach

Start

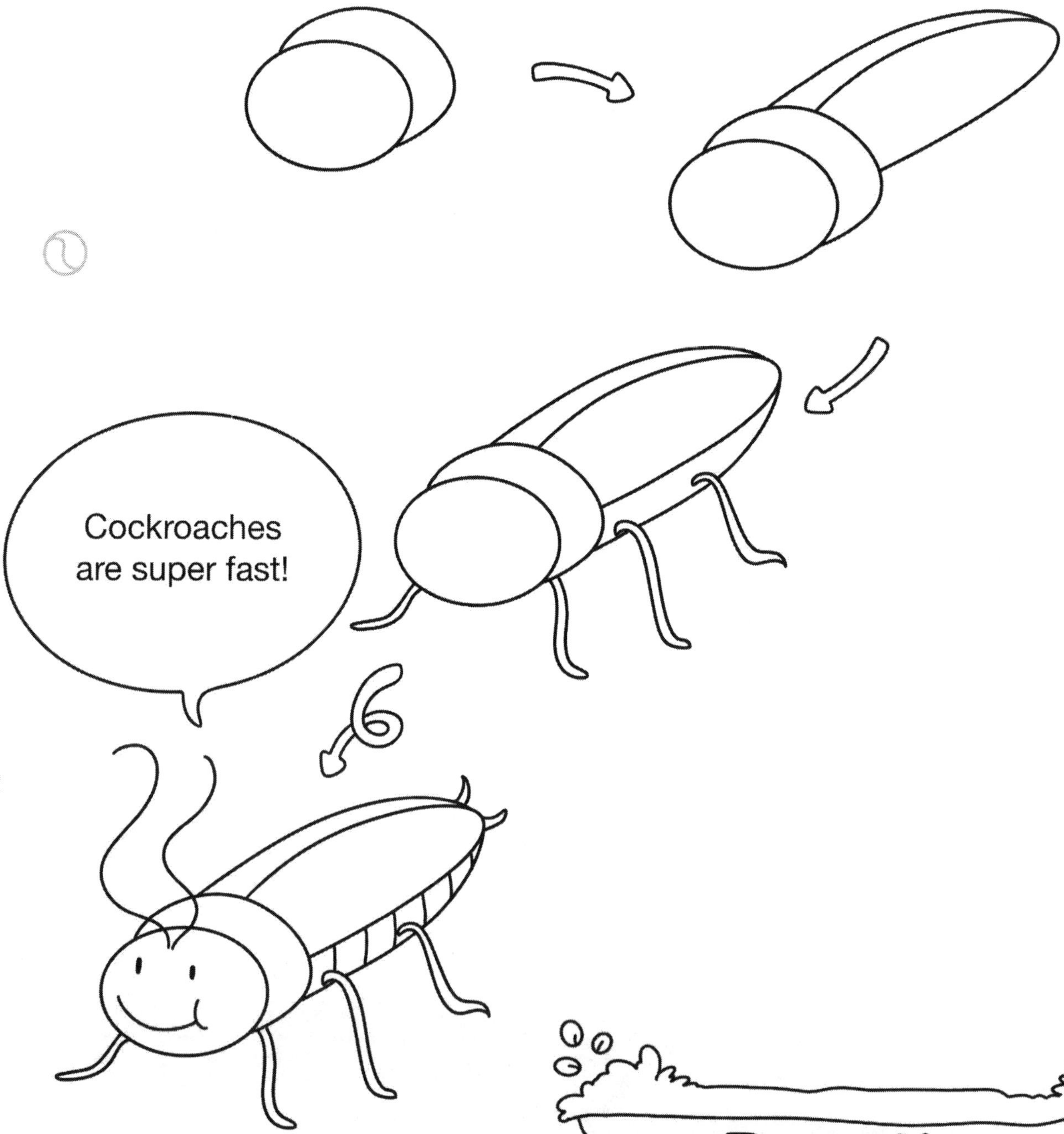

Practice

Bee

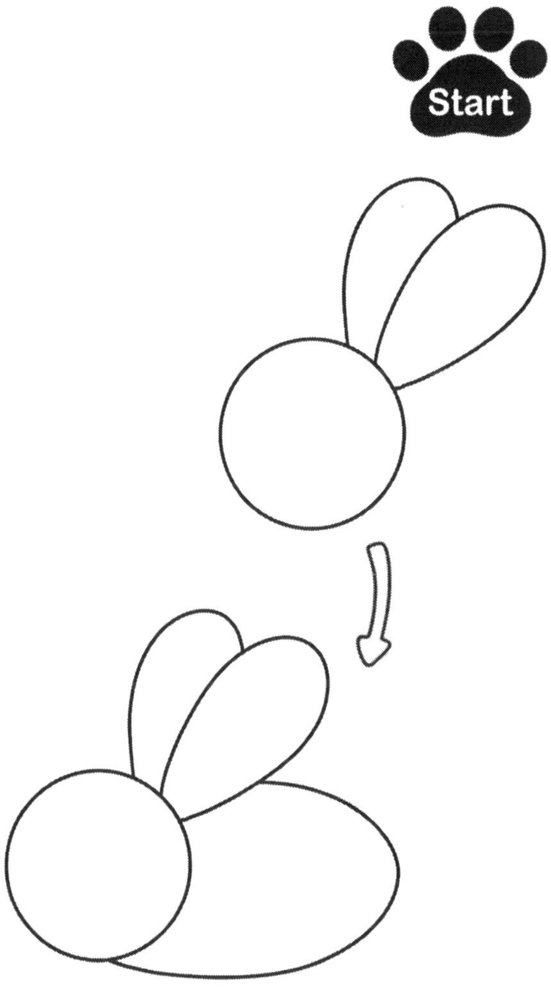

Practice

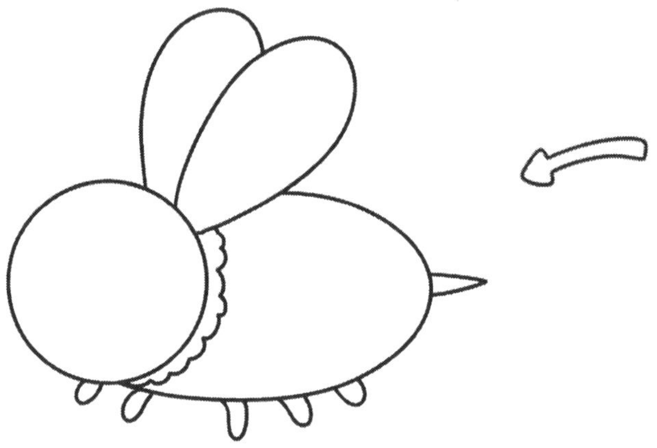

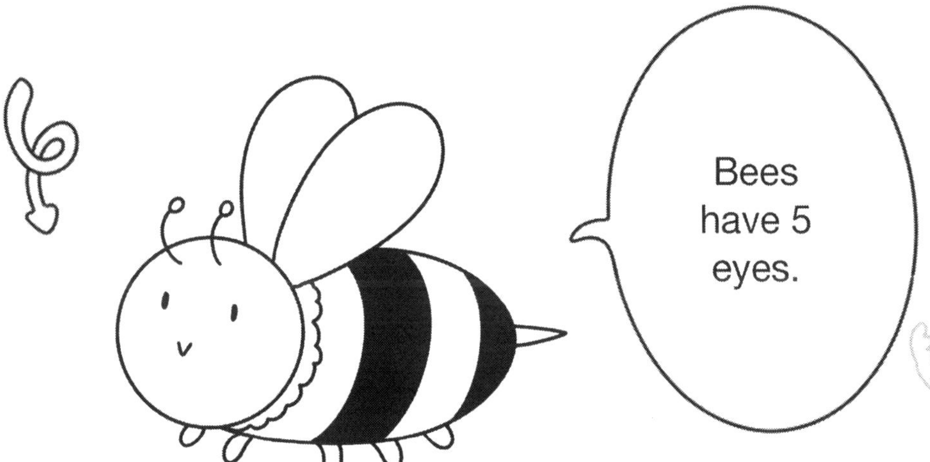

Goose

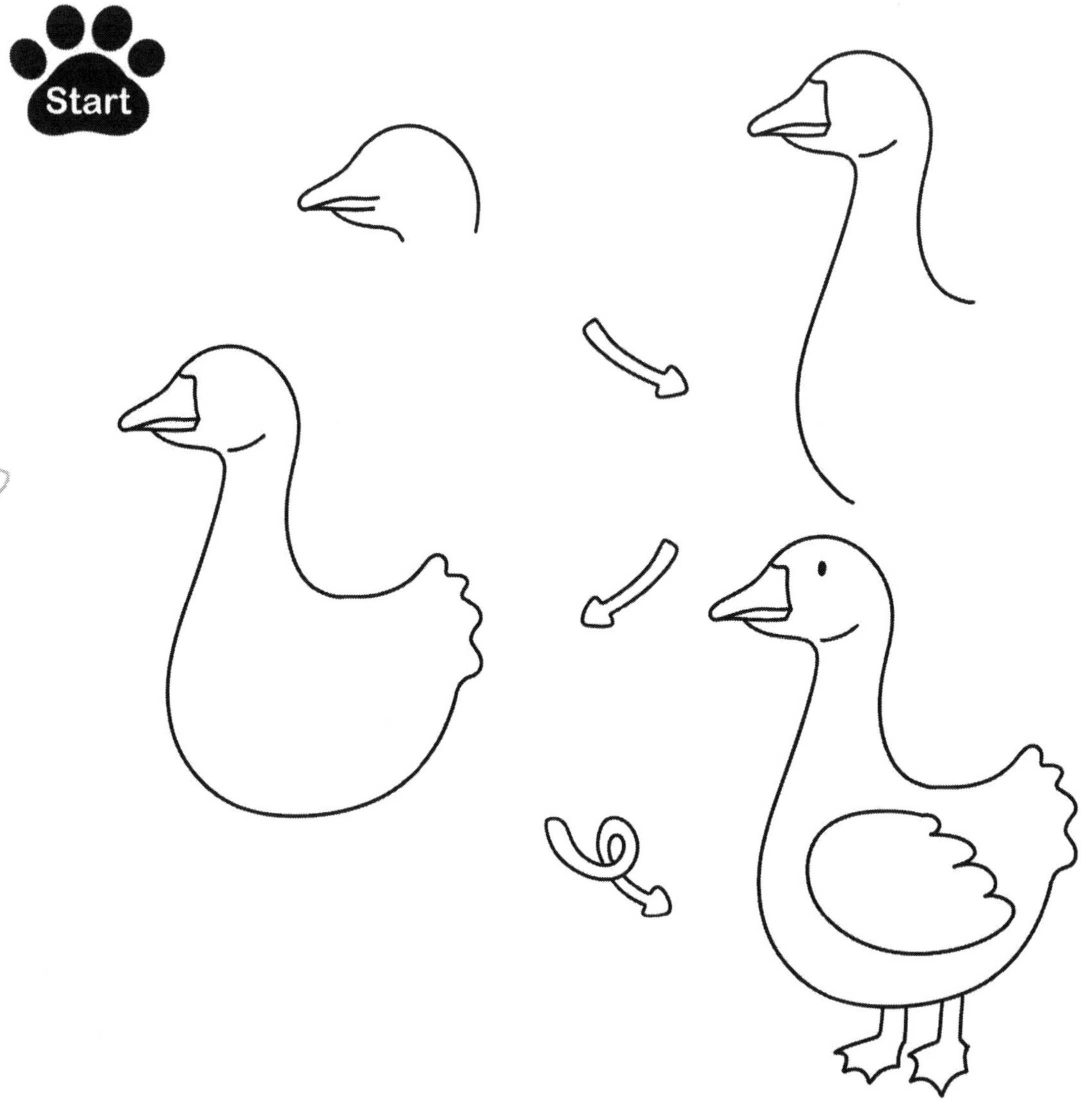

Geese fly in a "V" formation.

Practice

Hippopotamus

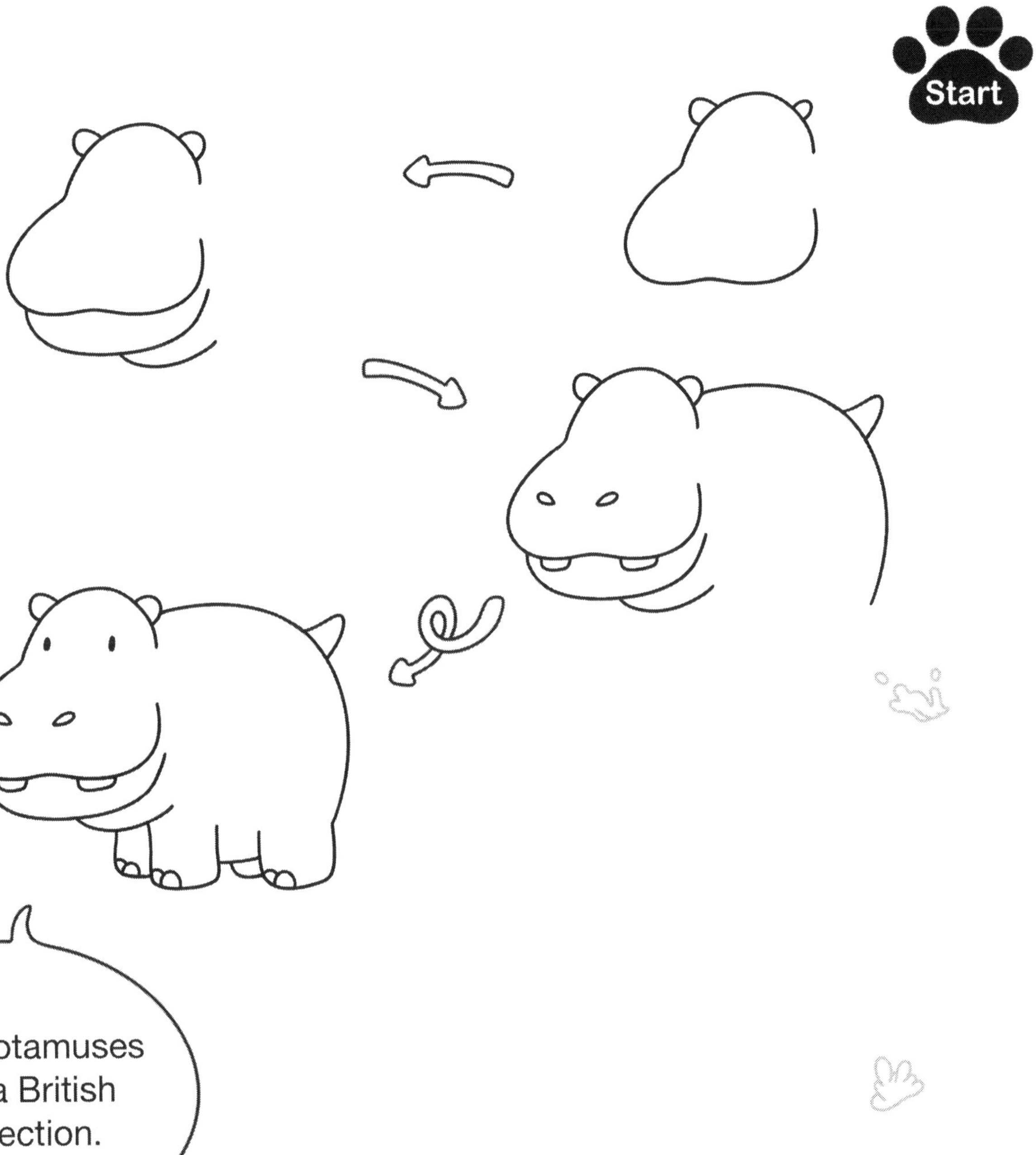

Hippopotamuses have a British connection.

Practice

Coral

Start

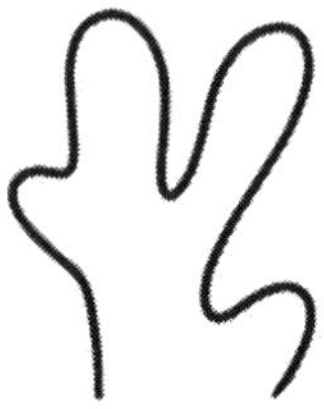

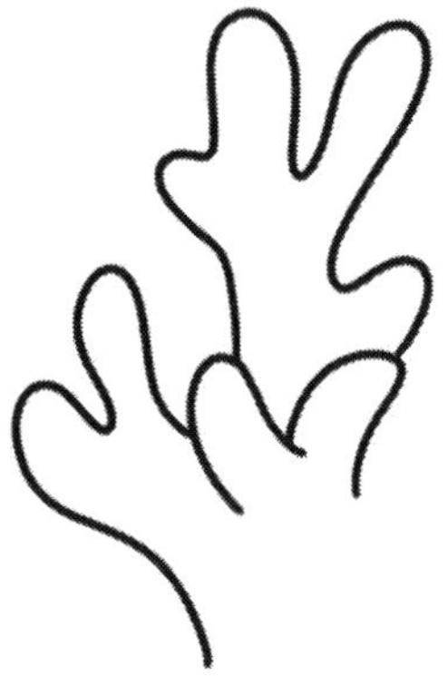

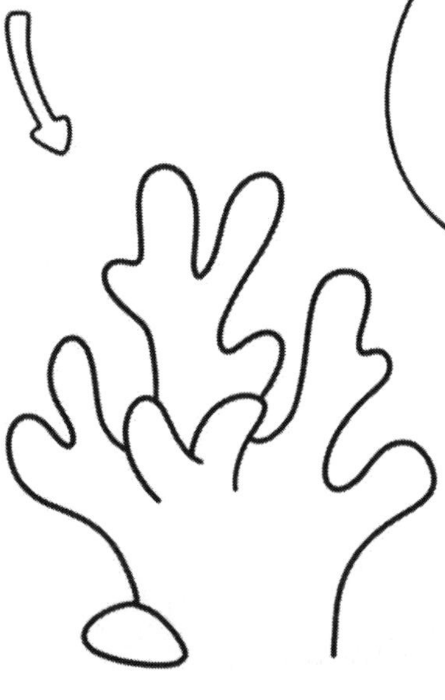

Practice

Coral are animals, not plants.

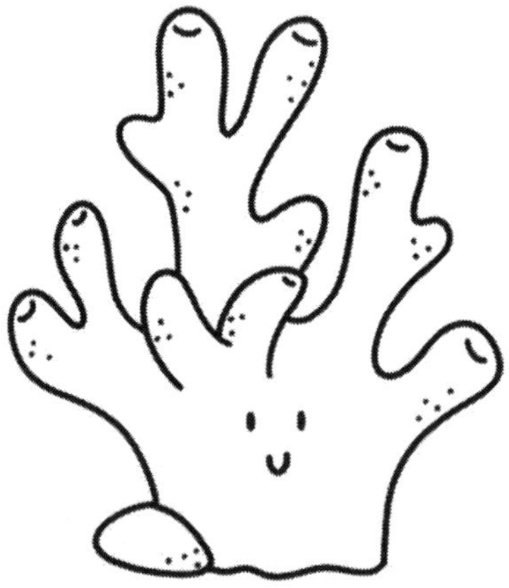

Butterfly

Start

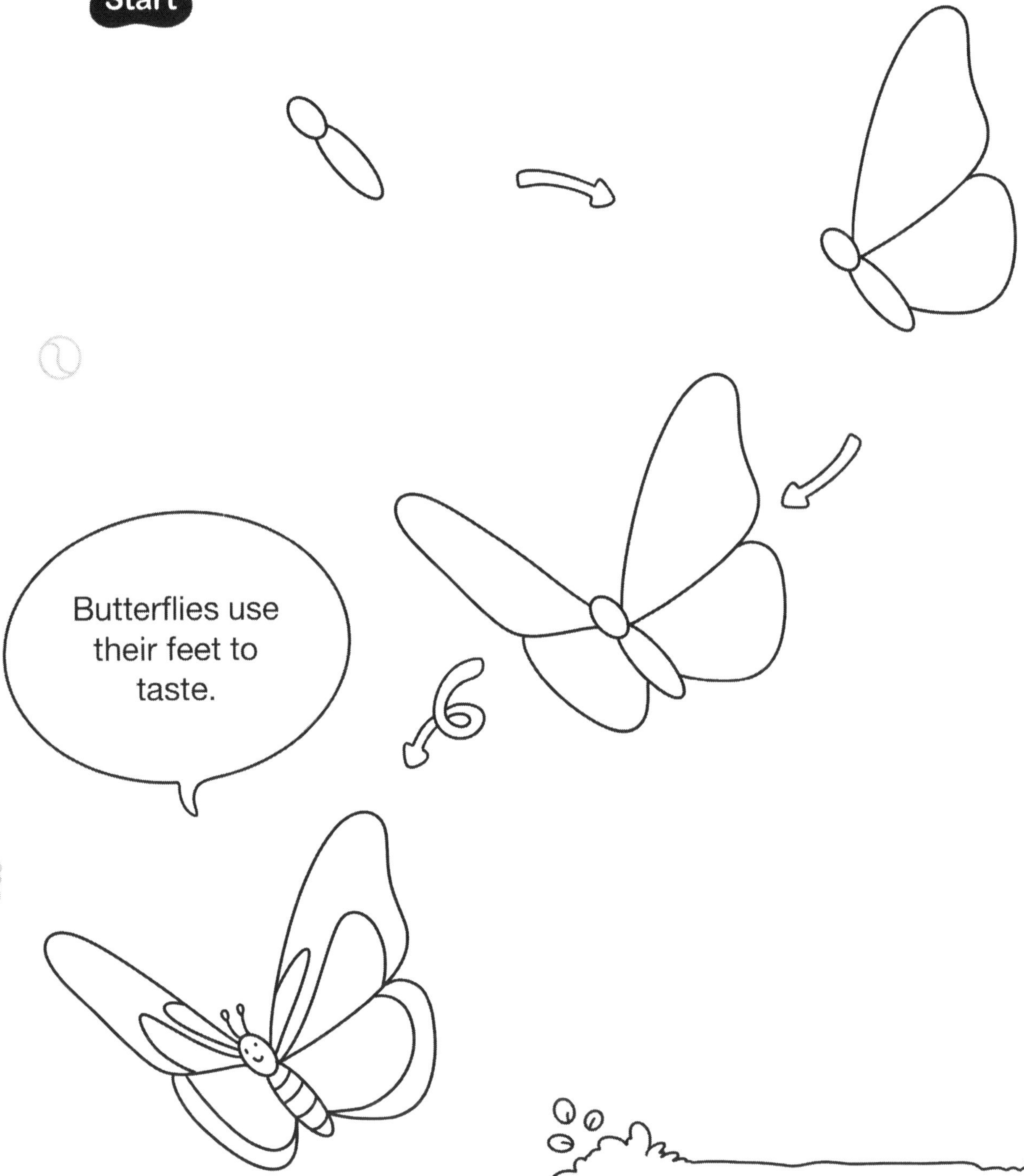

Practice

Goat

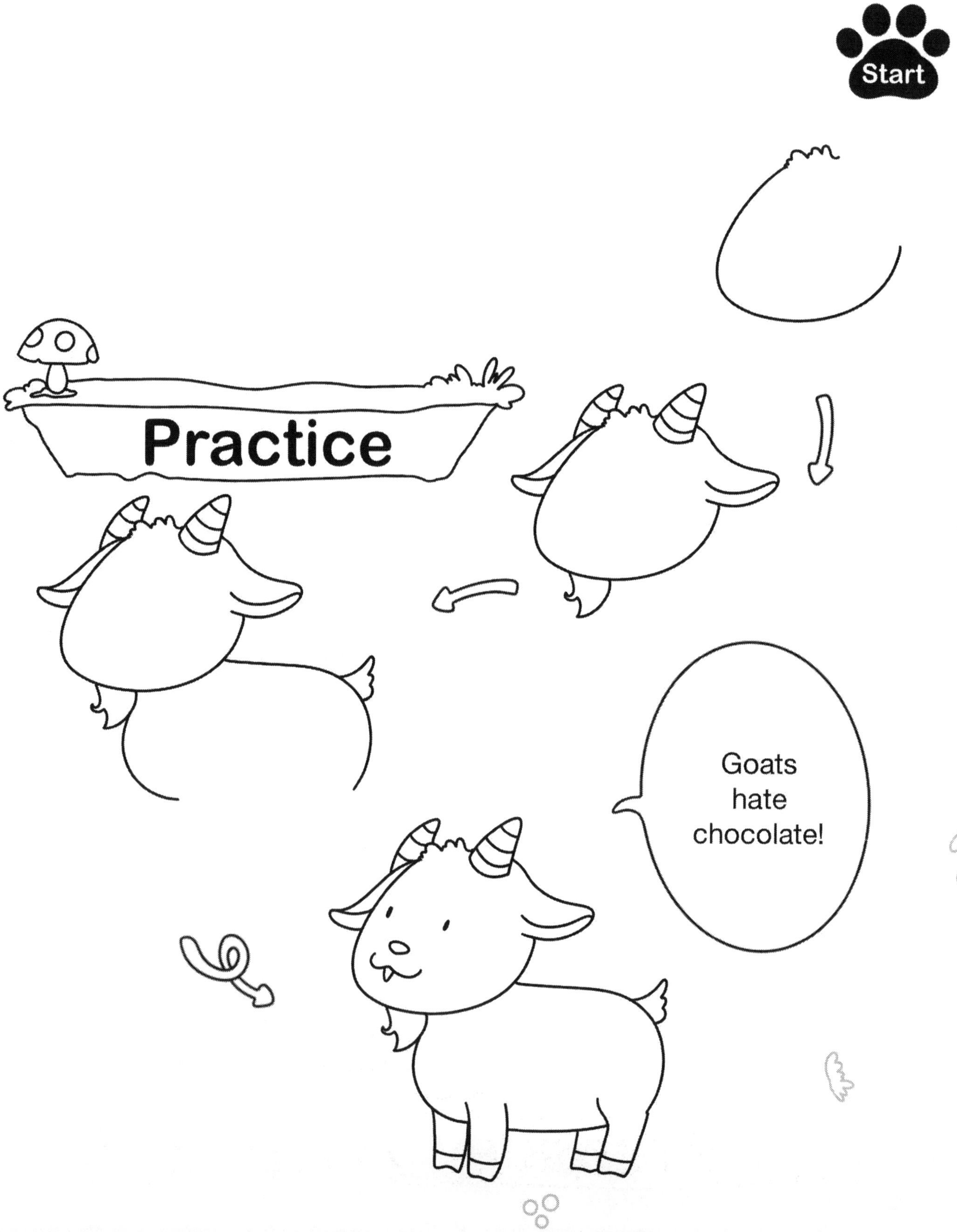

Practice

Unicorn

Start

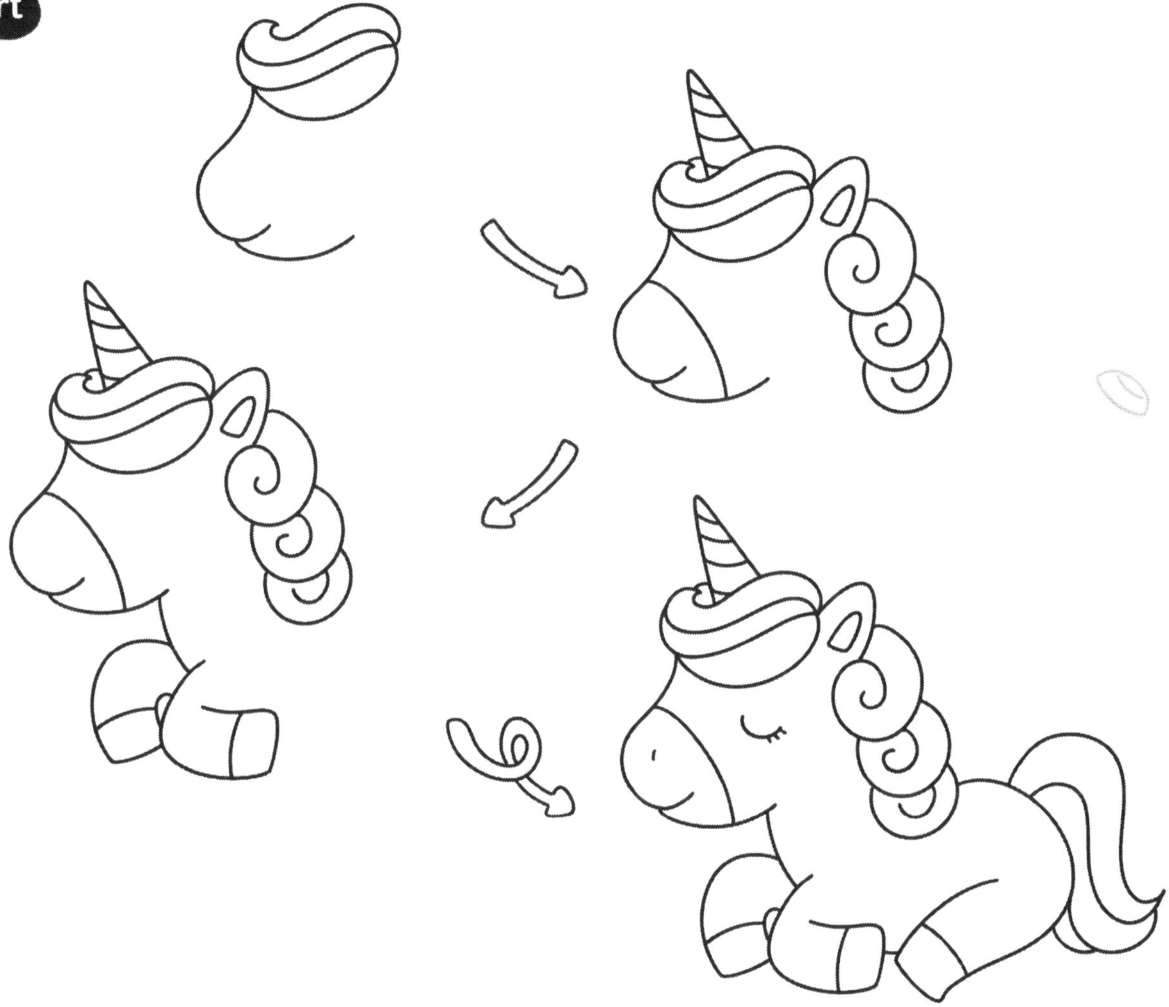

Unicorns are earthbound and do not have wings.

Practice

Flamingo

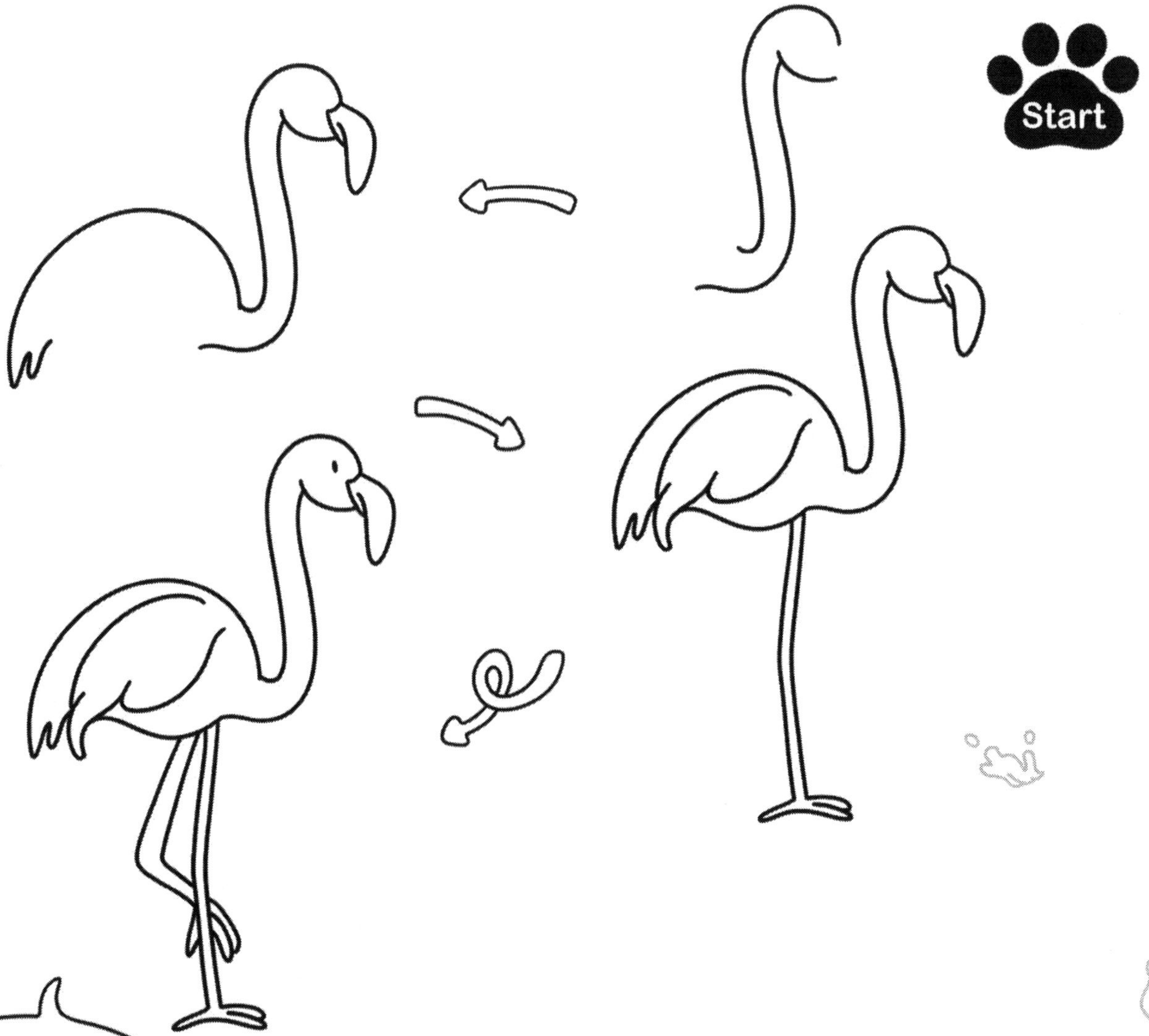

Flamingo get their pink color from their food.

Practice

Stingray

Start

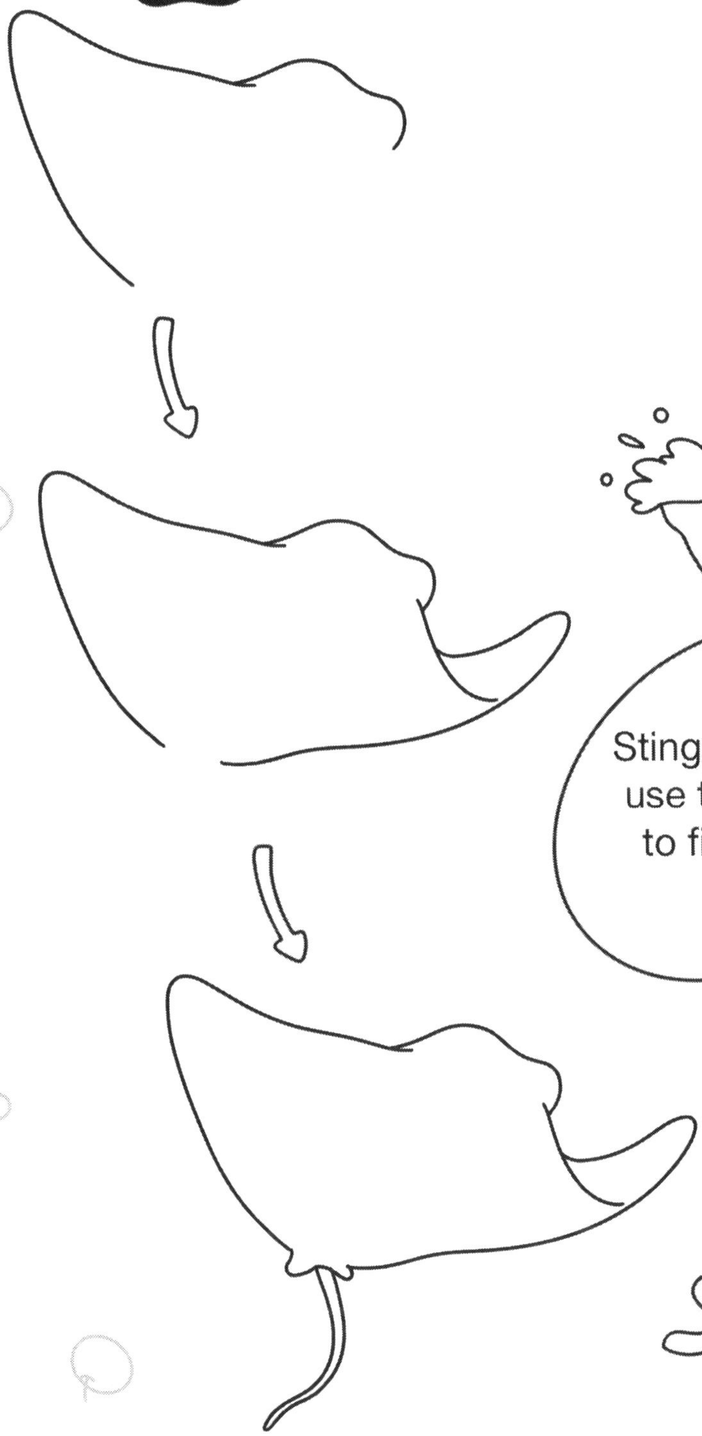

Practice

Stingrays don't use their eyes to find prey.

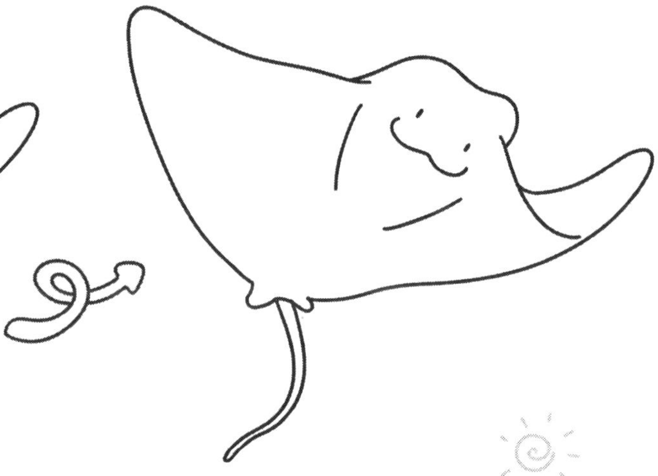

Fly

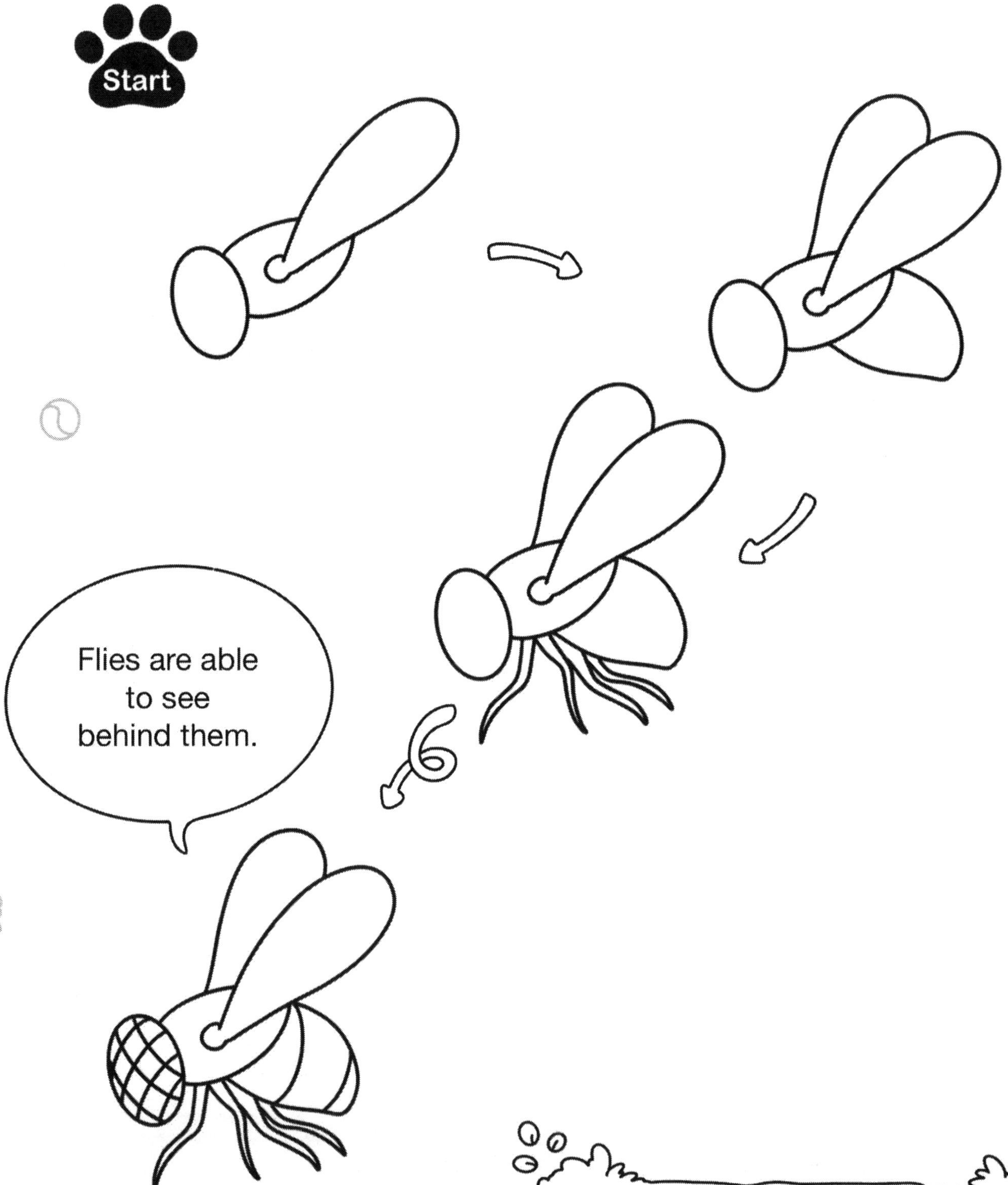

Practice

Gasshopper

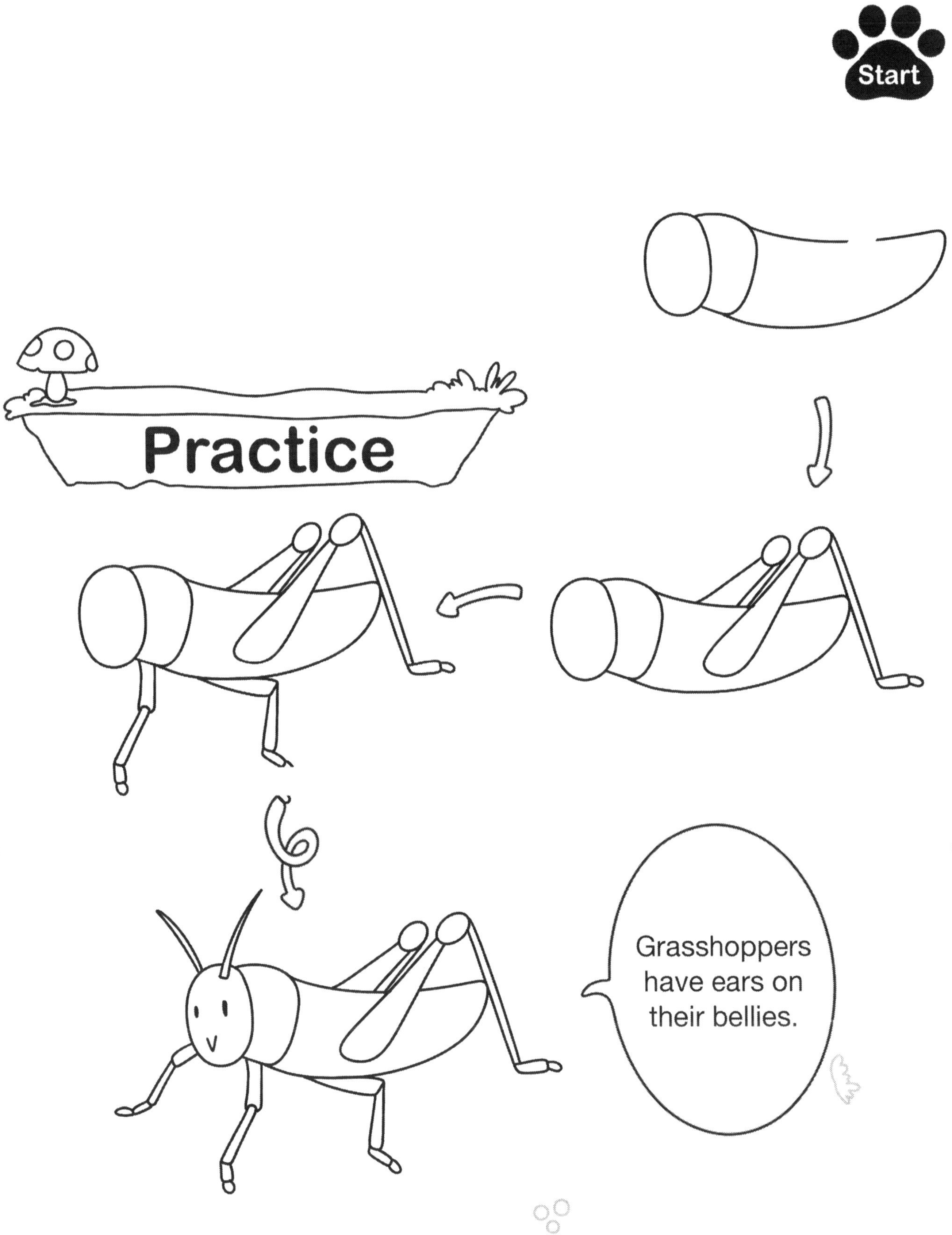

Spider

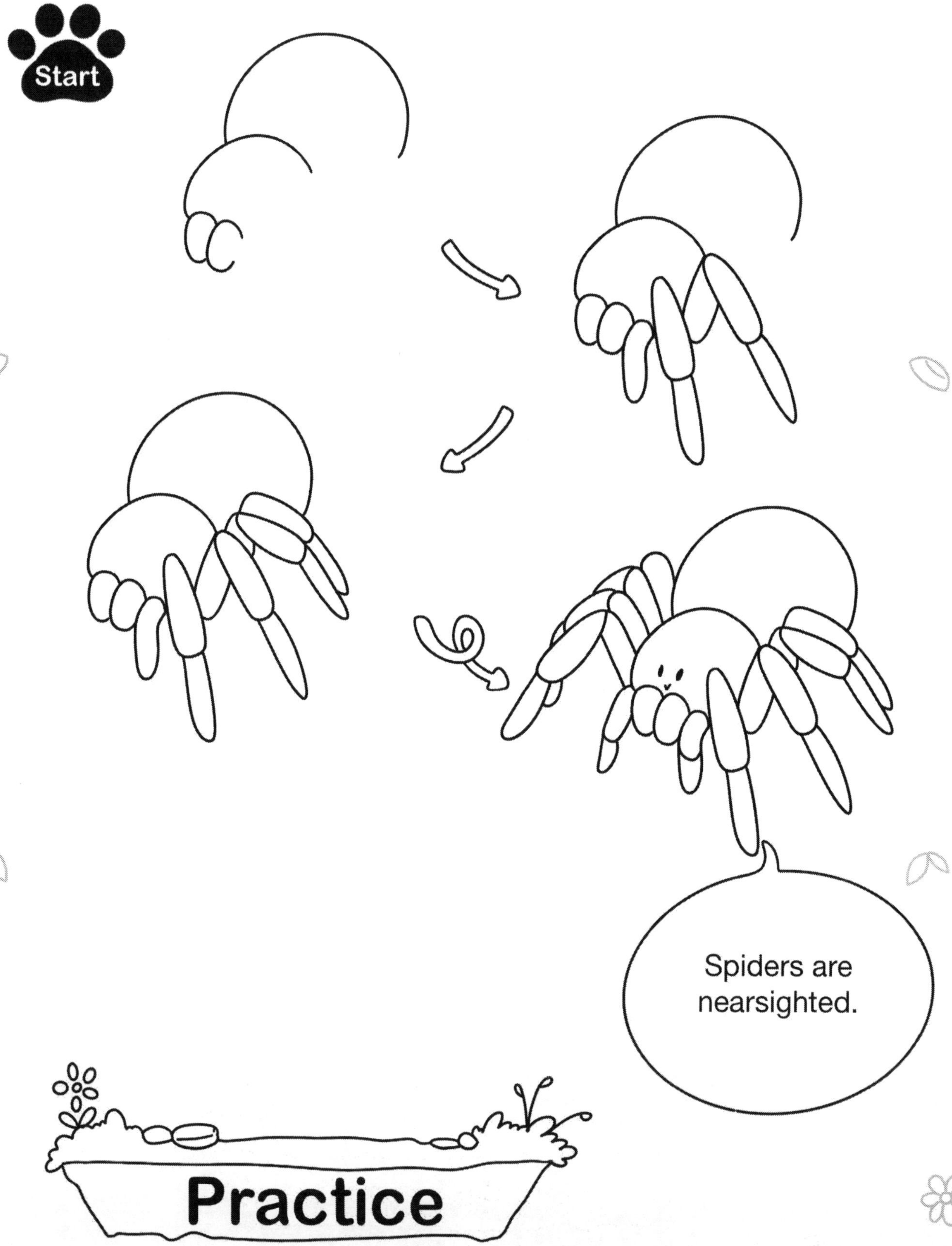

Practice

Cricket

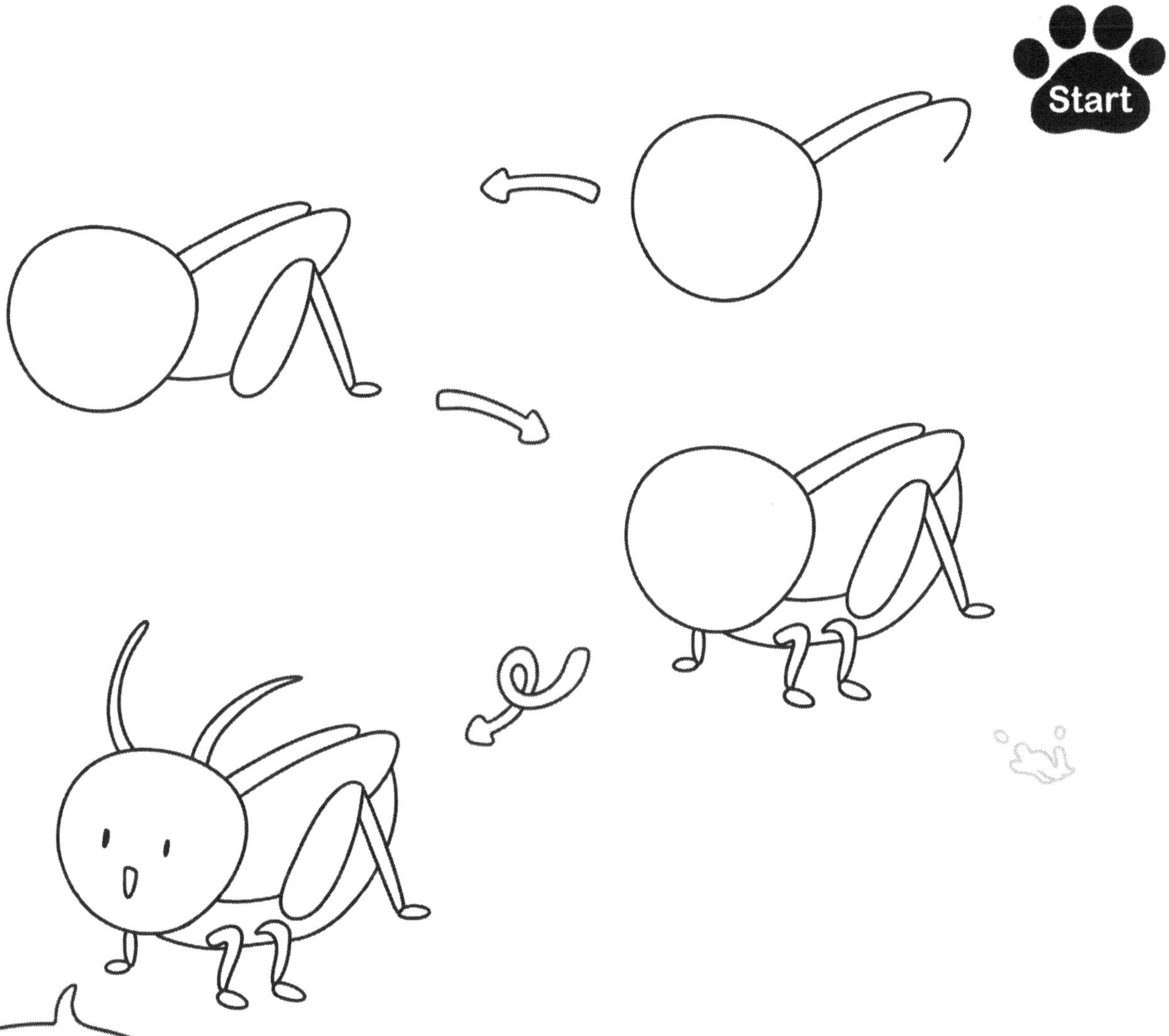

Crickets are a symbol of good luck.

Practice

Whale

Start

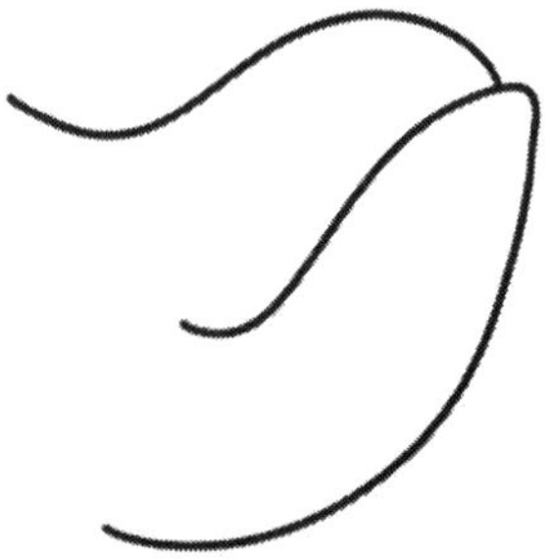

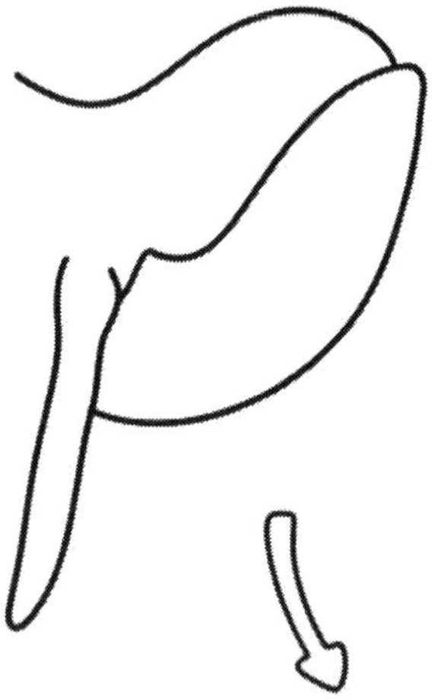

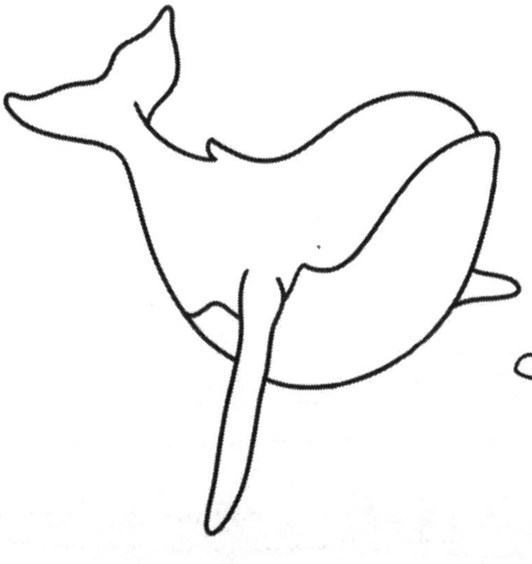

Practice

Each whale tail is unique.

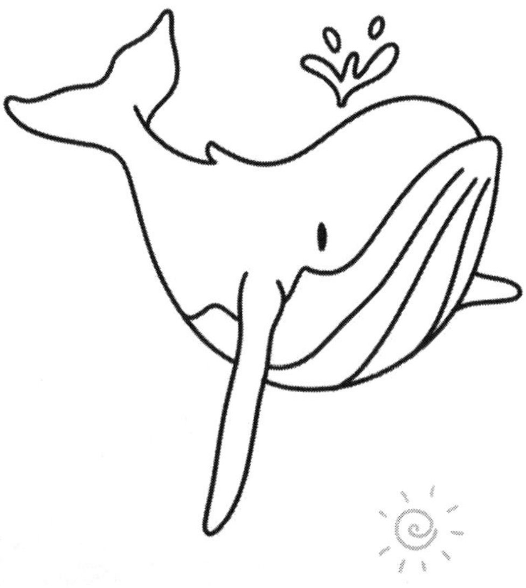

Tiger

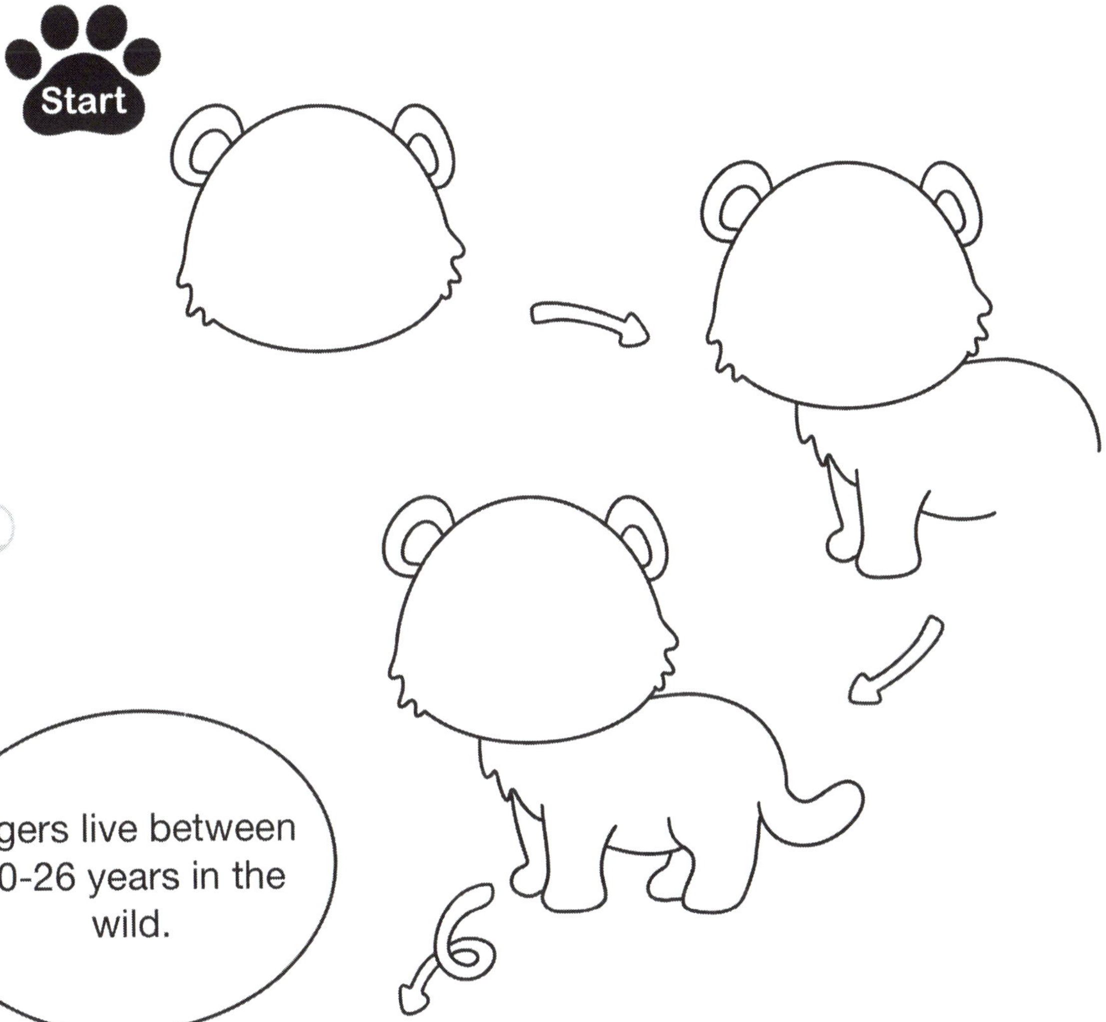

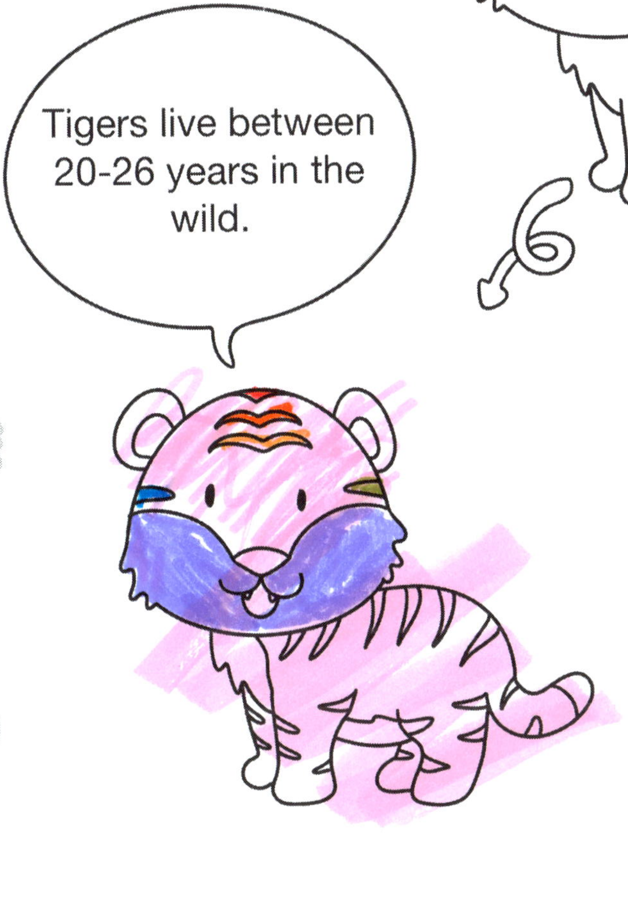

Practice

Turkey

Practice

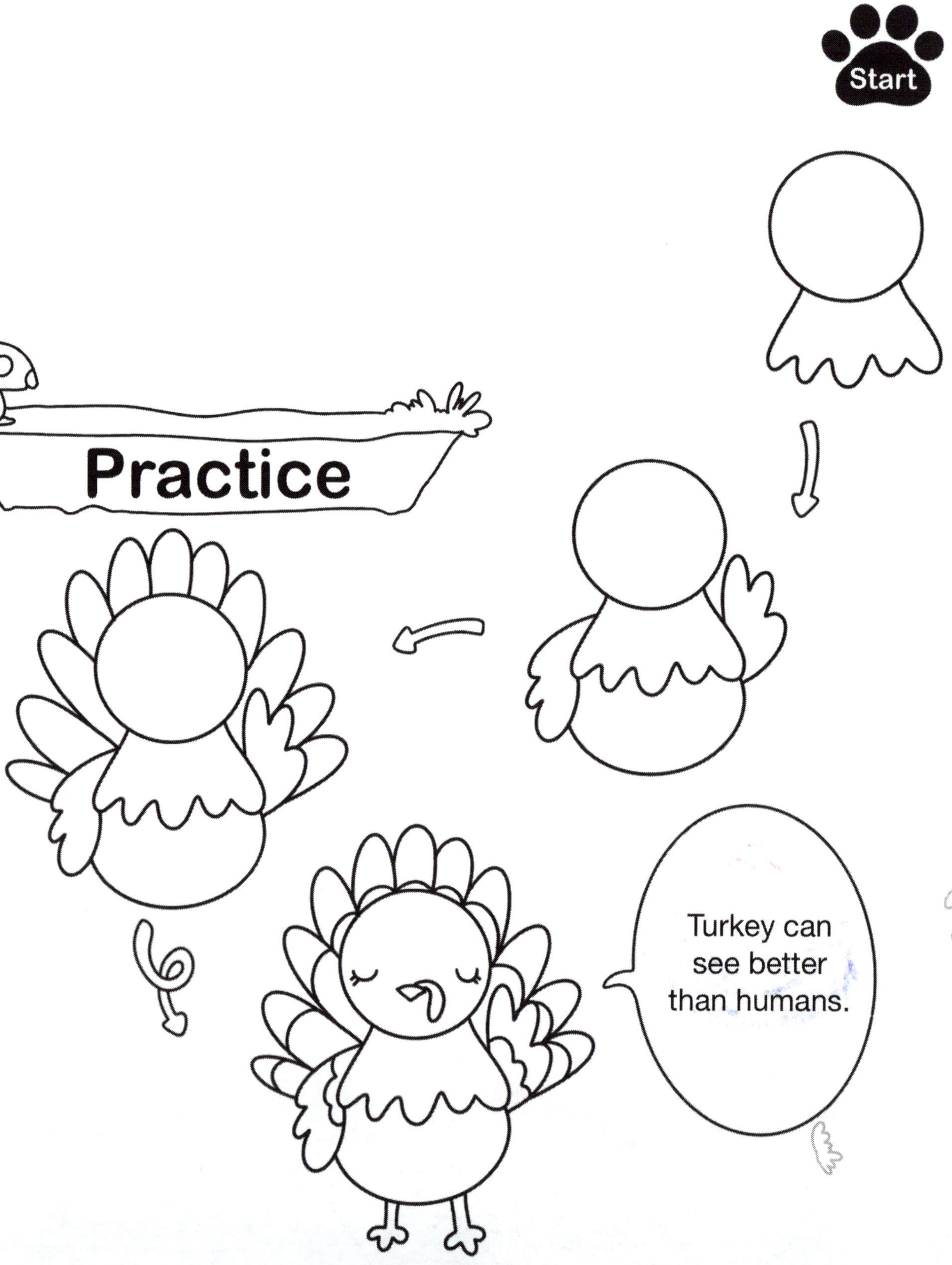

Deer

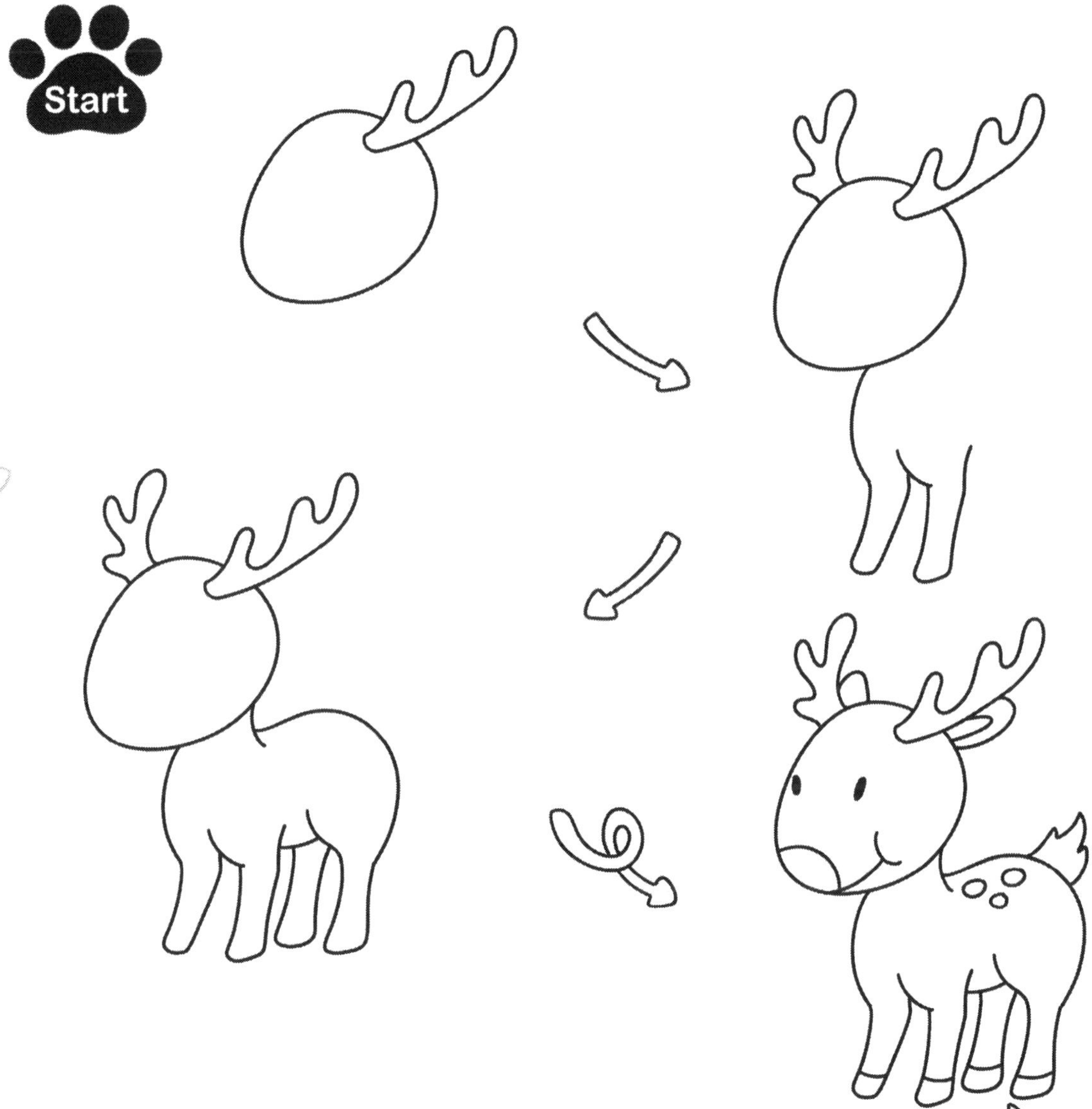

Deer have great hearing senses.

Practice

Monkey

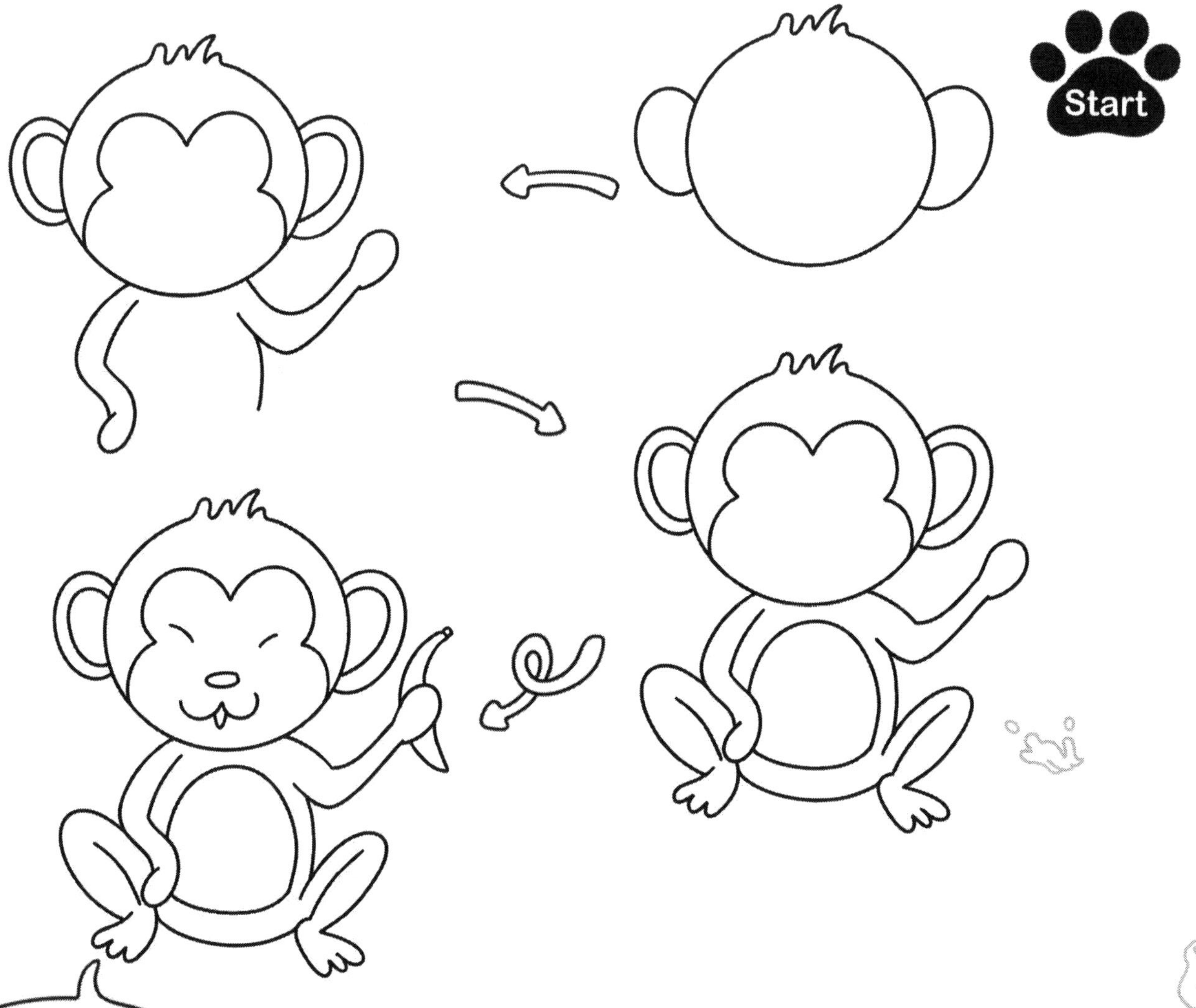

Monkeys have forward facing eyes and flat noses.

Practice

Otter

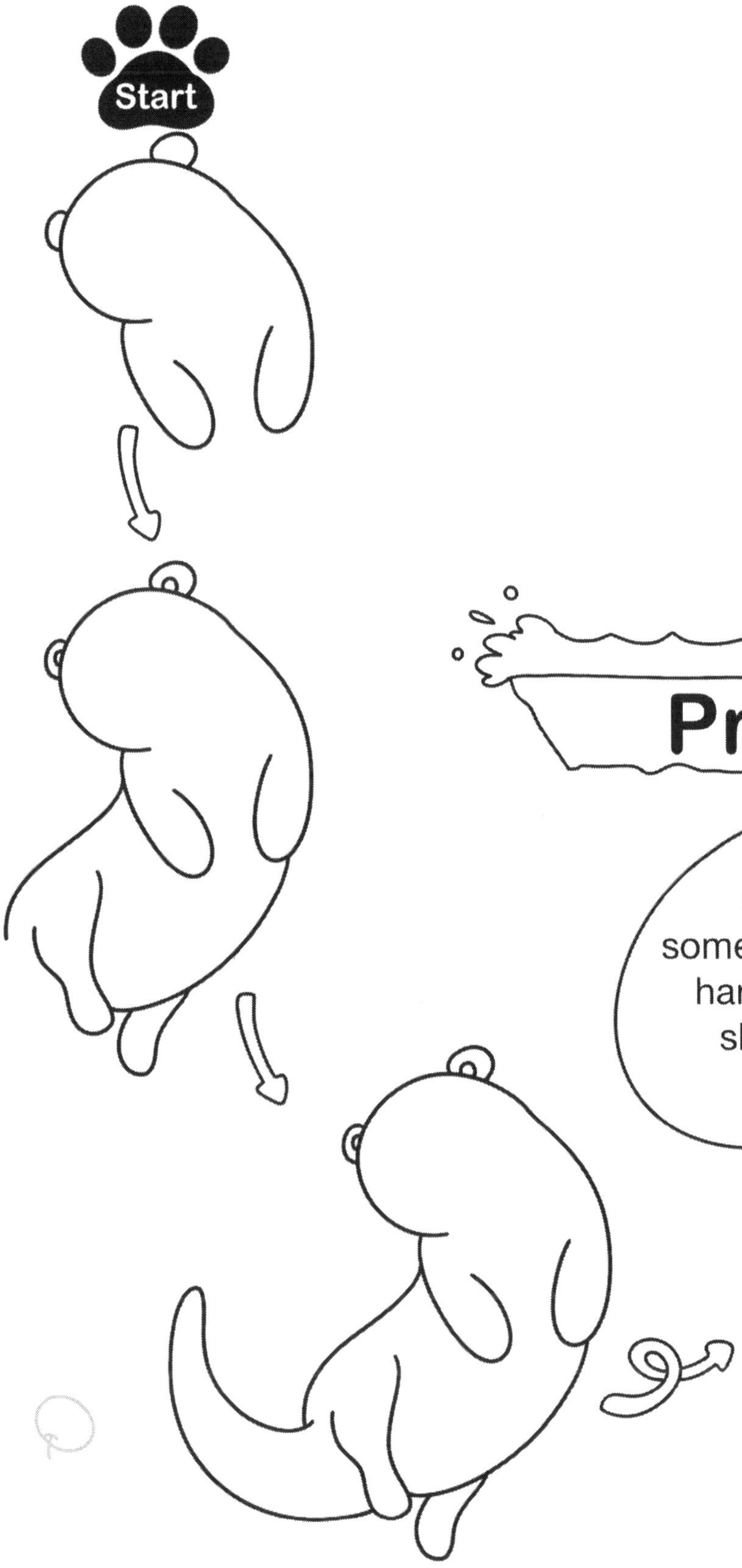

Practice

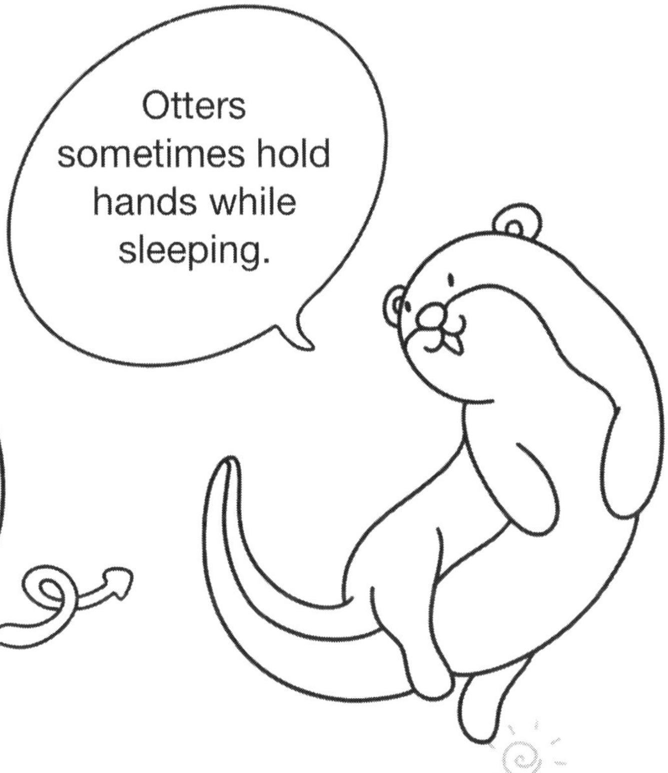

Rooster

Start

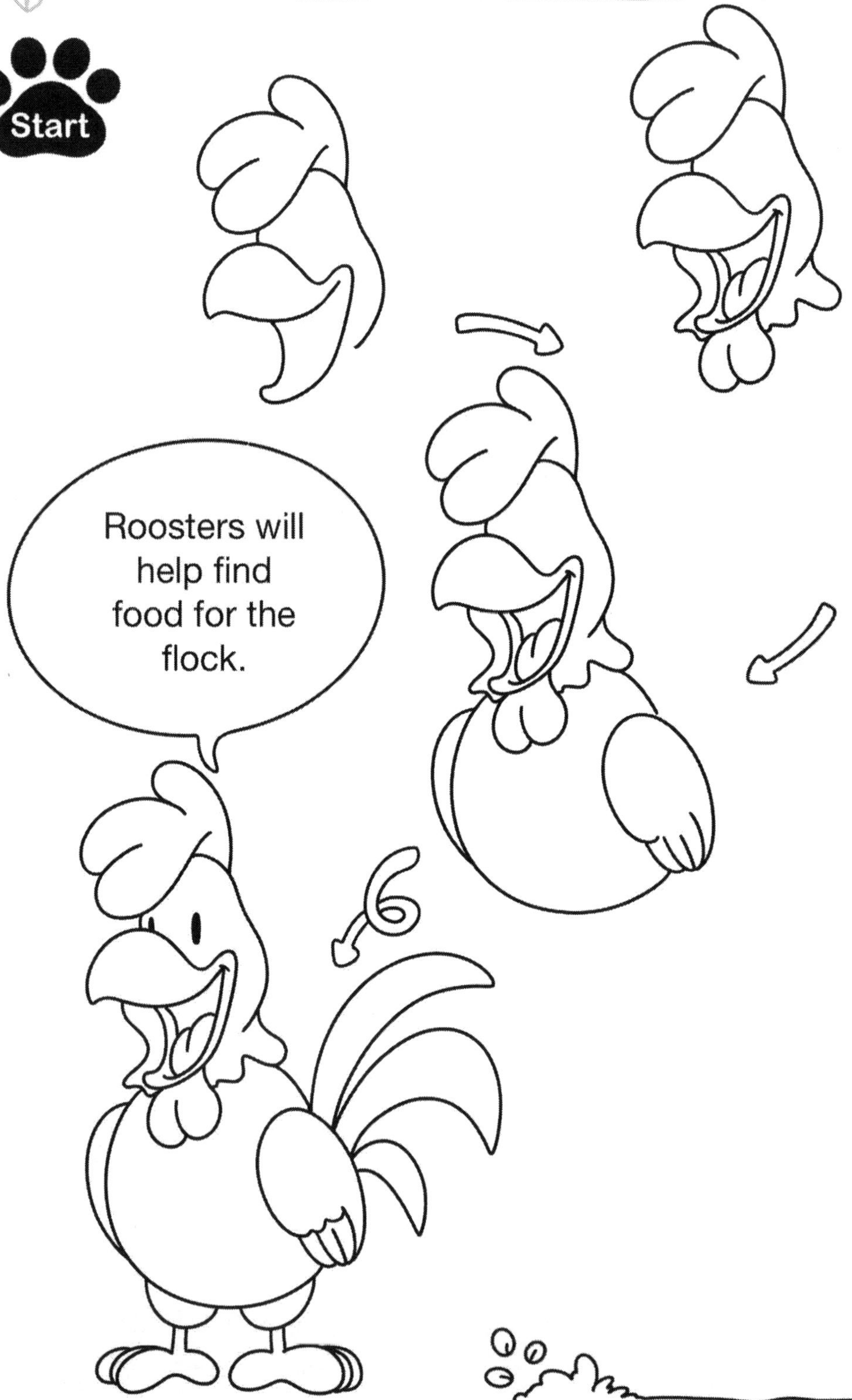

Practice

Rabbit

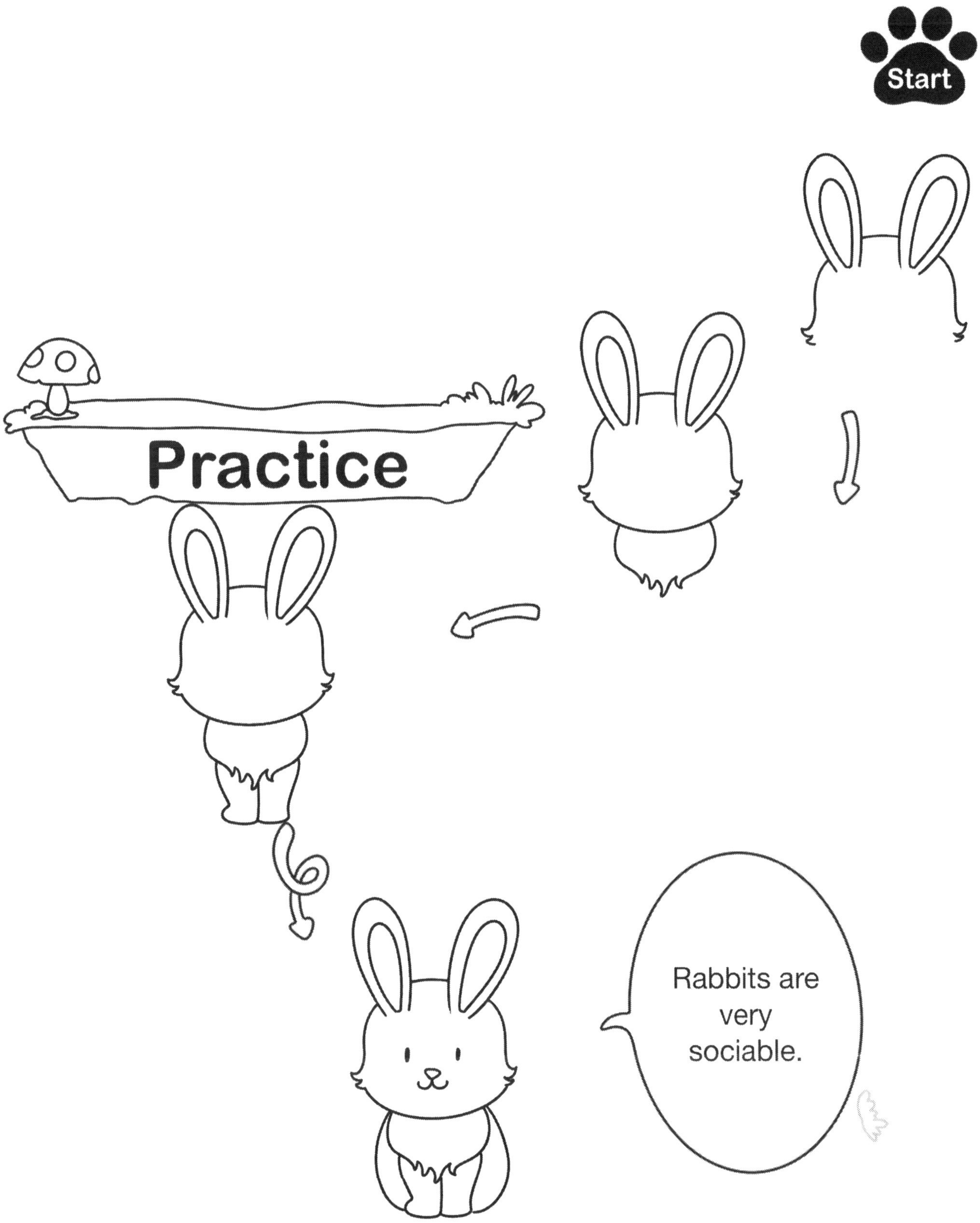

Worm

Start

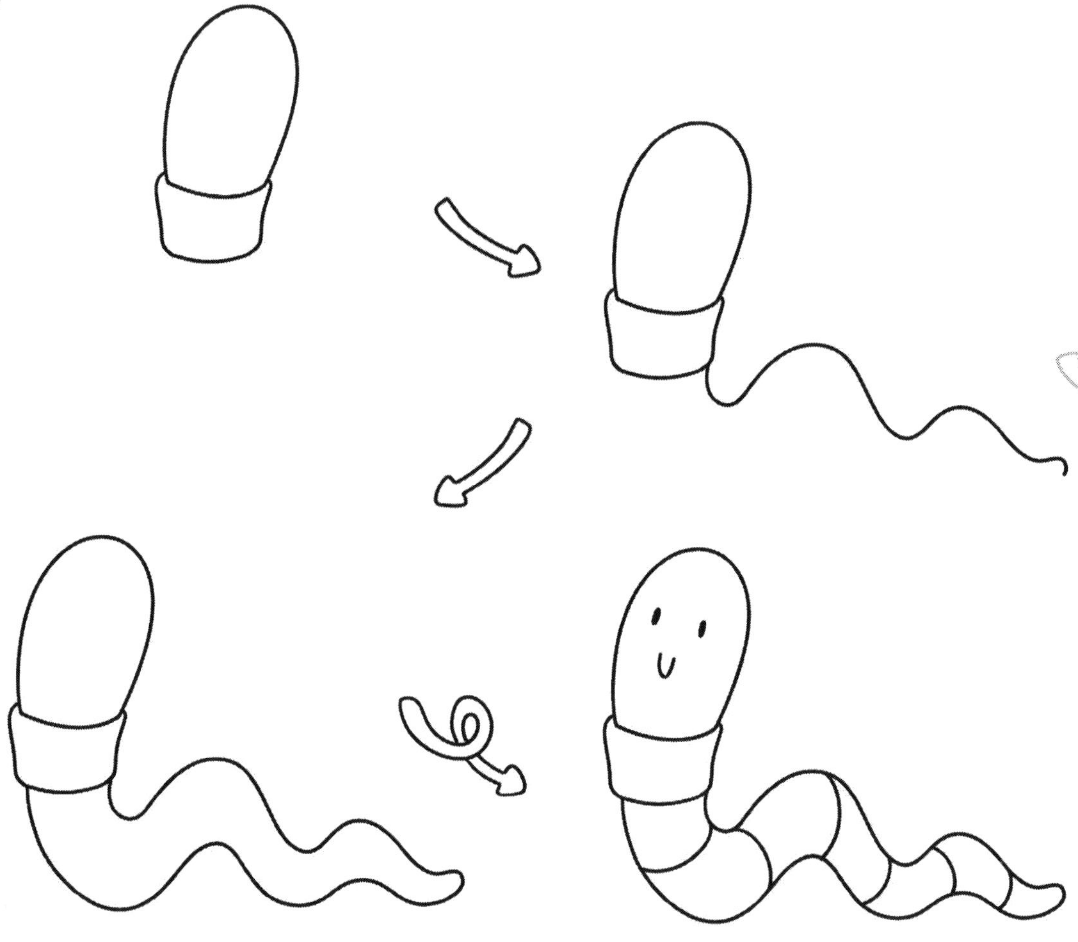

Worms have five hearts.

Practice

Woodpecker

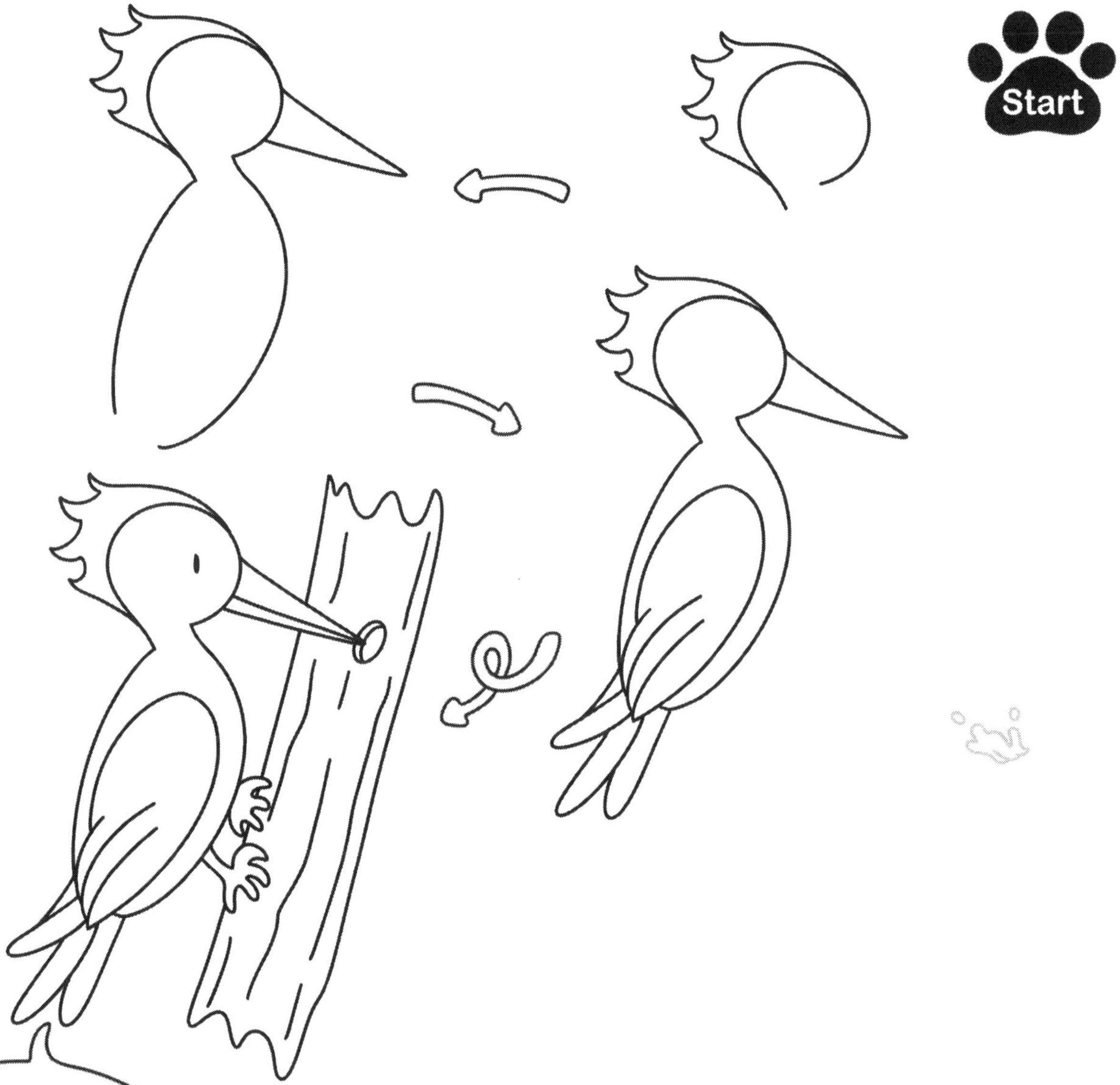

Woodpeckers have super long tongues.

Practice

Swan

Start

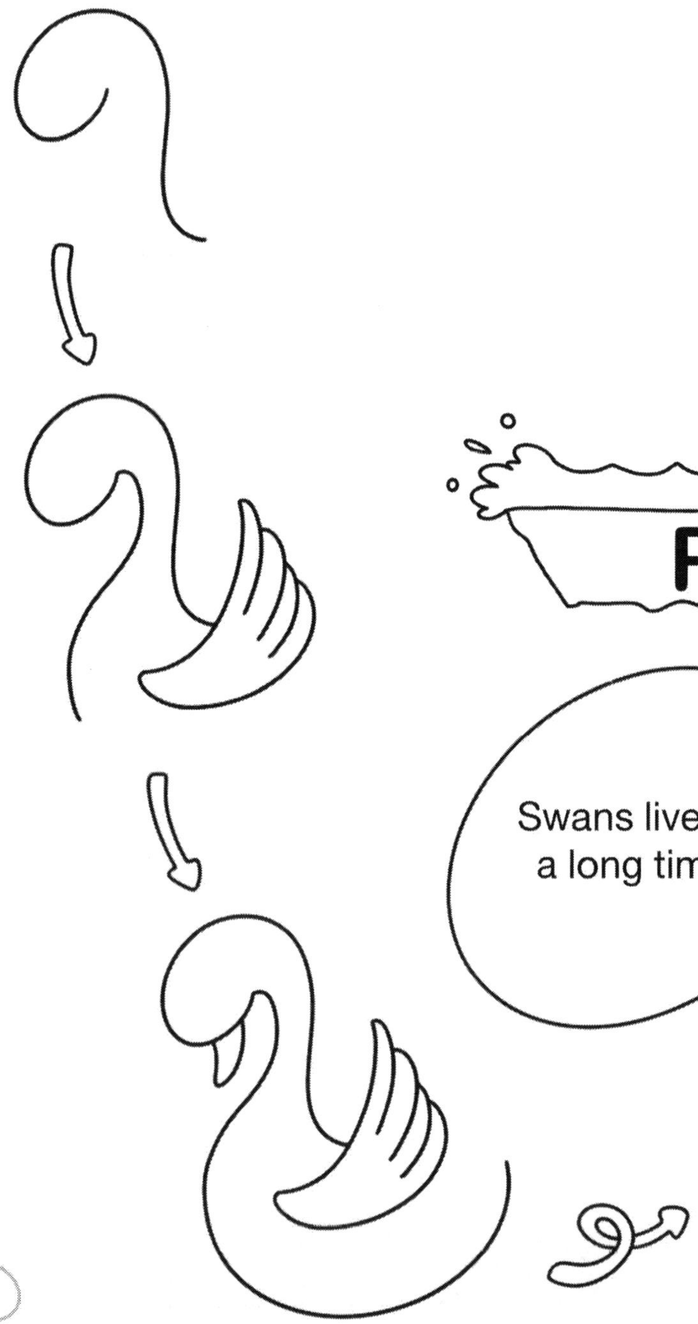

Practice

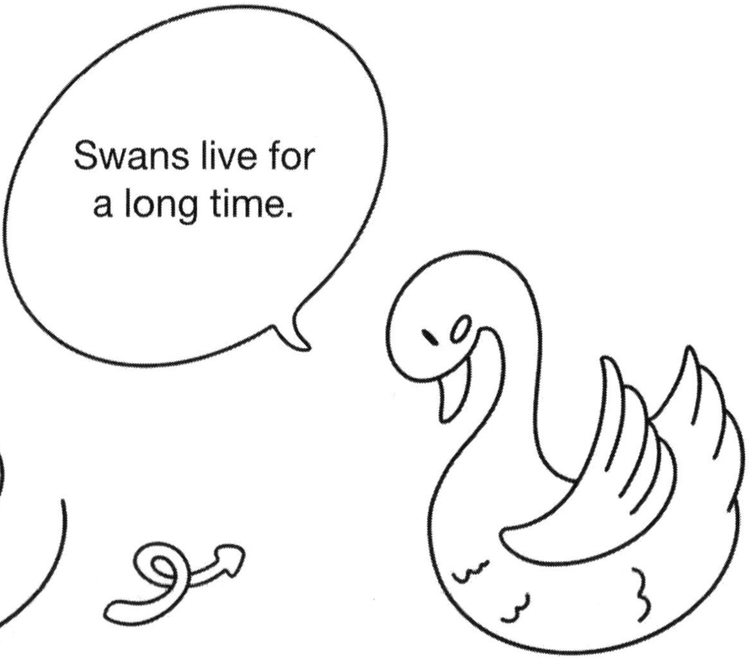

Peacock

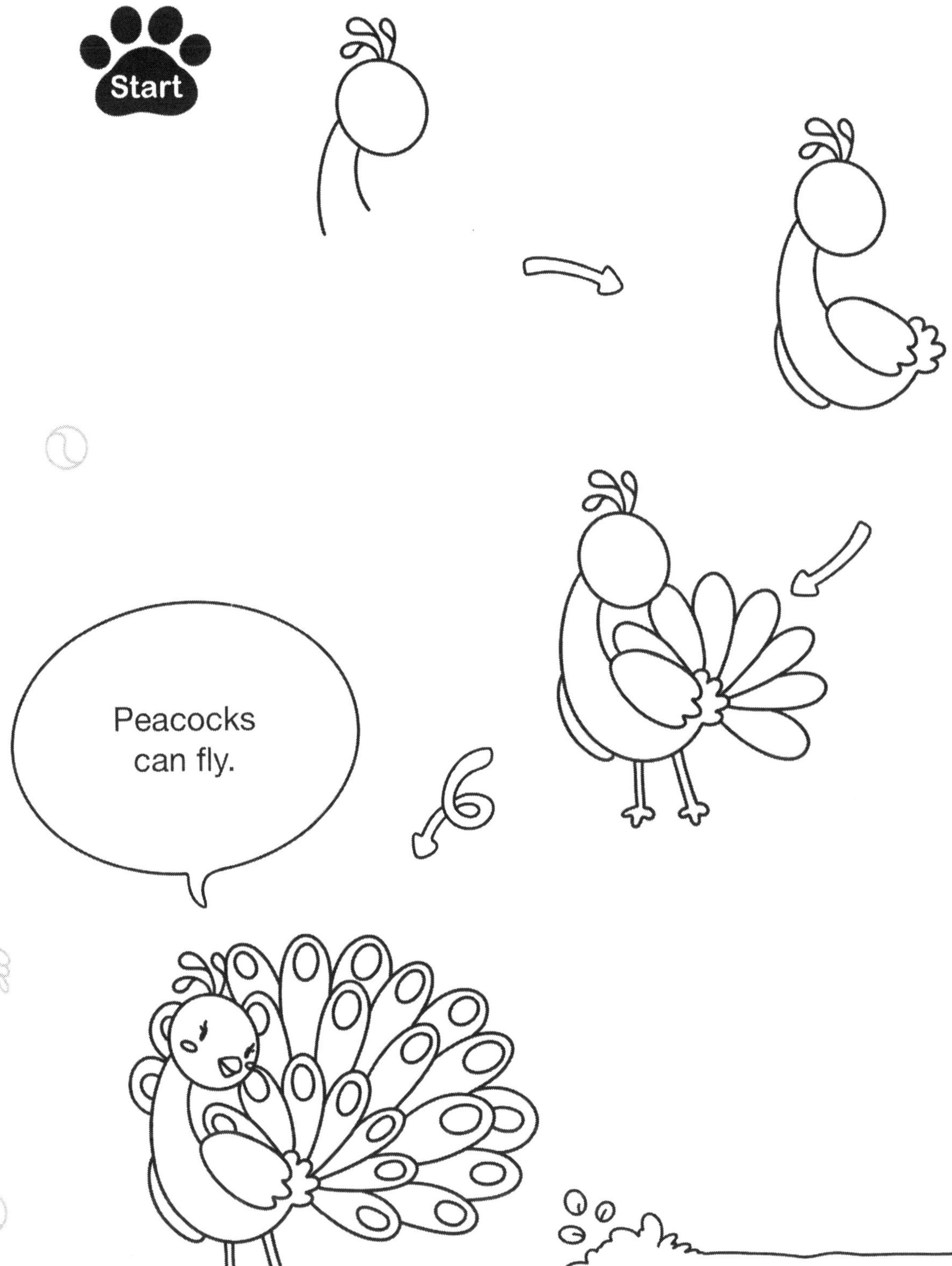

Practice

Ant

Start

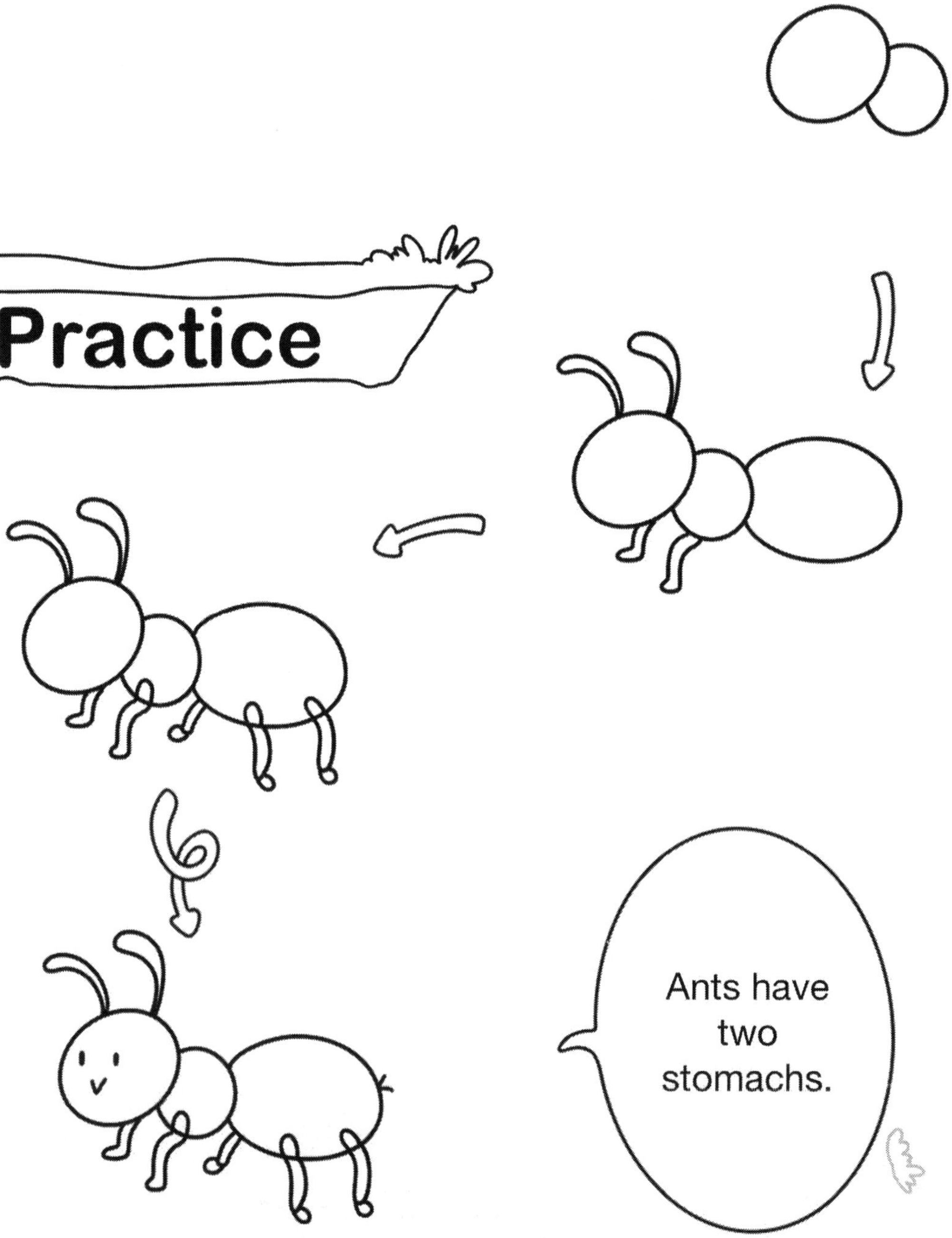

Practice

Ants have two stomachs.

Millipede

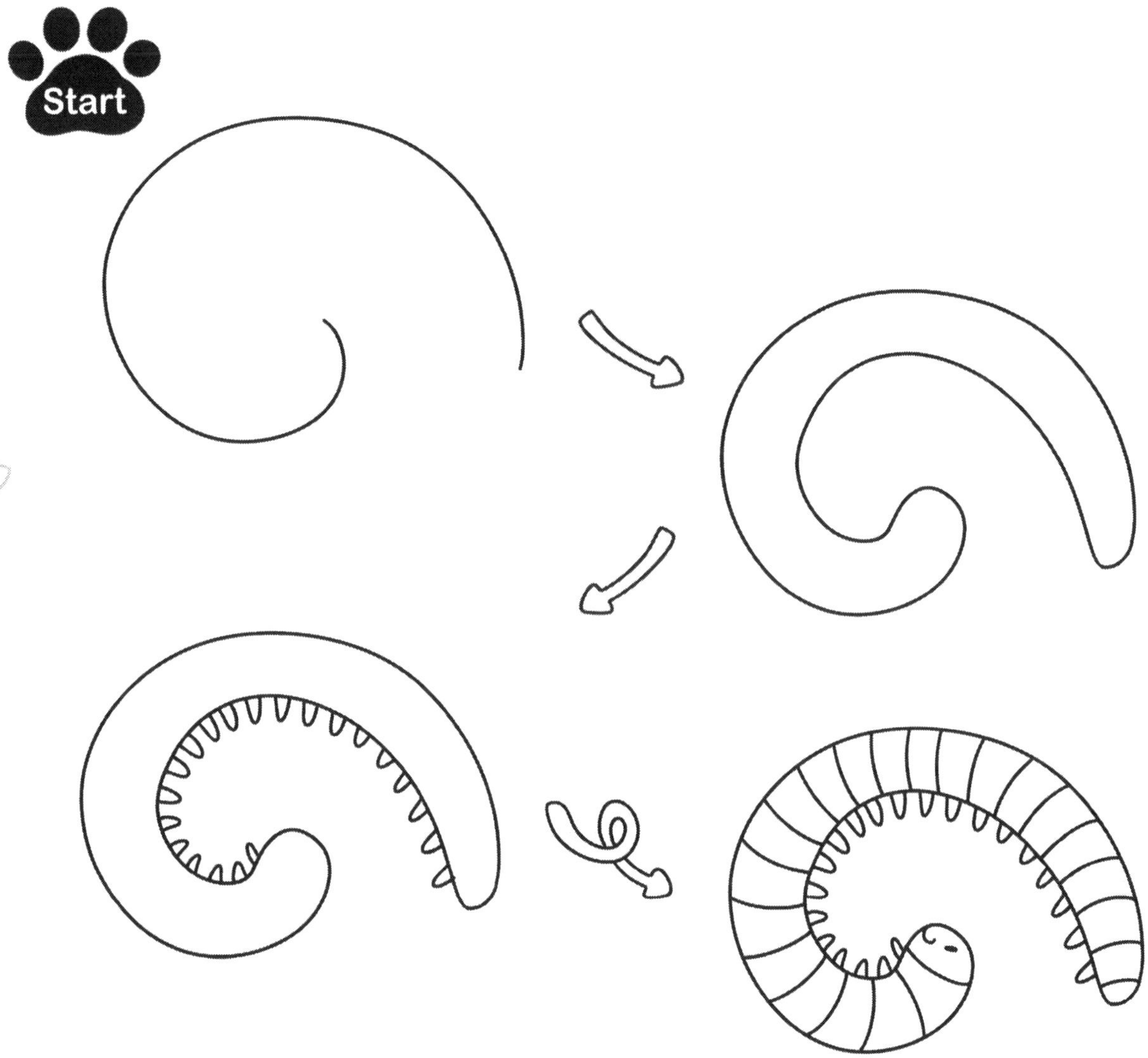

Millipede do not have 1000 legs.

Practice

Dragonfly

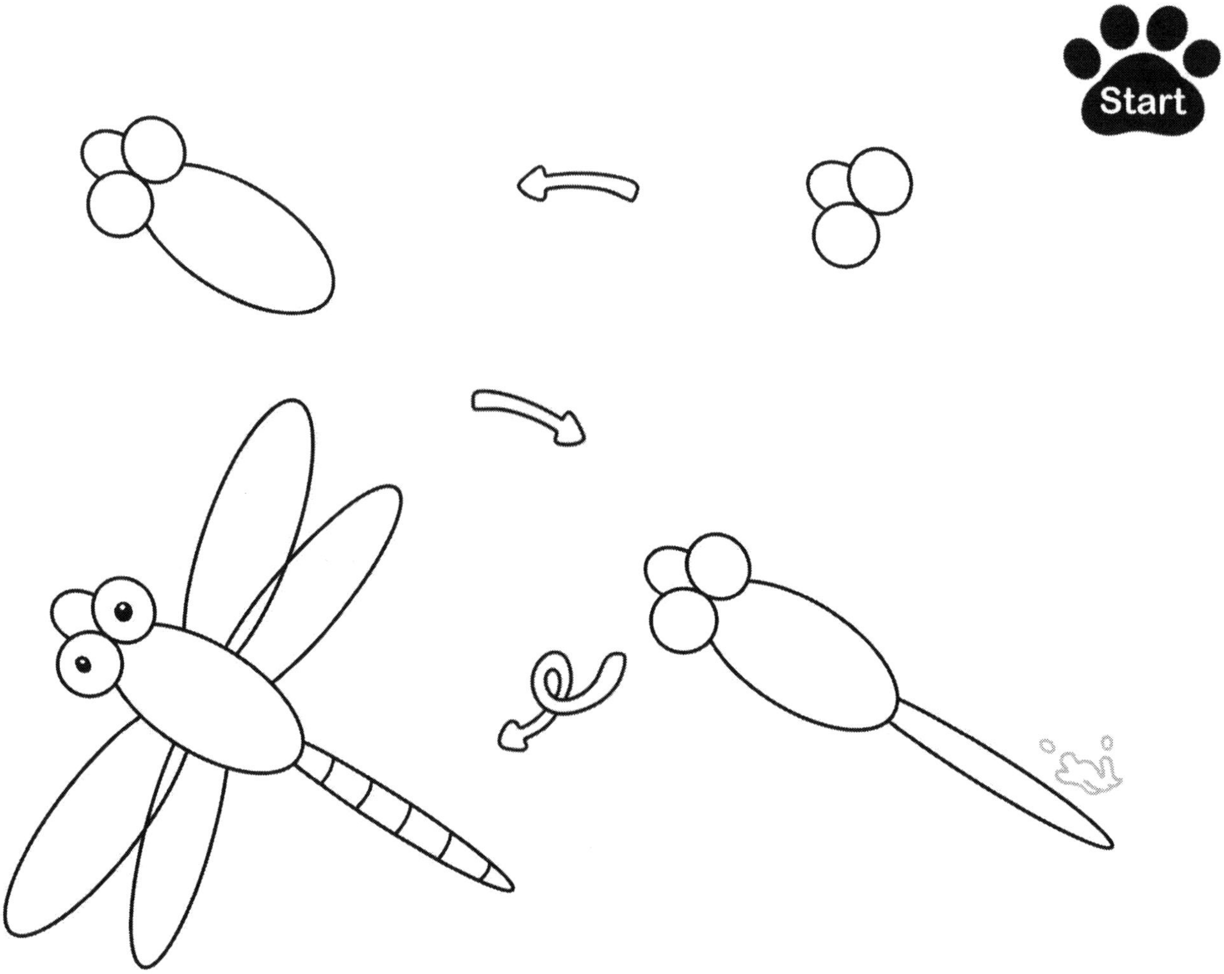

Dragonflies are freaky fliers.

Practice

Narwhal

Start

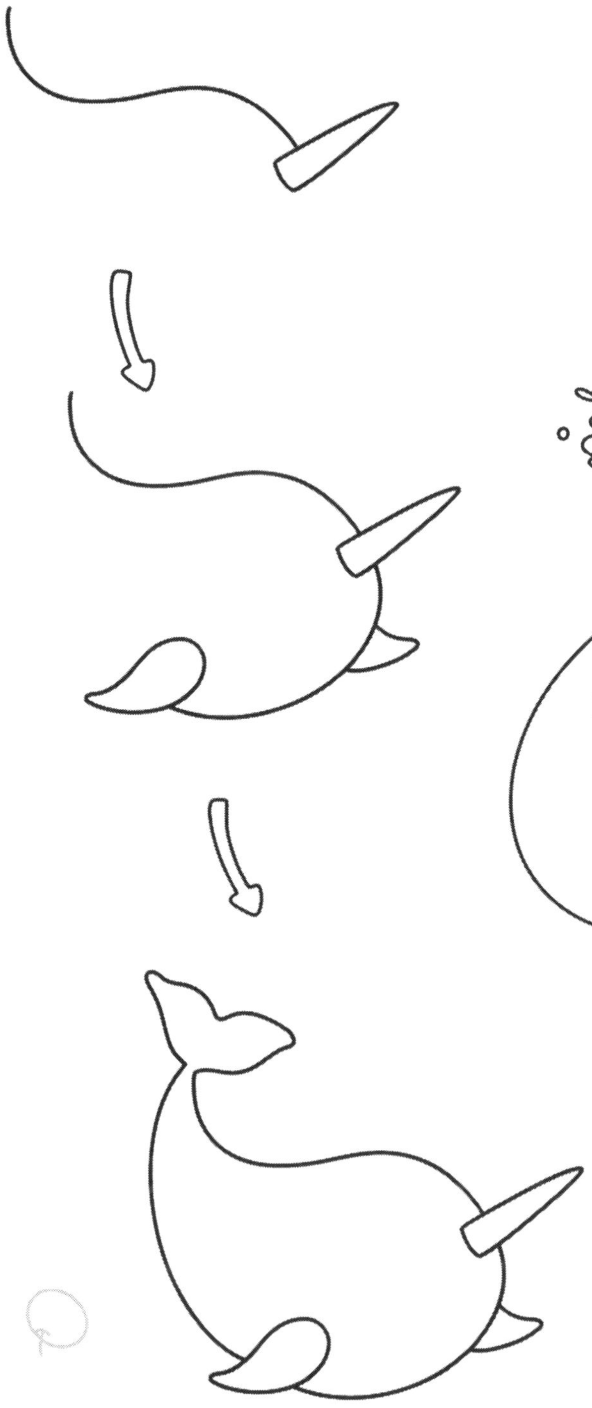

Practice

Narwhals live up to 50 years.

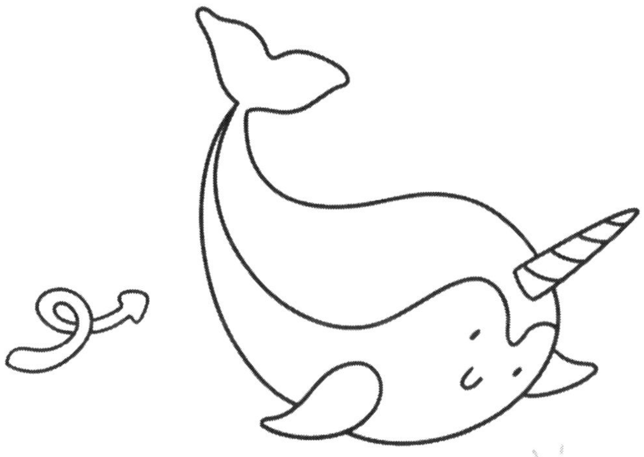

Beetle

Start

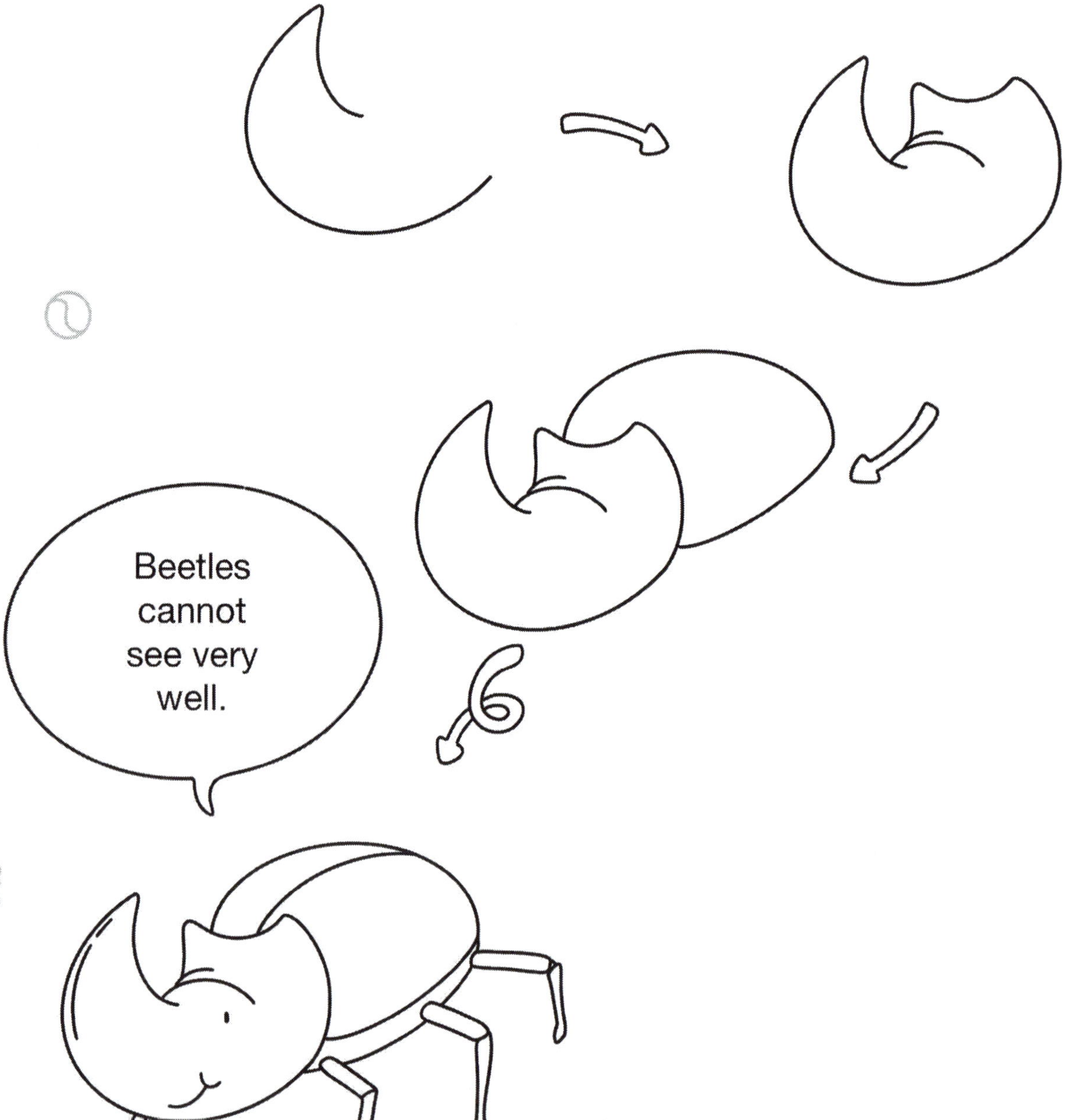

Practice

Cicada

Practice

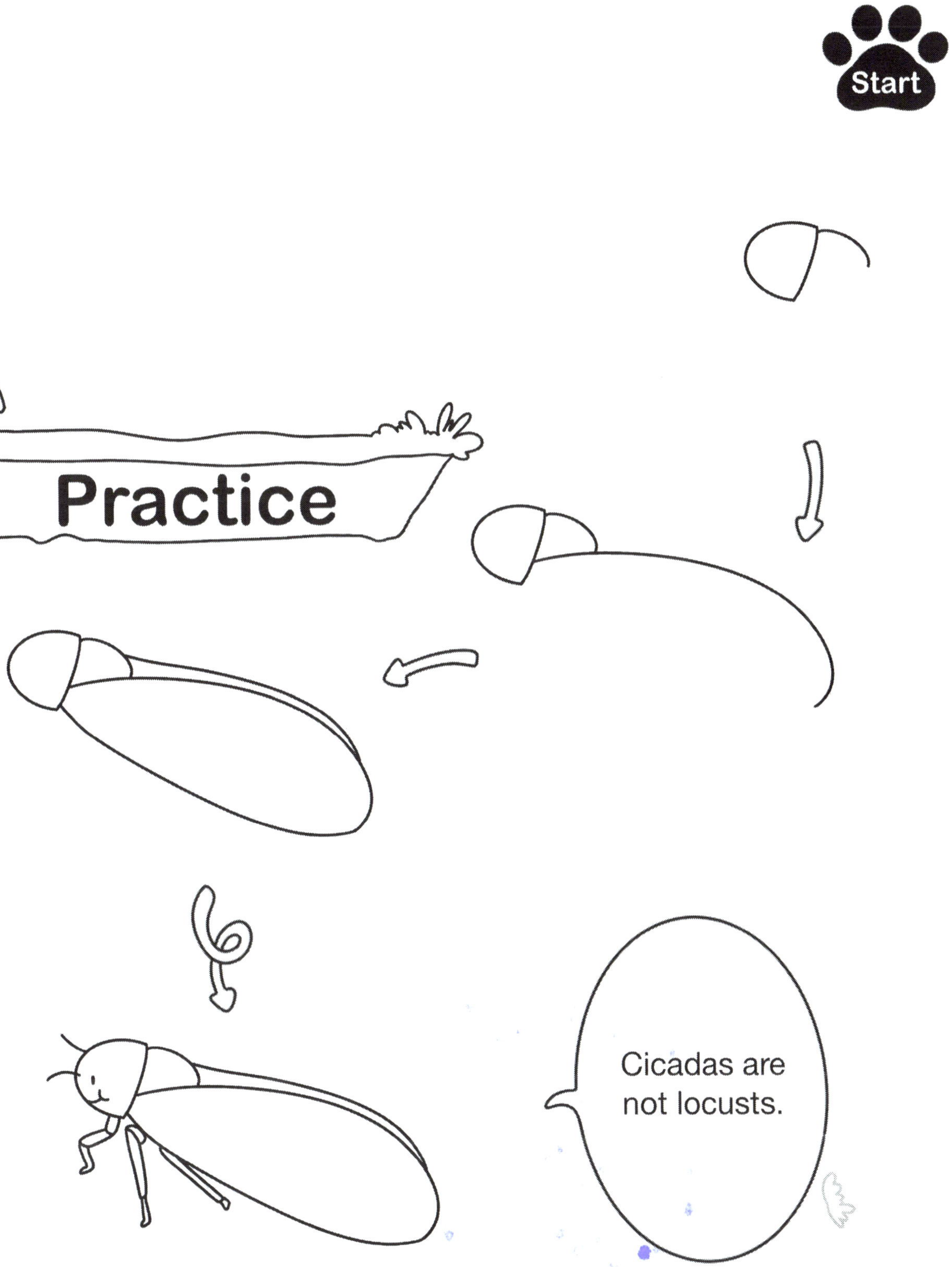

Hamster

Start

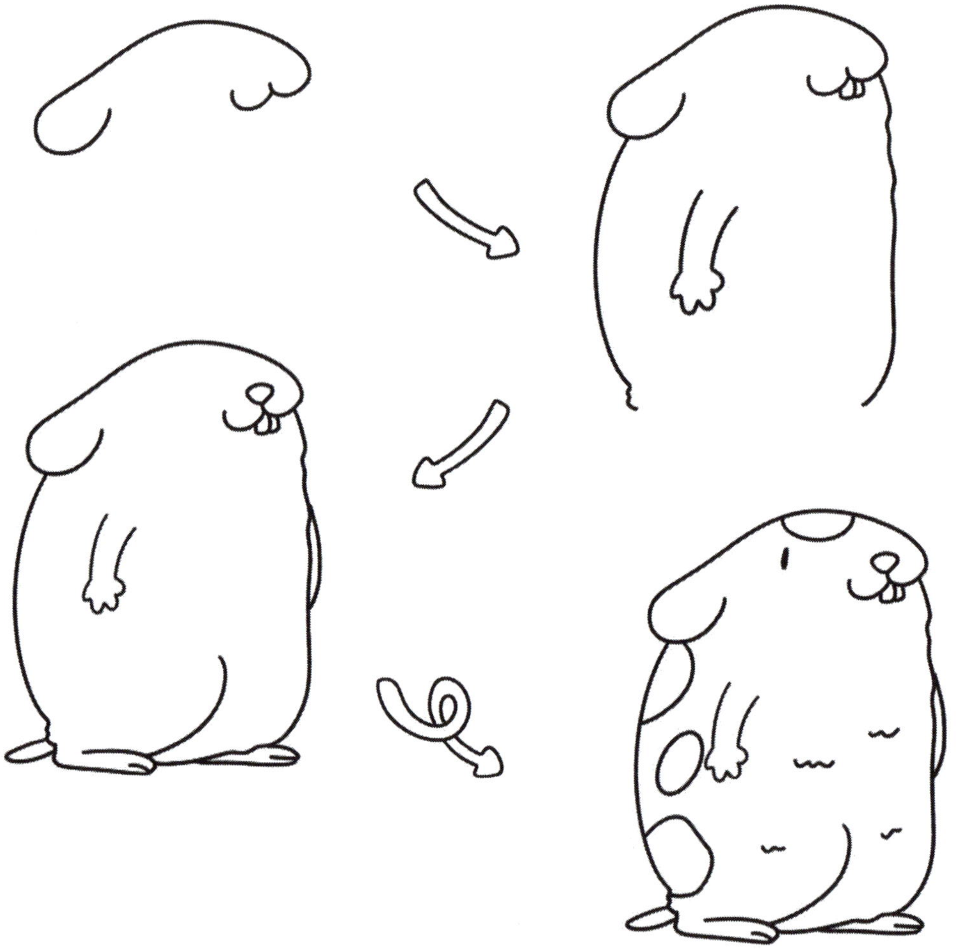

Hamsters love to hoard their food.

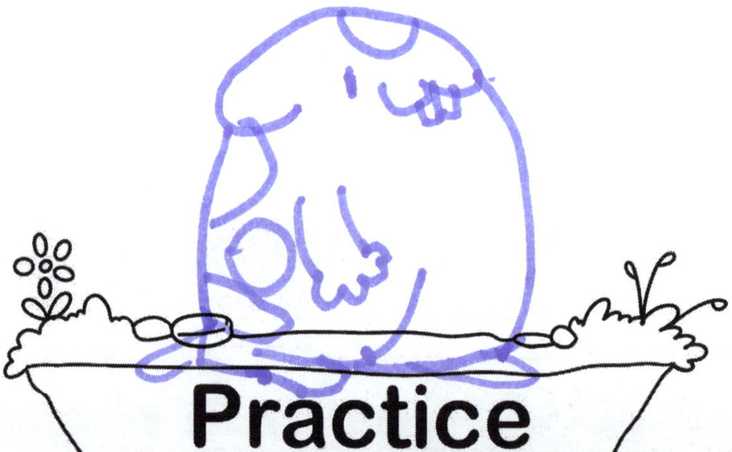

Boar

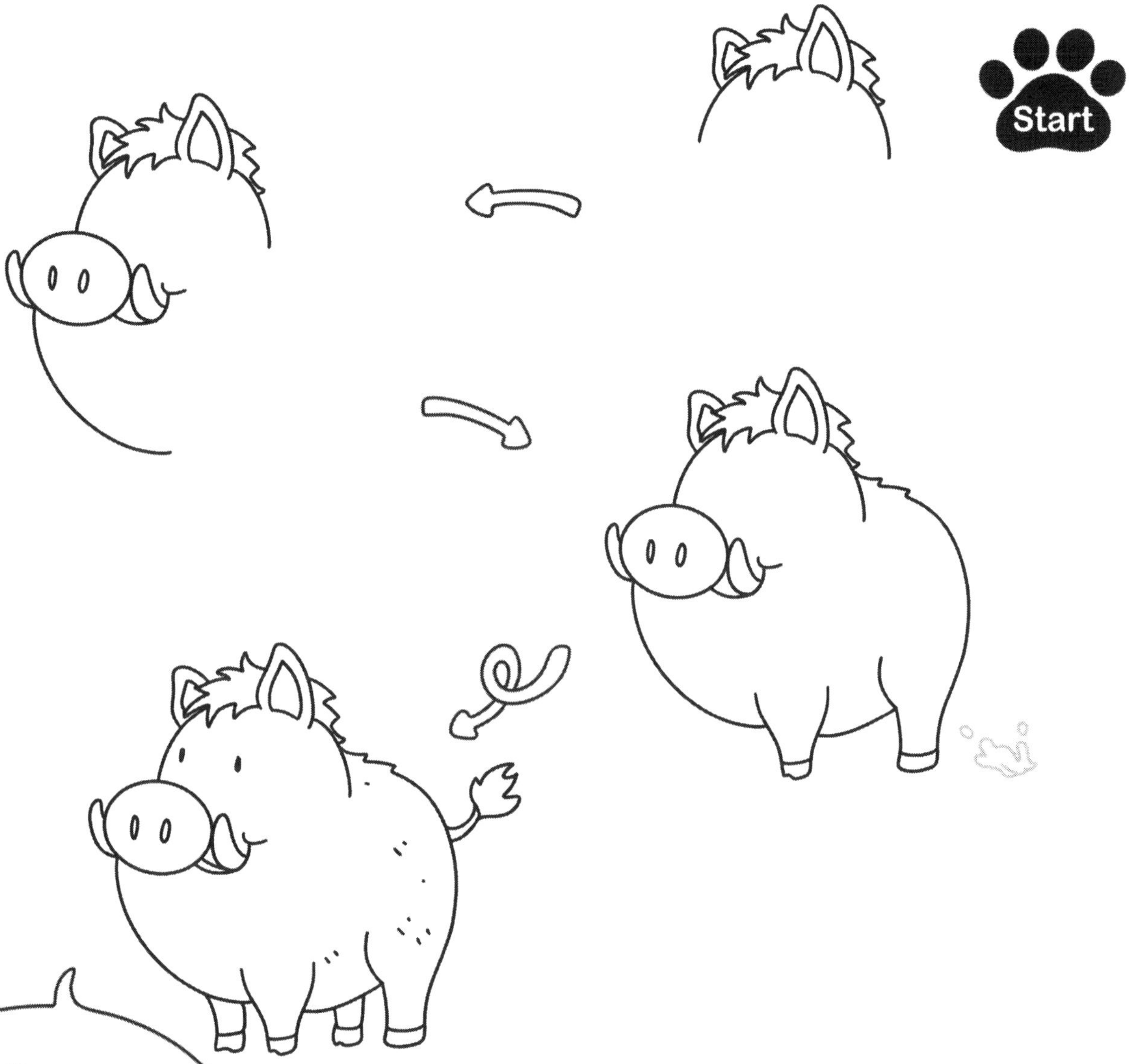

Boars often eat green plants.

Practice

Dumbo Octopus

Start

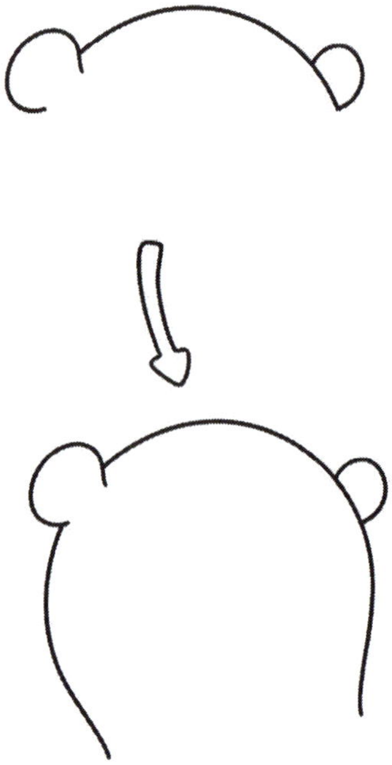

Practice

Dumbo octopuses have big eyes.

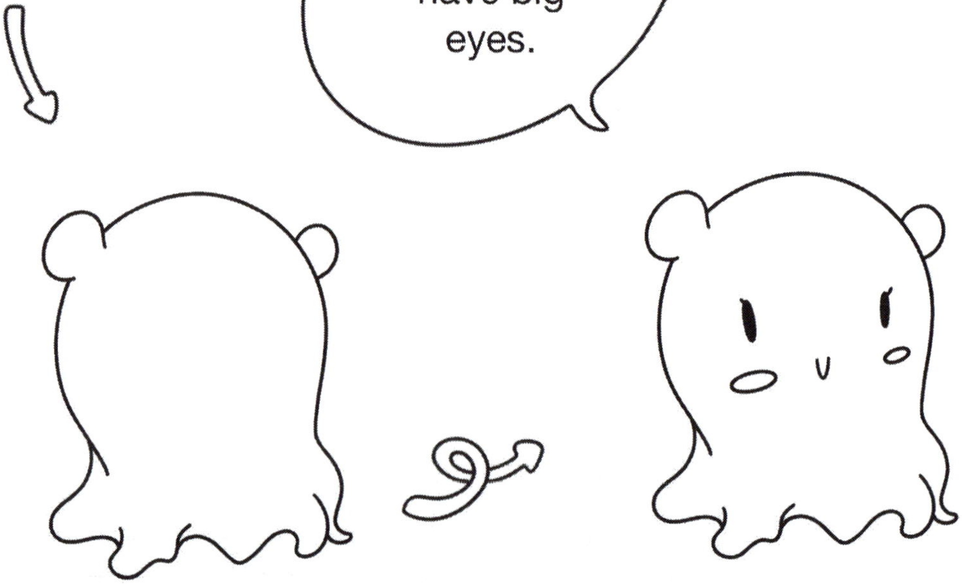

Cobra

Start

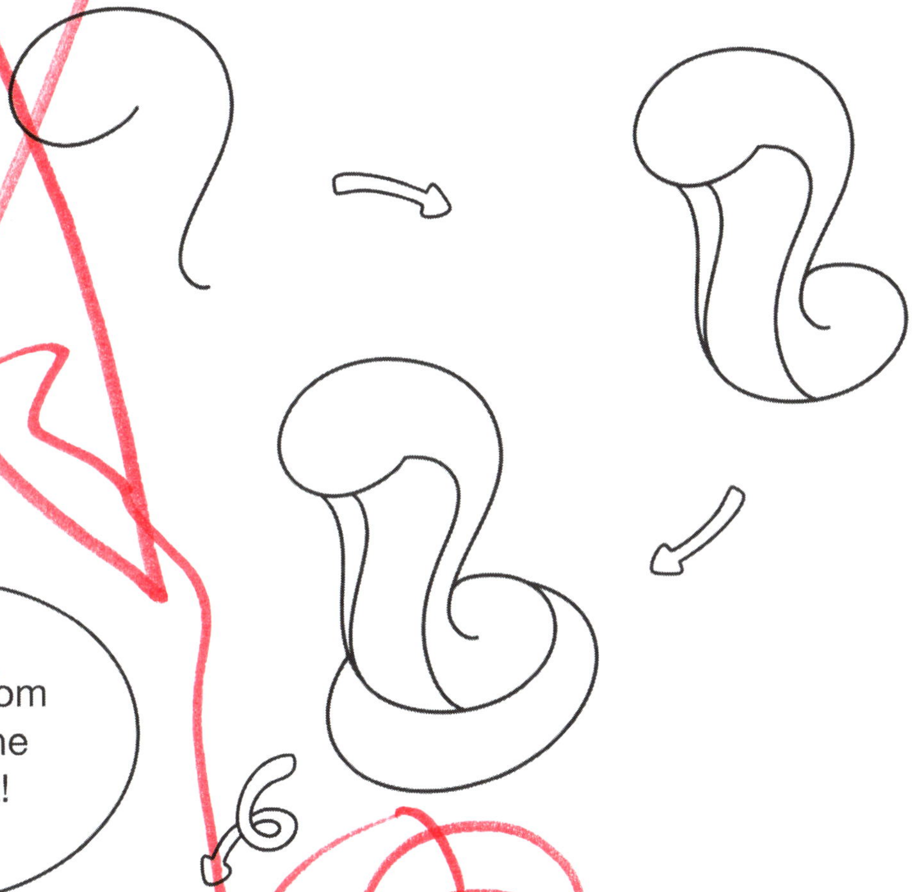

Cobra venom can kill one elephant!

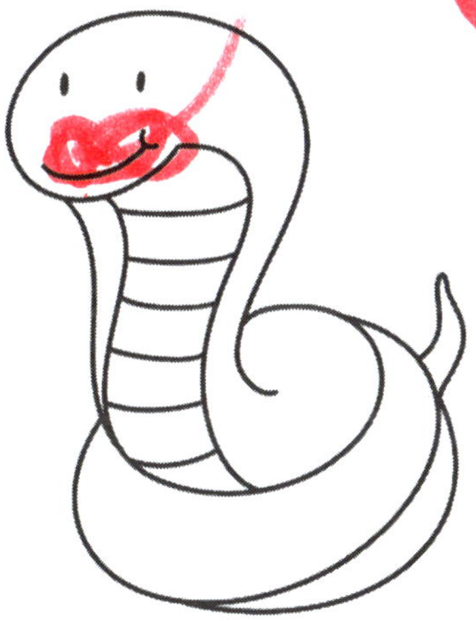

Practice

Flea

Practice

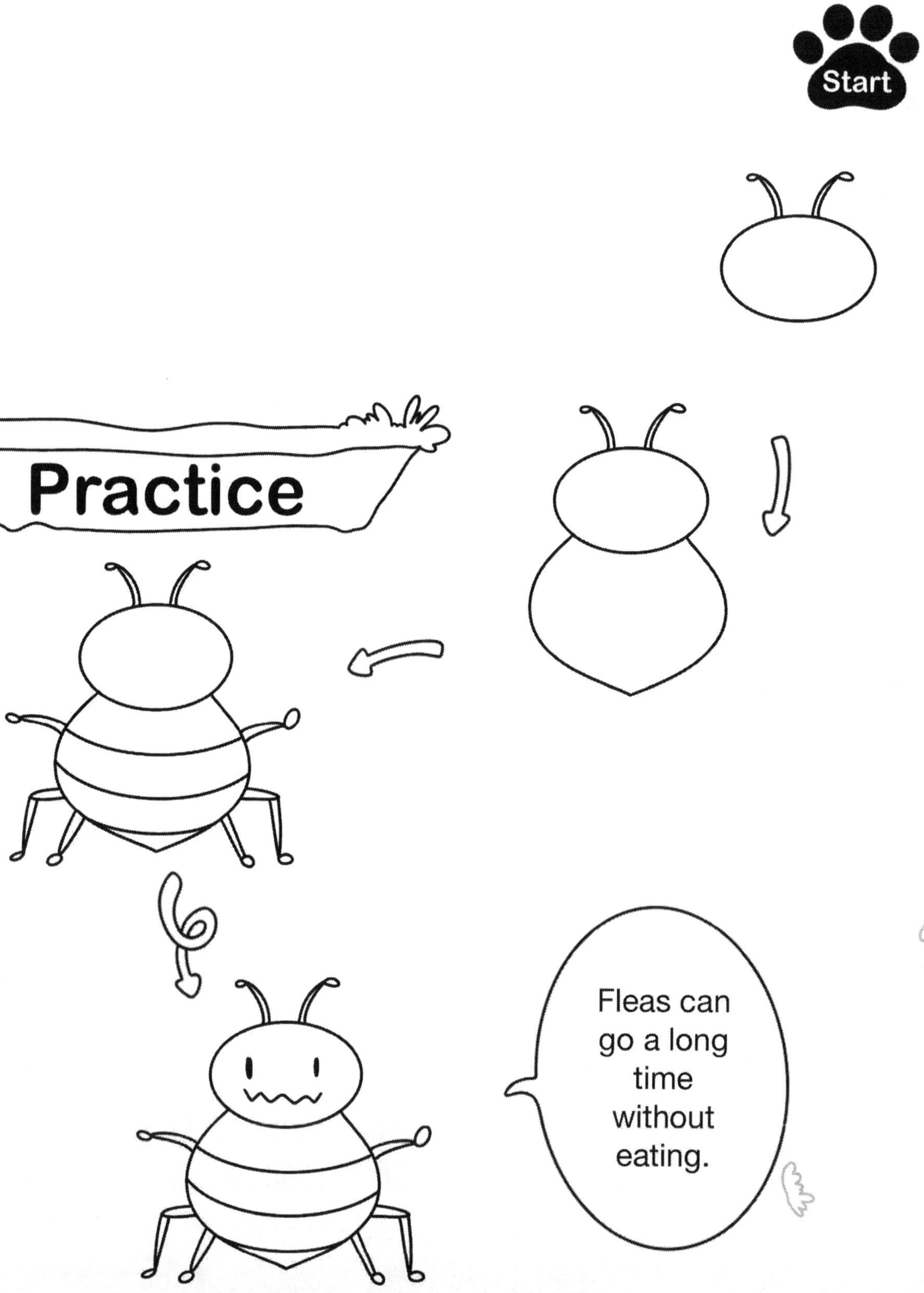

Falcon

Start

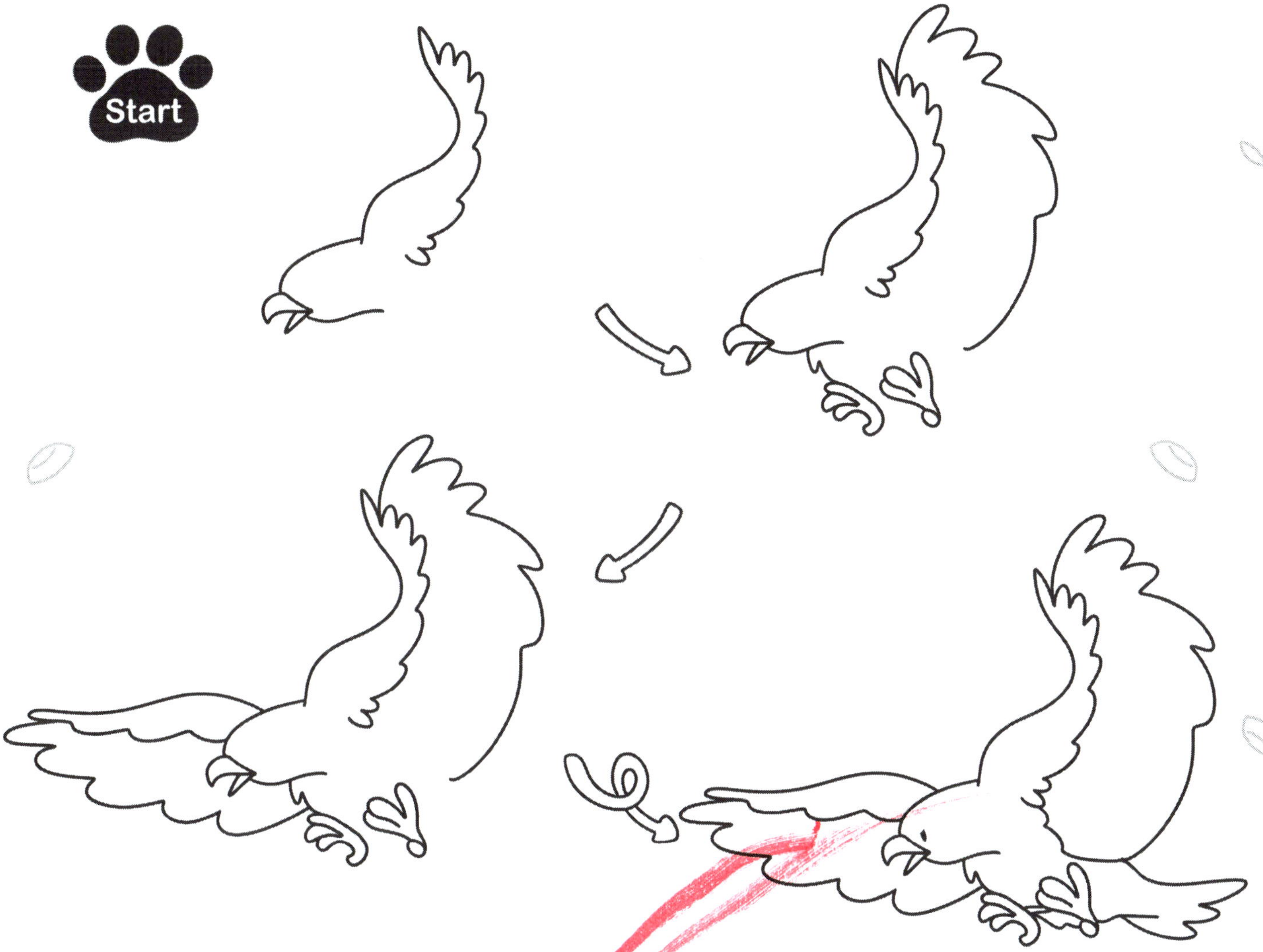

Falcons are really fast.

Practice

Gibbon

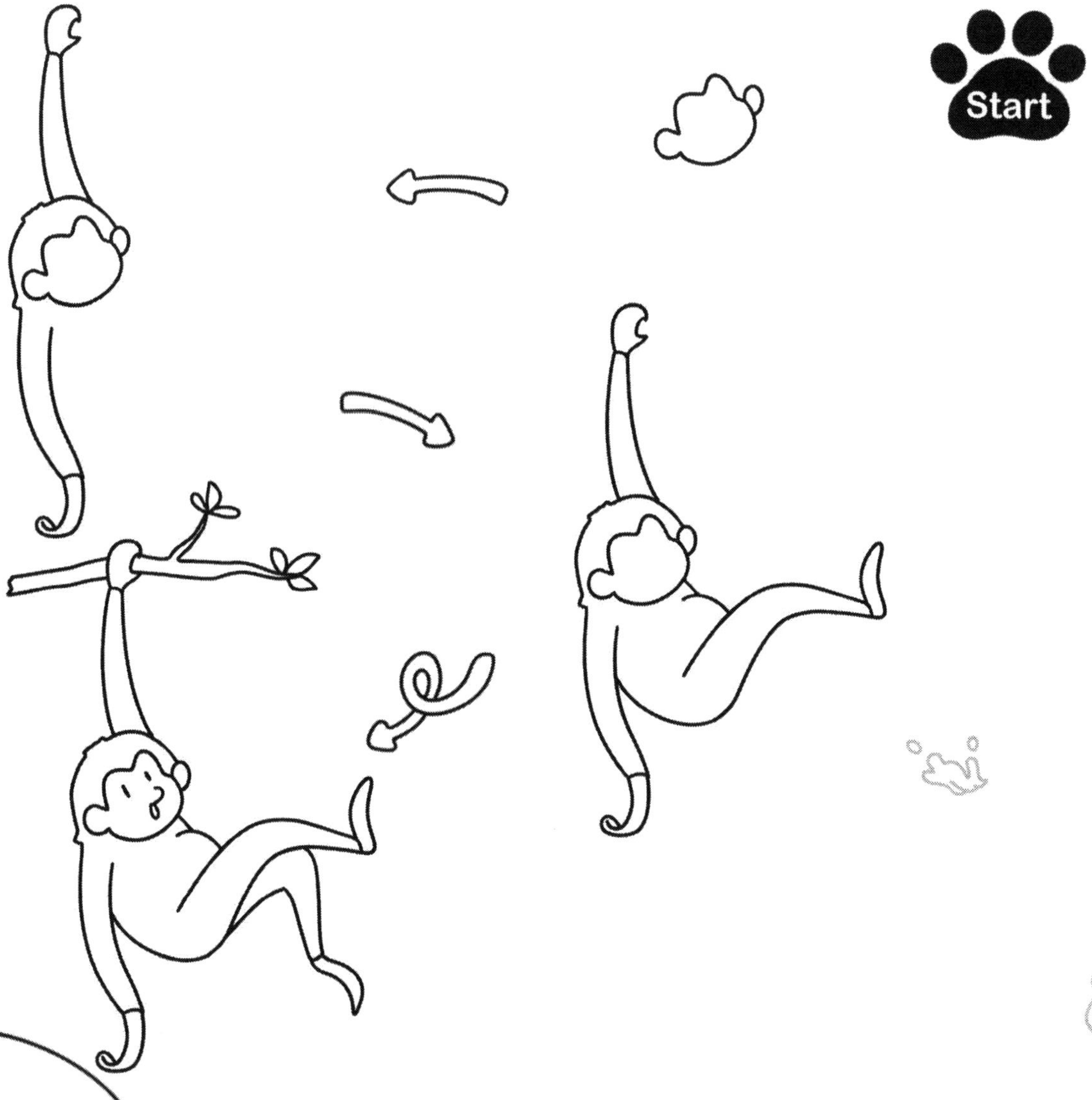

Gibbons cannot swim.

Practice

Swordfish

Start

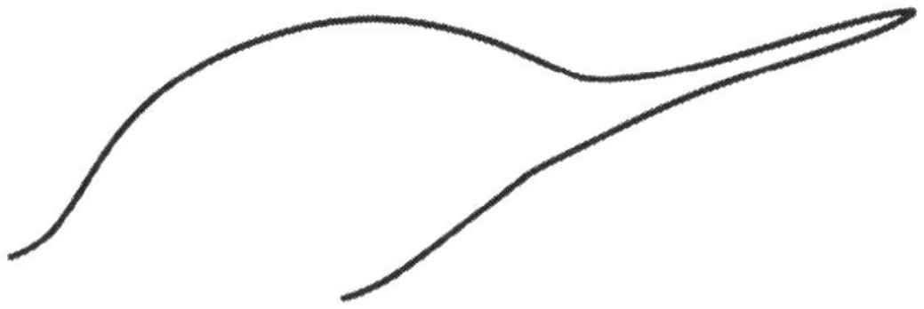

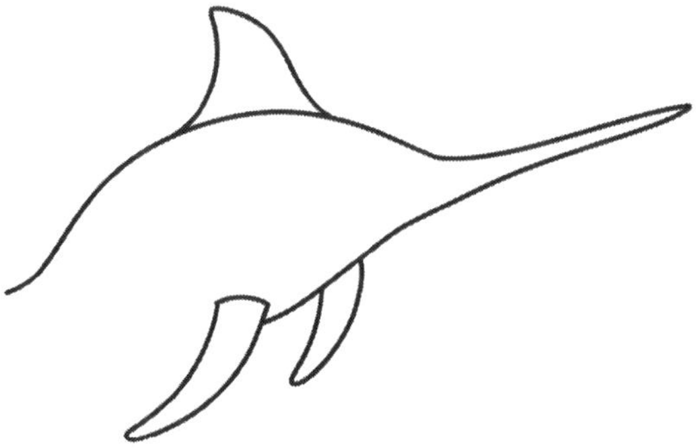

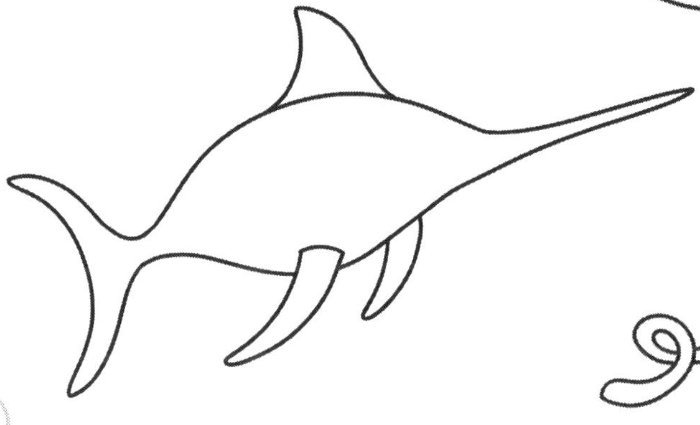

Practice

Swordfish
mostly eat at
night.

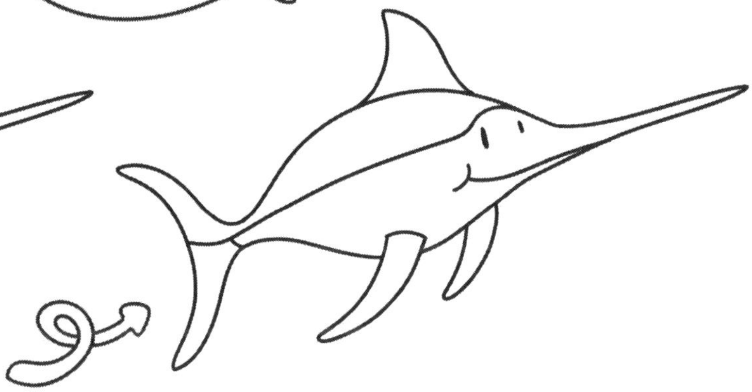

Mantis

Start

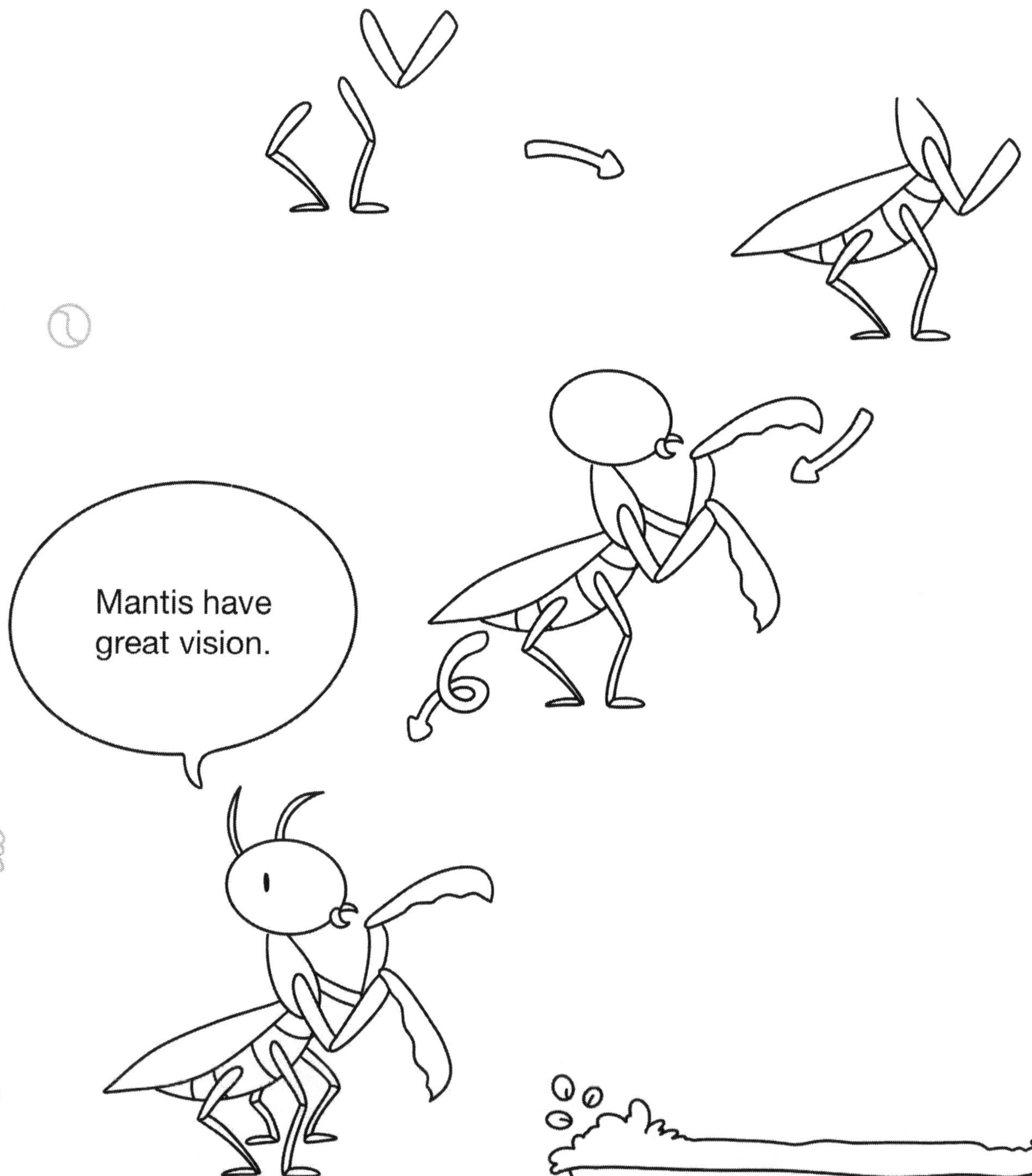

Practice

Iguana

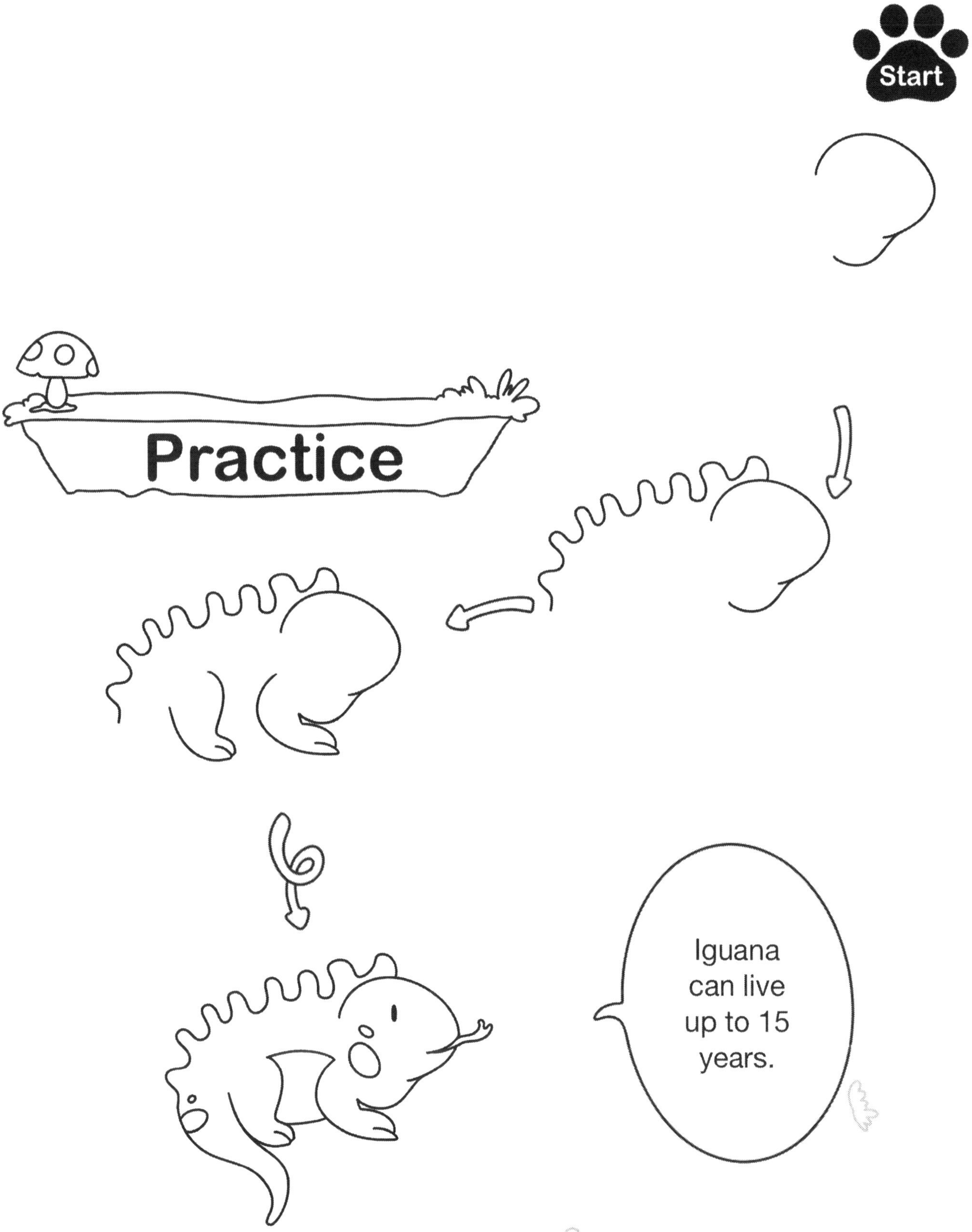

Pangolin

Start

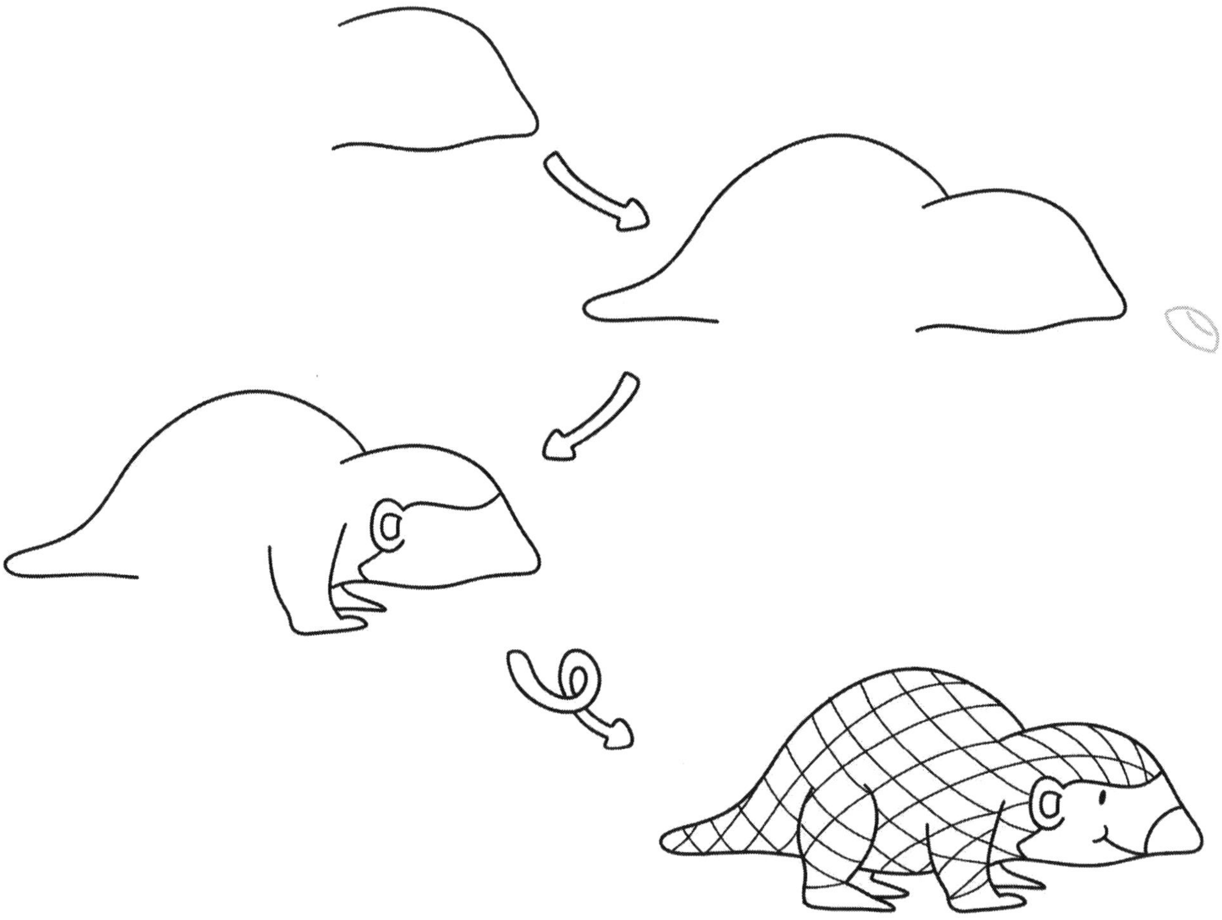

Pangolins are unable to chew.

Practice

Scorpion

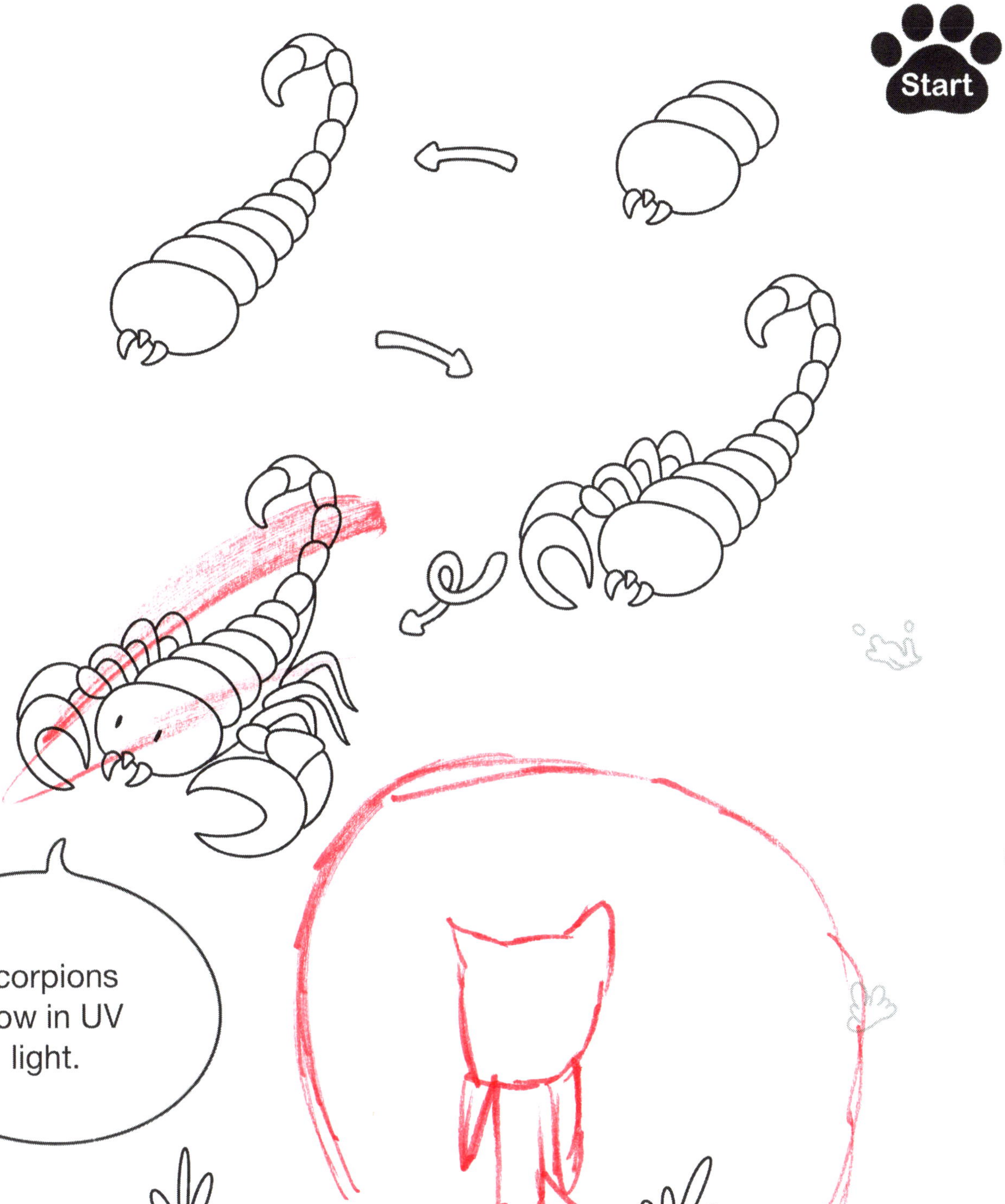

Scorpions glow in UV light.

Practice

Pufferfish

Start

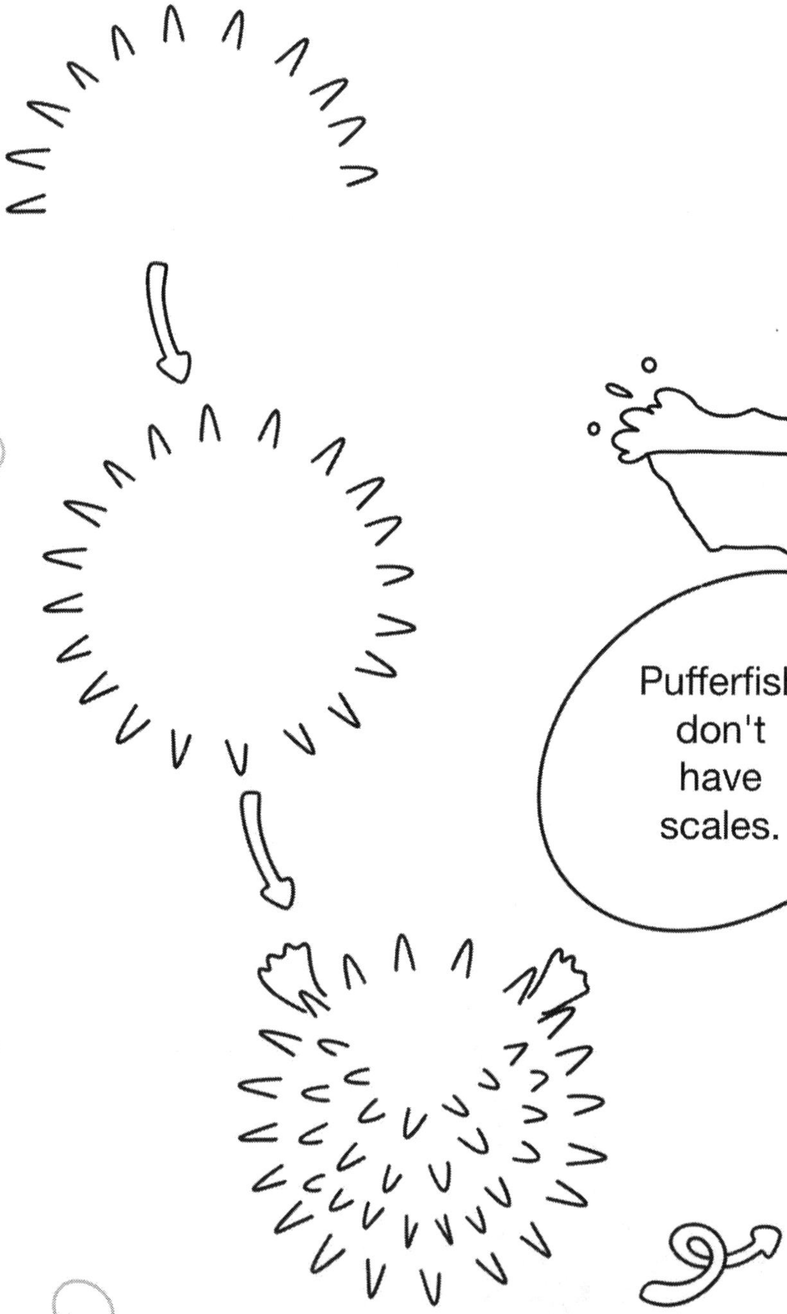

Practice

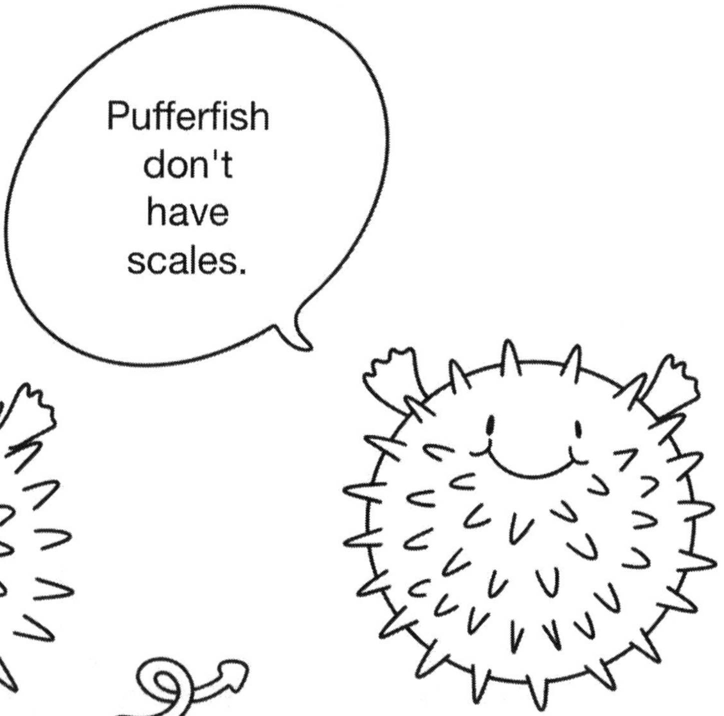

Mammoth

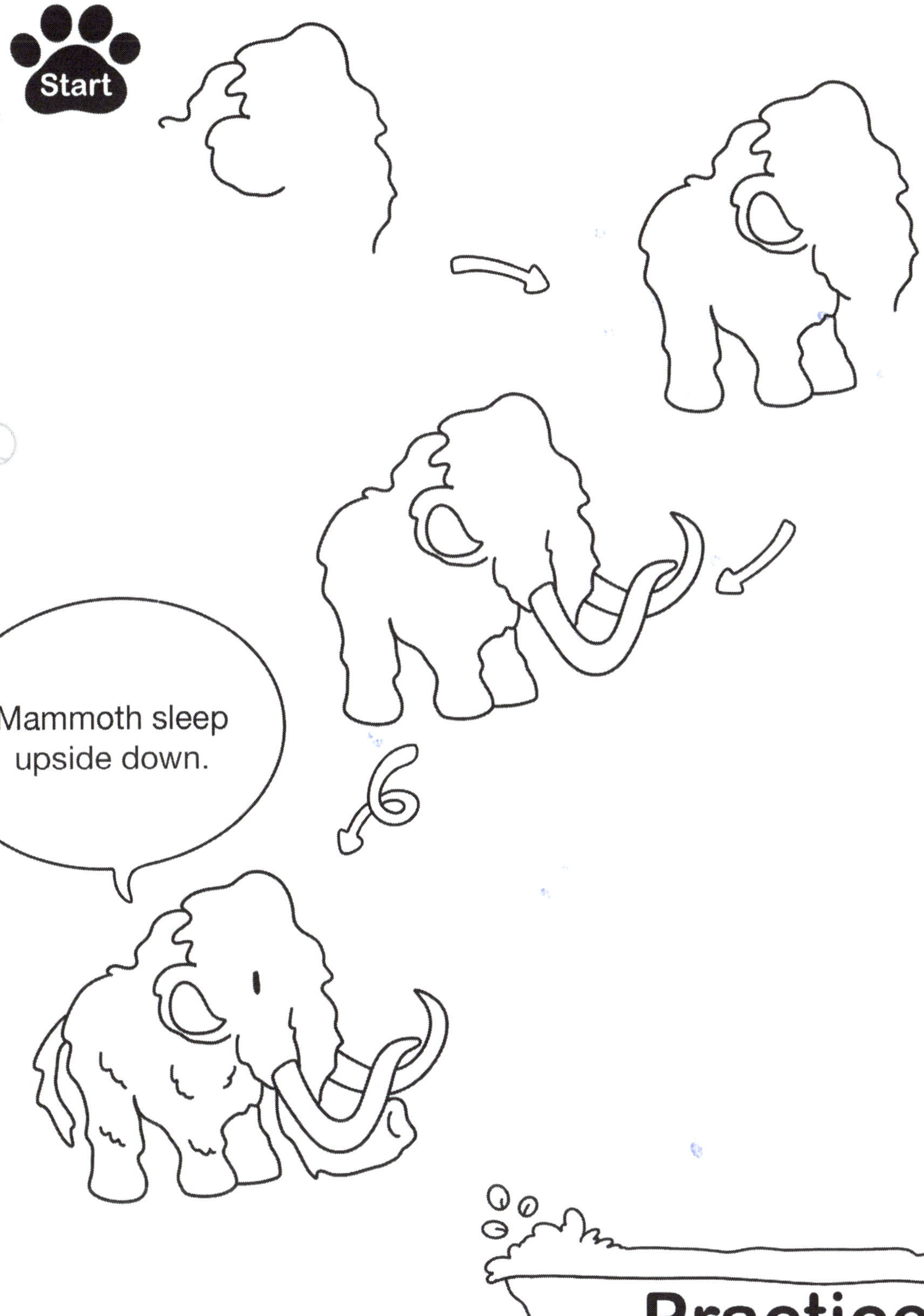

Practice

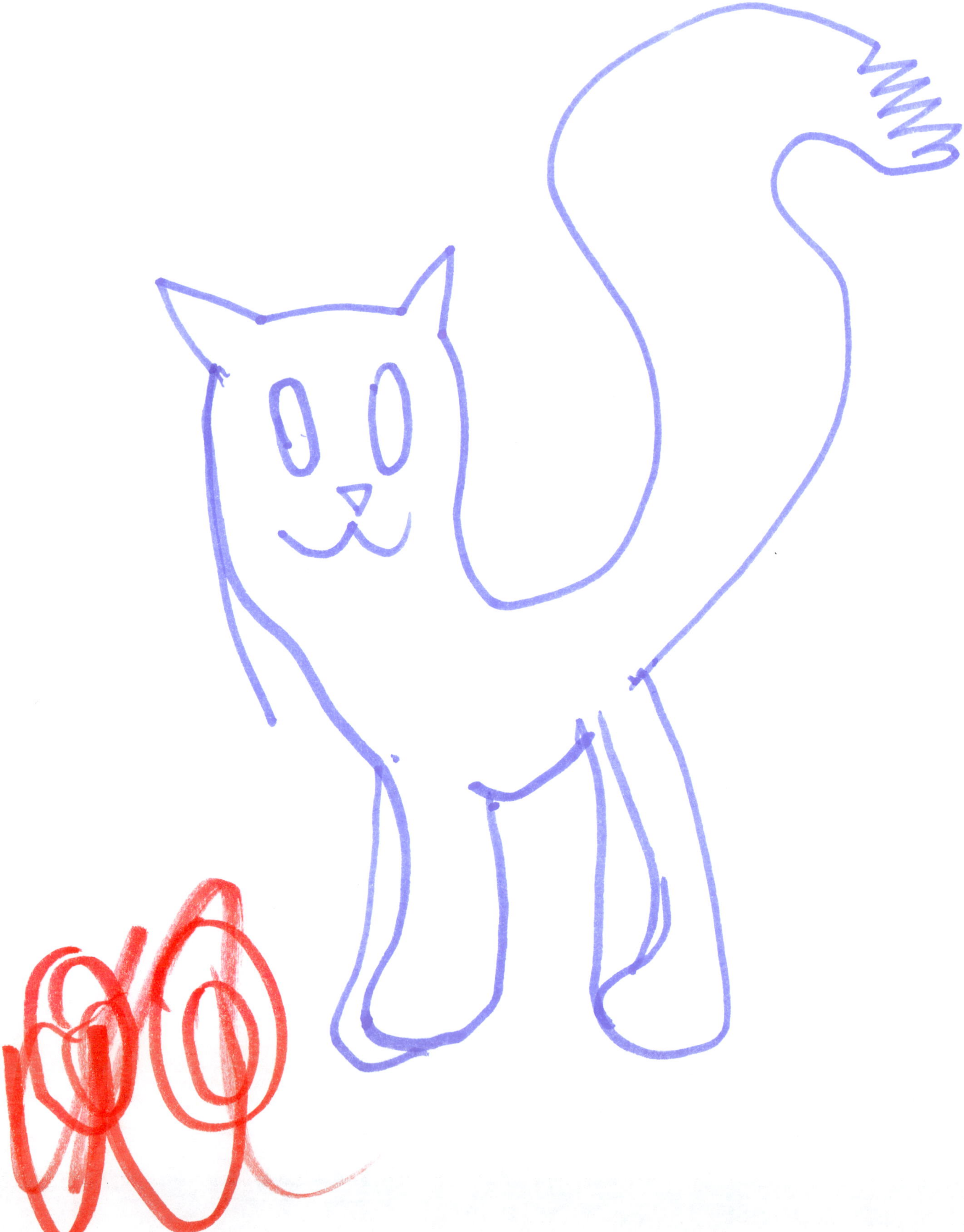

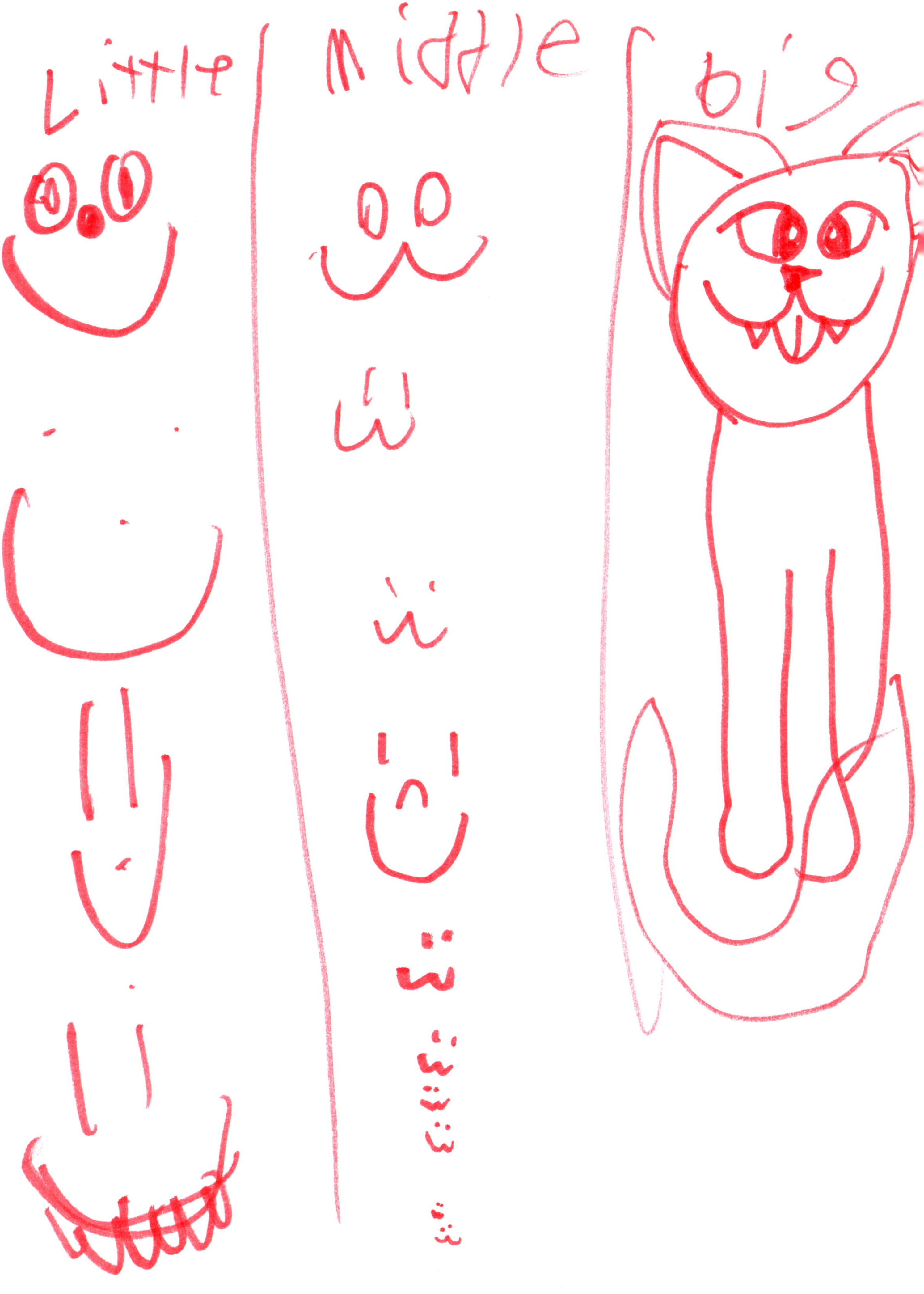Little
middle
big

hi

Made in the USA
Columbia, SC
18 December 2023

28877502R00061